CR

Localities at the Center

Native Place, Space, and Power in

Late Imperial Beijing

Harvard East Asian Monographs 258

CR

Localities at the Center

Native Place, Space, and Power in

Late Imperial Beijing

Richard Belsky

Published by Harvard University Asia Center
Distributed by Harvard University Press
Cambridge (Massachusetts) and London, 2005

Printed in the United States of America

The Harvard University Asia Center publishes a monograph series and, in coordination with the Fairbank Center for East Asian Research, the Korea Institute, the Reischauer Institute of Japanese Studies, and other faculties and institutes, administers research projects designed to further scholarly understanding of China, Japan, Vietnam, Korea, and other Asian countries. The Center also sponsors projects addressing multidisciplinary and regional issues in Asia.

Library of Congress Cataloging-in-Publication Data

Belsky, Richard.
    Localities at the center : native place, space, and power in late imperial Beijing / Richard Belsky.
        p. cm.
    Includes bibliographical references and index.
    ISBN 0-674-01956-3 (alk. paper)
    1. Sociology, Urban--China. 2. Associations, institutions, etc.--China --Beijing--History. 3. Rural-urban relations--China--Beijing--History. 4. Community development, Urban--China. 5. City and town life--China --History. 6. Country life--China--History. 7. Kinship--China--History. 8. China--Social conditions—1644–1912. I. Title.
    HT147.C6B45 2005
    307.76'0951'156--dc22

                                                                    2005020523

Index by the author

♾ Printed on acid-free paper

Last figure below indicates year of this printing

15 14 13 12 11 10 09 08 07 06 05

Endpapers: see Fig. 1.1, p. 2.

To Ted and Laura Belsky

ᘒ

Acknowledgments

Funding for research on this project was provided by a PSC/CUNY Research Grant, a fellowship from the Committee for Scholarly Communication with the People's Republic of China and a Frederick Sheldon Traveling Fellowship.

I am very grateful to the faculty and staff of the Institute of Qing Studies (Qingdai lishi yanjiusuo) at Renmin University of China, most especially my advisor, Li Hua, and to Chong Chengde, who was helpful in many different ways. I would like to thank the staff of the libraries and archives whose help was instrumental to my work, including those associated with the Beijing University Library, the Qinghua University Library, the National Library of China, the Capital Library of Beijing, the Library of the Chinese Academy of Science, the Anhui Provincial Library, Fujian Provincial Library, Hunan Provincial Library, Guangdong Provincial Library, the Number One Historical Archives, the Beijing Municipal Archives, the Library of Congress, the Starr Library of Columbia University, the Yale University East Asia Library, and the Yenching Library of Harvard University, where Raymond Lum generously arranged for the use of the map of Beijing presented on the cover and endpapers of this book.

I want to thank Philip Kuhn and William C. Kirby for their mentoring, support, and encouragement throughout graduate school. I would also like to thank all those who read, commented, and contributed to the various sections and versions of this work over the years, including William T. Rowe, Susan Naquin, David Strand, R. Bin Wang, Vincent Goossaert, Rebecca E. Karl, Peter Zarrow, Tobie Meyer-Fong, Li Xiaocong, Peter Carrol, Kenneth Chase, Adam Schneider, Chen Shiwei, Karl Gerth, C. Pat Giersch, Richard Horowtiz, Caroline Reeves, Dex Wilson, the members of the Columbia University Modern East Asia: China, and the Traditional China Seminars, and the Beijing as a Holy City: Historiographical Survey and New Material Conference. I am very grateful to the many residents of former huiguan sites who welcomed me into their homes and shared their stories with me, and I am thankful to He Zhenqiang for his drawing of the Zhaoqing lodge that is used in this book. I also want to give special thanks to Kong Xiangji, who encouraged me in my study of Beijing lodges early on and generously shared with me his detailed knowledge of the late imperial political world, and to my friend Li Qiao, who shared his knowledge of Beijing history and spent many hours making site visits to huiguan locations with me over the years.

I would like to thank Barbara Welter and my colleagues in the History Department for their support, and thank Hunter College for the one semester leave I was granted. I would also like to thank the two anonymous readers selected by the Harvard University Asia Center for their helpful suggestions for revisions. Finally, I would like to thank Kang and all the members of my family for their support throughout this project.

                                                        R.B.

℞

Contents

CR

Figures and Tables

Figures

Tables

☙

Localities at the Center

Native Place, Space, and Power in

Late Imperial Beijing

℃

Introduction

Let us begin with an image of Beijing during the last years of Qing rule, a map of the capital that dates to 1909 (see Fig. 1.1).[1] Reproduced in black and white here, when seen in full color the map is strikingly attractive (see the endpapers to this volume), with waterways shown in blue; official buildings and notable princely residences of the Manchu nobility in red; and major temples in yellow. Indeed, although I first came upon an original copy of the map in the rare-book collection of the Yenching Library at Harvard University (and the image here has been generously provided by that library), a poster version of this same map has become a popular tourist item in Beijing in recent years and is sold at bookstores and souvenir stands throughout the city.[2]

Presumably, those who buy the map as a casual souvenir today are attracted to it as an image of "old Beijing," and that is certainly how it is packaged. But a closer look reveals the city depicted as the center of a forward-looking project. Despite the humiliations and disastrous upheavals of the preceding sixty years and unaware that the dynasty would fall within two years, in the first decade of the

---

1. *Zui xin xiangxi dijing diyu.*
2. *Lao Beijing hutong xiangxi tu.*

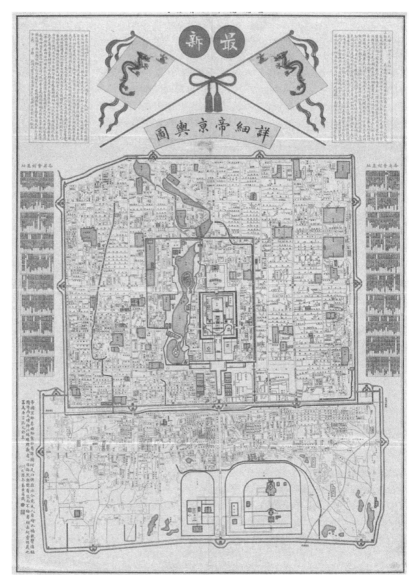

Fig. 1.1 Map of Beijing, 1909 (image courtesy Harvard-Yenching Library,
Harvard University; reproduced by permission;
see endpapers for a color version).

new century the cartographers found it possible to imagine a reformed and reinvigorated Qing imperial order. Far from a nostalgic image of the past, the map presents Beijing as a symbol of Qing-led modernity. The original title assures us that this is the "newest detailed" map of the imperial city, and true to its word the cartographic accuracy of this image is unsurpassed for a map intended for a popular audience; previous maps tended to smooth out the irregularities of the northwest and southeast corners of the city, distort the relative proportions of the northern and southern walled sections of the city, and less faithfully depict the layout of streets and other urban features. At the top of the map are two crossed banners, each depicting a dragon on a field of yellow, the official flag of the Qing empire.[3] Most significantly, bracketing the banners is the text of the well-known edict of August 27, 1908, in which the Empress Dowager laid out a vision of a reinvigorated, forward-looking dynasty and promised a sweeping political reform including the implementation of constitutional government, complete with a national parliament, within nine years.

Given the mapmakers' presentation of this image of a modernizing Qing capital, it is telling that they chose to place two long blocks of densely written text along the eastern and western sides of the city, containing the names and street locations of nearly 400 native-place lodges, or *huiguan*. The space devoted to the list of lodges says much about the vital role they had come to play in the social and political life of the city. Although native-place lodges had been an integral part of the capital for hundreds of years, they had taken on new functions in recent decades as Chinese elites rethought and renegotiated the respective roles of the imperial center and provincial peripheries.

In hindsight, the prominent association of the lodges with a modernizing Beijing in 1909 is also notable because the native-place lodges of Beijing and the native-place ties they represented would

---

3. One might suggest that the flags were in themselves symbols of Chinese efforts to participate in the modern world order of interacting nation-states, since the Qing dynasty did not adapt an official national flag until 1872. Originally triangular in shape, the rectangular version of the Qing flag presented here dates to 1890; see Crampton, *Flag*, 58–59.

soon come to be widely seen as backward remnants of a benighted Chinese past that were at best irrelevant and at worst actual obstacles to China's efforts to modernize. This negative reassessment of the Beijing lodges became the predominant view of them during the Republican period and helped set the stage for the eventual abolition of the lodges by the Communist government in the 1950s. This view has tended to color perceptions of the lodges to this day. The map thus helps us to see that the negative view of the lodges is itself a historical artifact and suggests we re-examine these assumptions. Seen in this light, I think, the map does us a service, for, as I will argue, the lodges not only developed during the final centuries of the imperial period into an essential feature of the late imperial political system but also served as vitally important elements in the construction of modern China. Ironically, as I will show, although the native-place lodges of Beijing came to be seen as unwanted remnants of China's backwardness during the twentieth century, they played an enormously important role in shaping the modern nation that came to reject them.

What were these native-place lodges? Whom did they serve? How did they develop over time? How did they fit into and help shape the urban ecology of the city? How did they further the multifaceted roles of native-place ties to China's late imperial capital? These are some of the questions addressed in this work. Making sense of this map will ultimately lead us to consider how native-place ties functioned as channels of communication between China's provinces and the political center, how sojourners to the capital used native-place ties to create solidarity within their communities of landsman, how the state co-opted these ties as a means of maintaining order within the city and controlling the imperial bureaucracy, how native-place ties transformed the urban landscape and social structure of the city, and how these functions were refashioned in the decades of political innovation that closed the Qing period.

ONE

Placing This Work

Native-place lodges are known in Chinese as *huiguan* 會館.[1] Previous works by English-speaking scholars refer to them variously as "provincial clubs," "guilds," "provincial guilds," and "*Landsmannschaften*." Of these terms, the one that best approximates the sense of the Chinese institution may be *Lansdsmannschaft*, which describes a fraternal organization of people originating from the same region and, in the United States at least, is closely associated with Jewish emigrants to the New World. It is this term that Ho Ping-ti (He Bingdi) chose as a translation for "huiguan" in his now-classic Chinese-language work on the topic. However, the *Landsmannschaften* of European immigrants to America now exist in far fewer numbers than they once did, and consequently fewer and fewer

---

1. The most authoritative and influential work on Chinese huiguan to date remains He Bingdi, *Zhongguo huiguan shilun*. Other major works (arranged in chronological order) include K, "Chinese Guilds and Their Rules"; MacGowan, "Chinese Guilds or Chambers of Commerce and Trade Unions"; Morse, *The Gilds of China*; Dou Jiliang, *Tongxiang zuzhi zhi yanjiu*; Niida Noboru, *Chūgoku no shakai to girudo*; Negishi Tadashi, *Chūgoku no girudo*; Golas, "Early Ch'ing Guilds"; Kwang-ching Liu, "Chinese Merchant Guilds"; Wang Rigen, "Ming-Qing shidai huiguan de yanbian"; and Zhongguo huiguan zhi buanzuan weiyuanhui, ed., *Zhongguo huiguan zhi*.

people are familiar with the term. Since there is little point in translating a Chinese term into another term that means nothing to most readers, no matter how accurate, I have opted instead to use the term "native-place lodge." Although inelegant, the term is, at least, to some degree self-explanatory.[2] As it happens, the word "lodge" fortuitously reflects two salient features of Beijing huiguan: they provided temporary living quarters (lodging) and meeting spaces (in the manner of, say, a Masonic lodge). Much is said of both of these functions in the chapters to come. For the sake of variety, I employ "native-place lodge" and "huiguan" interchangeably.

Native-place lodges were established in Chinese cities by and for those who came from and intended to return to some other region in China. In addition to lodging, huiguan provided places to socialize, to celebrate festivals, to discuss events at home, to debate affairs affecting personal or regional interests, and to network with others in order to facilitate acting on such interests. Well-funded lodges boasted posh banqueting facilities, and some of the finest and most opulent opera stages of late imperial China were found on huiguan premises. The lodges also invariably contained ritual spaces in the form of altars for the worship of regional deities, beatified local notables, and patron spirits held in particular reverence by the people of the regions represented. In Beijing and other administrative centers, many lodges provided study halls for examination candidates to use as they prepared for the civil service examinations. Some lodges featured elegant landscaped gardens through which native-place fellows and their guests might stroll and relax. Others established libraries on their grounds. Many huiguan also operated extensive cemeteries and mortuaries to serve the needs of departed landsmen. Native-place lodges were, in short, a vitally important social institution established to promote a host of mutual-assistance activities among the numerous sojourners of China's late imperial cities.

---

2. Naquin independently also opts for "lodge" as a translation, noting that the term "conveys (though imperfectly)" the sense of a huiguan as both an organization and a place; see Naquin, *Peking: Temples and City Life, 1400–1900*, 599.

Review of Previous Scholarship

The seminal social theorist Max Weber made an early and influential case for the historical significance of the ties of Chinese urban sojourners to their native places.[3] Weber argued that, compared with their Western European counterparts, Chinese cities lacked political, military, and organizational autonomy from the imperial government, and this had hampered their development. He attributed this condition to the historical inability of Chinese city dwellers to combine in citywide "oath-bound communities" or other representative bodies, which in the West had fought for the autonomy of their city. The fault, according to Weber, lay largely in the strong kinship and native-place ties between the Chinese urban resident and his home area.[4] As Weber described it: "Gaining a charter . . . was hardly possible along occidental lines because the fetters of the sib were never shattered. The new citizen . . . retained his relations to the native place of his sib, its ancestral land and temple. Hence all ritual and personally important relations with the native village were maintained."[5]

In Weber's eyes the Chinese city remained, throughout history, primarily a center of imperial administration and bureaucratic activity, because the development of a fully articulated social and political urban community was impeded by the centrifugal pull of overwhelming extramural ties. Weber further argued that these ties had thwarted China's social and economic development insofar as the merchant huiguan that represented these ties engaged in monopolistic practices.[6] The explanatory power of Weber's brilliant if not unerring insights contributed to their general acceptance within the Western academic community for more than half a century. The contemporary urban historian of Asia Rhoads Murphey, for example, describes traditional Chinese cities in highly Weberian terms:

---

3. Weber, *Religion of China*, 13–20. See also idem, *The City*, 81; and idem, "Citizenship."

4. Weber, *Religion of China*, 13–20.

5. Ibid., 13–14.

6. Ibid., 18.

Traditional cities were primarily centers of imperial authority imposed in a uniform plan on a varied landscape, symbolic monuments of the power and majesty of the Chinese state and of Chinese culture over which it presided. Functionally, they were in most cases predominantly agents of the imperial bureaucracy. . . . Urban elites were drawn in the first instance, in each generation, as much from the countryside as from the cities and retained close ties with their rural origins.[7]

Although not directly inspired by Weber's arguments, many Chinese intellectuals of the early twentieth century also came to believe that strong native-place ties hampered the development of a modern national identity. Figures as diverse as Liang Qichao 梁啓超 (1873–1929) and Sun Yatsen 孫逸仙 (1866–1925) had earlier argued that the Chinese penchant for particularistic allegiances undermined commitment to greater (especially national) causes. Native-place ties did have their intellectual defenders, though. Lin Yutang 林語堂 (1895–1976), for example, writing in English in 1935 put forward a more positive appraisal of provincial consciousness. While accepting the received wisdom of the day concerning an "absence of social mind" in China, Lin defended such ties insofar as he attributed the widespread philanthropy that existed in Chinese society to native-place allegiances:

"Provincialism," in Chinese called *tongxiang guannian*, . . . is responsible for the existence of district schools, public grainage, merchant guilds, or-phanages, and other public foundations. Fundamentally, they spring from the family psychology and do not depart from the family pattern. It is the family mind enlarged so as to make some measure of civic cooperation possible.[8]

The Weberian take on the historical importance of native-place ties was called into question by two important works on native-place networks and lodges by Chinese scholars, one written in the 1940s and the other in the 1960s. Both of them indicated short-

---

7. Murphey, "City as a Mirror of Society." However, this vision of the city has not been universally accepted; see DeGlopper, "Social Structure in a Nineteenth-Century Taiwanese Port City," esp. 633, for a specific refutation of Weber's char-acterization of urban dweller ties to native place.

8. Lin Yutang, *My Country and My People*, 203 (pinyin romanization substituted for original Wade-Giles).

comings in the Weberian model. Dou Jiliang's 竇季良 work, which focused on the huiguan and native-place associations (*tongxiang hui* 同鄉會) of Chongqing, discussed the psychological, cultural, kinship, and social origins of the "provincialism" (*xiangtu guannian* 鄉土觀念) that tied sojourners to their home region and served as a cohesive agent within their native-place organizations.[9] Dou was not primarily interested in how these organizations related to the historical development of capitalism. To some degree, however, his views on the regressive nature of native-place ties concurred with Weber's insofar as he underscored their potentially atomizing effect on larger group cohesion, both urban and national.[10] Dou differed from Weber, though, in suggesting that the sojourning/home community relationship was not an unchanging one. A central tenet of Dou's analysis is that the dissaggregative force of native-place ties had diminished over time. Dou believed a "natural tendency" increasingly replaced particularistic provincial interests with a community spirit (*shequ guannian* 社區觀念) that united all those in the city of residence.[11]

In his influential book on huiguan, Ho Ping-ti moved away from Dou's emphasis on social psychology, returning instead to Weber's original focus on economic development.[12] But the influence of Dou's evolutionary model is clear. Ho adopted and developed Dou's model as he refuted Weber's conclusions. Interestingly enough, in regard to one of his most central arguments, Ho's own brief English-language abstract provides a slant significantly different from that found in the more nuanced, fully argued Chinese text.

---

9. Dou Jiliang, *Tongxiang zuzhi zhi yanjiu*, 1–8.

10. Ibid., 14–16. Next to nothing is known of Dou's academic training. Weber's main works had not yet been translated into English, and although it is possible that Dou had access to the original German publications, it seems more likely that Dou was responding to domestic concerns.

11. Ibid., 16–20, 80.

12. He Bingdi, *Zhongguo huiguan shilun*. He was, perhaps, also responding to Japanese academic discourse on Chinese sojourner ties, which depicted strong native-place ties as a feudal or medieval characteristic but placed less emphasis on their ability to thwart progressive economic tendencies. Some of the major Japanese works relevant to this issue are Imahori Seiji, *Chūgoku no shakai kōzō*; Niida Noboru, "The Industrial and Commercial Guilds of Peking"; Negishi Tadashi, *Shina girudo no kenkyū*; and idem, *Chūgoku no girudo*.

Ho's abstract states: "Contrary to impressions of previous writers that the prevalence of *Landsmannschaften* reflected the existence of unusually strong local particularism in China and has hence hindered China's modernization . . . detailed case-studies . . . reveal that the institution of *Landsmannschaften* has in fact facilitated interregional economic and social integration."[13] This is a delicately worded statement, but the implication appears to be that particularistic native-place ties furthered, rather than impeded, modernizing economic dictates (read carefully, Ho attributes a positive role only to native-place *lodges*; although he raises the issue of the native-place *ties* that underlay the lodges, he does not directly refer to them again). Some scholars have taken this to mean that Ho was, in fact, proposing a "separate model of 'rational economic activity' based on the particularities of the Chinese case."[14] But Ho's argument for the positive contribution of huiguan did not go that far. Ho unwaveringly accepted Weber's standards of economic rationality; he differed only in believing that China could have ultimately achieved that standard on its own and that huiguan played a transitional role in that historical transformation. The argument was much more fully presented in the chapter "Huiguan and the Gradual Dissolution of Territorialism."[15] As the title indicates, Ho borrowed and expanded on Dou's model of the gradual dissolution of the pull of native-place ties over time. Like Dou, Ho saw the inexorable influence of social and economic rationalization shaping a process whereby narrow native-place allegiances were inevitably undermined and gradually melded into a greater synthesis with the resident community:

Within the smelting furnace of a single city, economic and social forces never cease to dissipate and weaken the territorial particularism (*zhenyu guannian* 畛域觀念) originally characteristic of every kind of geographically based association (*diyuan zuzhi* 地緣組織). Common economic benefit facilitates the incorporation of organizational trade-based princi-

---

13. He Bingdi, *Zhongguo huiguan shilun*, "English Abstract," 4. See also Ho Ping-ti, "The Geographic Distribution of Hui-Kuan," 122.

14. See Goodman, *Native Place*, 44. Goodman, indeed, criticizes William Rowe for "ignoring" Ho's argument in this regard, although, as I will show, Goodman herself misread just what Ho's argument is.

15. He Bingdi, *Zhongguo huiguan shilun*, 101–14.

ples that transcend territorial principles. Over the long term, complete social interaction aids in the manifestation of social homogenization between locals and non-locals.[16]

Ho's thesis differs from Dou's earlier work primarily in its greater emphasis on economic forces and its more fully developed evolutionary model, which postulates an inevitable transformation of huiguan organizational principles from those based on native place to those based on non-territorial-delimited trade:

Generally speaking no matter how deeply or firmly established the principles of territorialism (*diyuan guannian* 地緣觀念) are in the beginning, the economic benefits of a single trade, sooner or later will overcome the original narrow territorialism within that same trade; therefore, in the end there always will be a trend toward supra-territorial forms of organizations organized according to principles of trade.[17]

Ho provides numerous examples as evidence of this proposed trend, and he explains away those cases that do not accord with his evolutionary hypothesis in the following way:

Of course, those who wish to bring order to history cannot but pay attention to both sides of a single issue. Among the hundred plus several tens of huiguan and *gongsuo* 公所 in Suzhou, although there is proof of the dissolution of the principles of territorialism, there is likewise no lack of examples of territorial organizational principles being preserved from beginning to end. . . . The causes for the preservation of territorial organizational principles within these trades, although very complex, are still not difficult to explain in principle. . . . In all [of the above cases] due to superior commercial or technical conditions, other regional groups could not compete; therefore there was no need to expand the original territorial character.[18]

---

16. Ibid., 114. Note Ho refers to "social homogenization between locals and non-locals." Compare Dou Jiliang's (*Tongxiang zuzhi zhi yanjiu*, 82) description of assimilation or "nativization," a process in which, according to Dou, the social community becomes increasingly unified in terms of blood, dialect, cultural customs, habits, and so on. Ho uses this term as well elsewhere; see, e.g., He Bingdi, *Zhongguo huiguan shilun*, 111. Ho's notion of "homogenization" allows for a less unidirectional cultural transformation. This is a useful paradigm that recognizes the adoption of sojourner cultural characteristics by local communities.

17. He Bingdi, *Zhongguo huiguan shilun*, 102.

18. Ibid, 104.

This explanation highlights the differences in Weber's and Ho's understanding of the monopolistic practices of huiguan. Whereas Weber saw outright economic monopoly, which paralyzed economic development, Ho argued that in practice, generally speaking, competition with other groups was unavoidable. Such competition then acted as the engine of rationalization. Where specific conditions allowed for complete monopoly, however, competition was averted and traditional forms were maintained. Such conditions merely served as the exceptions that prove the rule. Ho was one of the earliest scholars to propose a territory-to-trade evolutionary model of Chinese associational organization. It is a formula that was subsequently widely adopted, although it is rarely attributed to him.[19]

Ho, like Weber, viewed native-place particularism as essentially regressive in nature, but he argued that economic forces ultimately transformed the organizational expression of these ties. Even though huiguan initially facilitated interregional social and economic integration, the very rationalizing and modernizing forces this contribution helped unleash inevitably undermined the territorial allegiances upon which huiguan were based. Ho refuted Weber by demonstrating that huiguan and sojourner ties to native place had not acted as impediments to modernization. China's modernization, Ho insisted, had not been dependent on the Western impact for initiation or development because China possessed an internally generated rationalizing dynamic that was already in

---

19. Niida, "The Industrial and Commercial Guilds of Peking," 202–3, seems to suggest with anecdotal evidence that some form of this evolutionary process had transpired among some of the commercial guilds of Beijing, but he did not develop the observation into a true model of a general tendency. Peter Golas ("Early Ch'ing Guilds," 557–58) follows Ho in seeing economic forces as the primary motive force behind an evolutionary transcendence of territorial organizational principles.

Bryna Goodman (*Native Place*, 43; see esp. note 67) discusses more recent Chinese scholarship echoing the transition from native-place orientation to more economically "rational" attitudes. In addition to the works cited by Goodman, see also Yu Heping, "Yapian zhanzheng hou tongshang kouan hanghui de jindaihua."

William Rowe seems to get the most "credit" for the "from native-place to trade" model of huiguan evolution, which has come under increasing attack. See, e.g., Kwang-ching Liu, "Chinese Merchant Guilds," 14–15*n*31. Ironically, this is not a model that Rowe ever fully embraced.

the process of producing a modern capitalism prior to the Western impact. As Ho put it:

Undoubtedly, the rise of modern shipping and ground transportation, the introduction of Western thinking, the prospering of national-ethnic consciousness, the promulgation of the new industrial and commercial organization laws, have all speeded the decline of small group organizations (*xiaoqun zuzhi* 小群組織). But it can be seen from the historical examples cited in this work, that even if the changes in the international state of affairs had not occurred, and ancient China remained closed and autonomous, internal economic and social forces would have certainly promoted the dissipation of territorial particularism and the rise of big-group consciousness. The best indication of this tendency is the transformational and metamorphosing history of the huiguan system over the [past] five hundred years.[20]

More recently, William Rowe's work on social and economic developments in Hankou has expanded the intellectual approach established by Dou and Ho.[21] Rowe also explicitly challenges Weber's thesis and does so by adopting many of the central tenets of the earlier Chinese scholars.[22] Of primary interest to this discussion is Rowe's treatment of sojourner ties to, and sojourner identity with, native place. Citing Dou and Ho's early work, Rowe depicts the growing acculturation of Hankou sojourners and demonstrates that a "corresponding growth of identification with the host locality was reflected in patterns of philanthropy and public service."[23] Contrary to Weber's contention that native-place identification prevented the formation of autonomous urban community consciousness, Rowe reveals a growing identification of sojourners as "Hankow men . . . [which] was gradually translated into a sense of locational solidarity and an impetus to communal self-nurturance."

---

20. He Bingdi, *Zhongguo huiguan shilun*, 114.

21. Rowe, *Hankow.*

22. Ibid.; see esp. "Introduction," 1–14, for Rowe's discussion of Weber in relation to his own work. Rowe, much more than Ho, frames his rebuttal of Weber within Weber's own framework of urban autonomy, but his conclusion that China might well "if left to itself, ultimately have developed into an industrial capitalist society comparable to that of the West" (ibid., 345) is strikingly reminiscent of Ho's conclusions.

23. Ibid., 250.

Parting from Dou and Ho, however, Rowe explicitly denied that increased "locational identity" necessarily implied the withering of original native-place bonds. "There is no reason to assume that the identification of a Chinese urban dweller with his native place . . . in any way precluded the development of a conception of himself as a full member of the community to which he had immigrated or in which he sojourned."[24] Instead, drawing on a model developed by political scientists in reference to other societies, Rowe suggests that a multiplication rather than a substitution of social identities was at work.[25] The final chapters of Rowe's book deal specifically with how these identities commingled and contributed to an emerging urban consciousness that embraced a sense of Hankou as an autonomous community, without denying native-place bonds.[26]

Bryna Goodman has returned to the subject of native-place ties and native-place organizations and in doing so has presented us with a work of exceptional nuance and complexity.[27] Goodman's work is concerned primarily with social-political history and the evolution of urban and national identities, not with economic problems. Uninterested in questions regarding the role of native-place ties in the promotion or suppression of native capitalist development, she dismisses the very premise of the question as misguided.[28] Goodman instead persuasively argues that native-place ties did not inherently conflict with "modernization," a concept she correctly maintains must be understood as culturally defined, although she seems to equate it with the adoption of national identity. Arguing that native-place organizations remained a persistent and vital feature of Shanghai even as the city "modernized" during the twentieth cen-

---

24. Ibid.
25. Rowe (ibid.) credits his understanding of "identity multiplication" to the article by Robert Melson and Howard Wolpe, "Modernization and the Politics of Communalism: A Theoretical Perspective," *American Political Science Review* 64 (Dec. 1970): 1112–30.
26. Rowe, *Hankow: Commerce*, chaps. 8–10 *passim*.
27. Goodman, *Native Place*. See also idem, "New Culture, Old Habits."
28. The themes discussed in this paragraph are developed throughout Goodman's *Native Place* but are cogently summarized in the introduction; see esp. 41–46.

tury, she demonstrates that native-place identities, far from stifling nationalist allegiances, actually contributed to their development. Goodman also emphasizes the variability and multiplicity of identities, arguing that "the transformation of urban identity was a process of accretion of identities, not the displacement of native-place identity for newer, more 'modern' ones."[29]

As this last statement (essentially a restatement of Rowe's earlier formula of identity multiplication) suggests, Goodman's approach is significantly indebted to Rowe's, although she goes to some length to deny this, ascribing to Rowe a position he explicitly rejected: "The findings of this study challenge those of Rowe which suggest the attenuation of native-place ties in the last decades of the nineteenth century and the displacement of native-place identity by an emergent urban 'Hankow' identity."[30]

Such disagreements aside, even this simple review of previous thinking about native-place ties in China reveals how much this scholarship holds together as a body of work, within which one finds developments, breakthroughs, and great continuities. The increasing sophistication of analytical models and the use of more fully grounded historically informed investigations of city-specific historical case studies perhaps best represent development in this scholarship. Each of the scholars highlighted above contributes substantially to our understanding of this multifaceted question, but the single biggest breakthrough in this discourse, perhaps, came from the obscure scholar Dou Jiliang, who first insisted that native-place identities are not static but complex social and psychological processes that evolve according to a dynamic logic. This was something Weber and other early scholars were unable to see, and Dou's evolutionary model influenced later scholars tremendously. Goodman, too, deserves much credit for her emphasis on simultaneous multiple identities and her insistence that modernity be defined in culturally sensitive ways.

For all the rethinking in our understanding of this subject, some continuities are striking. Driving much of the investigation of native-place ties is the question of whether these ties are progressive

---

29. Ibid., 46.
30. Ibid., 45.

or retrogressive: Weber saw native-place ties as obstacles to development; Dou argued that over time these obstacles withered away; Ho saw native-place organizations facilitating the very processes that eventually undermined native-place ties; Rowe challenged Weber on his own terms, by re-evaluating the character of China's late imperial economy (and the role of native-place organizations within it) and thus coming to very different conclusions; even Goodman, who insists that the definition of progress must be open to "new modalities," is concerned primarily with showing how these ties contributed to the process of "modernization." Thus, although she rejects the significance of the capitalist-development standard, and although she argues eloquently for culturally sensitive, multi-modal standards of modernity, she is still caught up in a measurement of historical progress based on contributions to a "modernity" closely associated with the development of a "national" identity.

My work builds on and breaks from the questions that have heretofore been brought to the study of native-place ties. Although this study rejects the measurement of historical significance according to teleological models framed in terms of capitalism or modernity, I am indebted to Ho for his path-breaking insights into how the act of institutionalizing native-place ties could over time create unintended historical dynamics. My work is also indebted to Bryna Goodman's authoritative demonstration of the positive contributions made by native-place identities to the construction of early twentieth-century national consciousness in Shanghai. Like Goodman, I find that native-place ties contributed to a new sense of national identity, although I argue that in Beijing this process had its roots in urban transformations that date to the eighteenth century, and that this consciousness emerged as a potent political force in Beijing by the 1890s, well before similar developments in Shanghai.

In other areas, too, this study returns to concerns addressed before. Like Weber, I explore the relationship between sojourners and the state and inquire into the effects native-place ties had on the character of the city in which they operated. However, if my concerns are in that sense Weberian, my findings certainly are not. To begin with, this study eschews taking the idealized western city as a standard by which to judge historical Chinese ones. Rather than decry the "failure" of native-place lodges to foster "oath-bound communities" that might stand in opposition to the state, I find great historical significance in the mutually beneficial relationship that evolved between the state and the sojourning communities. The reader will find much in this study concerning ways native-place ties among scholar-officials served to mediate between the interests of those men, the localities from which they came, and the interests of the state. Indeed, I show that native-place ties and their institutional expression were incorporated as constitutional elements of the late imperial political system. In order to address how native-place ties affected cities, I examine the spatial patterning of the lodges and explore the profound effects this had on the urban ecology of Beijing and on scholar-official identity. I then show how the particular urban context native-place ties helped to create affected the tumultuous events that accompanied the collapse of the old order and the search for a new one in the late nineteenth and early twentieth centuries.

Finally, while endeavoring for theoretical engagement, I have tried to keep this study empirically grounded. The native-place lodges of Beijing were far from typical, and the functions of native-place ties there were not representative of those elsewhere. In order to set the unique character of the Beijing lodges in a proper light, I provide a preliminary overview of native-place lodges in China outside Beijing, before moving on to examine the Beijing lodges and their relationship to the city and state and to political events. The lodges were indispensable links that bound China's localities with its political center during a period of enormous change and innovation. Although I am not especially concerned with whether the native-place lodges were a progressive institution that facilitated modernization, I am keenly interested in the role they played in China's evolution from a late imperial to a national social-political system. As we shall see, they played a dramatically important role, but let us first get a sense of how native-place lodges operated outside Beijing.

TWO

Native-Place Lodges

Beyond Beijing

This study is concerned primarily with native-place networks in Beijing, but to properly appreciate those functions of native-place ties that were and were not unique to the capital, we must first have a general sense of the nature of native-place networks in China, outside Beijing. Since native-place lodges served as the essential institutionalized expression of native-place ties in China, this chapter focuses on huiguan and provides an overview of both the origins of the institution and the regional variations in establishment of native-place lodges. For the past several decades, historical scholarship on China has reflected a growing appreciation of regional dynamics. Indeed, some of the most outstanding recent works on Chinese history have been local histories, and in some respects this study is a local history, too, albeit one that focuses on the interaction between the most central of central places and the various other localities of the realm. Although the value of recognizing the distinctiveness of regional dynamics cannot be doubted, we must keep in mind that there were many levels of regional interaction. Of course, no good local history can treat its subject as a completely autonomous unit, but clearly more work needs to be done to further our understanding of how material objects, people, and ideas moved from place to place in China. This chapter builds on previous work on native-place networks across China and hopes to contribute to that scholarly discussion, but it is clear to me that our understanding of native-place networks as a larger social/cultural system is still only at a preliminary stage, and more work calls out to be done on this topic.

Huiguan Defined

Since ancient times Chinese people have honored an affection for one's native place. This regard is expressed in many ways. It is, for example, striking that in classical Chinese poetry expressions of homesickness are far more prevalent than themes such as romantic love emphasized in other poetic traditions. Homesickness might entail nothing more than fondness for one's family, were it not that connections between family and place have also long been highly valued. Consider, for instance, the widespread traditional desire for one's bones and the bones of one's ancestors to be buried in native-place ground. It is not surprising therefore that the emotional bonds that tied people to their homes tended to extend not only to family but also to the customs, the speech, the food, the natural environment, or the "water and soil" of a place. It might be said that the "who" of Chinese folk traditionally has been deeply shaped by the "where" of their origins.

Given this respect for the connection between people and native place, it makes sense that Chinese people have sought to promote the bonds of affinity that unite those who also hail from the same place. The honoring of native-place ties has been reflected historically in many different levels of social behavior, from informal favors extended from one landsman to another to the formation of political cliques, but the quintessential institutional expression of native-place solidarity over the past five hundred years has been the native-place lodge. The lodges served as a physical representation of native-place solidarity, they regulated the "performance" of native-place-based rituals and social interaction, and they facilitated the ability of communities organized by native place to sustain themselves over time. Although not everything related to native-place ties was directly associated with native-place lodges, any evaluation of the historical significance of native-place ties must begin with a consideration of huiguan.

The Chinese native-place lodge was defined by two essential characteristics: (1) it was established and operated by and for native-place compatriots; and (2) it had corporately owned property. However, the term *huiguan* itself is not an infallible indicator of a native-place lodge. Such lodges were called by many names. This is not unusual. Anthropologists have observed that any attempt to define institutions by their native terms is problematic; names "are not unambiguous pointers to the precise nature of the groups and quasi-groups for which they are used."[1] To some degree, such variations reflected regional dialectical differences. It was not unusual in provinces along the mid and lower reaches of the Yangzi watershed, for example, to refer to native-place lodges as academies (*shuyuan* 書院).[2] Other huiguan established in that general area designated themselves with terms more often reserved for religious buildings, such as *ci* 祠 (shrine), *an* 庵 (monastery), *dian* 殿 (temple/hall) and *miao* 廟 (temple). One especially popular term in those central Yangzi provinces (though not exclusively confined to that area) was *gong* 宮, a word commonly used to denote palaces but also

---

1. Freedman, *Chinese Lineage and Society*. For a lucid discussion of this passage and the general problem of native terms as it relates to the study of Chinese lineages and kinship-based groups, see Sangren, "Traditional Chinese Corporations," 395–98.

2. Examples in Hubei province included the (Anhui) Qinxi shuyuan 琴溪書院 in Hankou; the E'cheng shuyuan 鄂城書院, also known as the (Hubei) Wuchang huiguan 武昌會館, in Shashi; the Qingchuan shuyuan 晴川書院 in that same city, which served sojourners from Hanyang in Hubei; the Wujun shuyuan 武郡書院, which represented Wuchang sojourners in Zhongxiang; and the Qi'an shuyuan 齊安書院 in Guanghua, which served sojourners from Huangzhou (Hubei). See "Appendix One: Chinese Native-Place Lodges in Cities Across China During the Late Nineteenth and Early Twentieth Centuries," in Belsky, "Beijing Scholar-Official Native-Place Lodges."

sometimes temples.[3] For example, the Temple/Palace of the River Lord (Chuanzhu gong 川主宮) was a common designation for huiguan established by Sichuan natives in central China. The name apparently refers to a spirit who presided over the four rivers associated with that province. Sojourners from Hunan and Hubei often called their huiguan the Palace of King Yu (Yuwang gong 禹王宮), a name that honors the "Great Yu," legendary founder of the Xia dynasty and mythic tamer of waterways. Jiangxi sojourners frequently established lodges under the name Palace of the God of Longevity (Wanshou gong 萬壽宮). By the late nineteenth century, at least, even Jiangxi natives were confused about what that name meant; the well-known official, reform advocate, and Jiangxi native Wen Tingshi 文廷式 (1856–1904) remarked on the general ignorance of origins of the name among Jiangxi people and explained that it came from a title bestowed by the early twelfth-century Song emperor Huizong on Xu Jingyang 許旌陽, a Daoist saint worshipped in many Jiangxi huiguan.[4] The names of lodges in northern Chinese cities, including Beijing, sometimes also featured terms associated with shrines and temples, particularly *ci* (shrine).

The term *huiguan* was occasionally but much less often applied to institutions that were not native-place lodges. In Panyu county, Guangdong province, for example, the Salt Affairs Office, an official bureau operating out of the county yamen, bore the name Yanwu huiguan 鹽務會館.[5]

Nomenclature aside, two other kinds of traditional organizations that should be distinguished from huiguan nonetheless shared important similarities with native-place lodges: temples and shrines serving particular sojourning native-place communities; and state residences or officially established lodges for sojourning officials, known as *di* 邸 or *jundi* 郡邸. Both institutions had been present in China long before the first huiguan were established. A brief consideration of the nature of these organizations will illuminate the differences between them and native-place lodges, as well as put into context any direct historical links.

---

3. See ibid. for numerous examples.
4. Wen Tingshi, *Wen Tingshi ji*, 2: 738.
5. *Panyu xian zhi* (1871), 5.24.

Shrines and temples dedicated to patron deities with special significance for a particular native place carried out many of the functions performed by huiguan. Shiba Yoshinobu, for one, has argued that shrines and temples to Mazu 媽祖, also known as the Heavenly Consort (Tian hou 天后), established in Ningbo by Fujian merchants as early as 1191 served as "clear prototypes" for later merchant huiguan.[6] Mazu was among the most popular folk deities in China, and her link to the people of Fujian was especially strong. According to the most common myth of her origins, Mazu was a fisherman's daughter born and raised along the Fujian coast. Many huiguan established by Fujian natives in cities across China featured shrines to the area's patron deity, and temples to the goddess often doubled as Fujian guild halls.[7] The close connection between Fujian native-place organizations and the worship of Mazu is reflected in the number of Fujian huiguan, especially in the provinces of the middle and upper Yangzi known by the alternative name Temple/Palace of the Heavenly Consort (Tian hou gong).

Ritual veneration of patron deities was an essential feature of native-place lodges in the late imperial period (see Chapter 6). Shiba's suggestion that such temples served as prototypes merits serious consideration, but too little is known about the functions and administration of such temples during earlier periods to settle the matter absolutely. We must exercise caution before too readily accepting a direct link between pre-Ming temples and later native-place lodges. For one thing, worship of the Heavenly Consort was by no means confined to Fujianese. The nineteenth-century Tian hou gong in Zhongjiang, Sichuan, served Guangdong not Fujian sojourners, for example.[8] Some non-Fujian-related merchant huiguan in late imperial and post-imperial times also worshipped her. Mazu served as the patron deity of several trades, including those of shipbuilding and fishing, that were not exclusively defined in terms of native-place origin. In modern times the Merchant Ship hui-

---

6. Shiba, "Ningpo and Its Hinterland," 416–17. For an excellent discussion of the many meanings of this deity, see Watson, "Standardizing the Gods," esp. 302.

7. Watson, "Standardizing the Gods," 303; Li Qiao, *Zhongguo hangye shen chongbai*, 311–16.

8. Belsky, "Beijing Scholar-Official Native-Place Lodges," Appendix One, 323.

guan (Shangchuan huiguan 商船會館) located in Shanghai, for example, boasted a prominent shrine to the goddess even though the men engaged in this trade came primarily from Hunan and Hubei provinces.[9]

State residences, on the other hand, were established to provide temporary lodgings exclusively for sojourners from specific regions, but they differed from huiguan in that they were not corporately owned. *Jundi* were found in imperial capitals as far back as the Han period (206 BCE–220 CE), if not before. In later times, such facilities were also called "submitting petitions halls" (*jinzouyuan* 進奏院), "gathering in the capital halls" (*chaojiyuan* 朝集院), and "examination graduate halls" (*zhuangyuanyuan* 狀元院). As the various terms indicate, these facilities were intended to serve regional officials and others who traveled to the capital on official business. A number of nineteenth- and twentieth-century Chinese texts portray *jundi* as precursors to huiguan. Indeed, this argument can be traced to as early as the seventeenth century.[10] One account from the annals of an early nineteenth-century lodge refers to the tradition of establishing *di* (called *dishe* 邸舍 in this text) in the capital. It suggests the custom dates to the Han and was continued throughout the succeeding ages. It then observes that although, unlike *di*, huiguan are not state run, the earlier institution may be considered the "actual prototype of the idea."[11]

Some recent literature on this subject follows a similar line. The Chinese scholar Wu Zhezheng refers to the earlier institution as *junguo gong di* 郡國公邸 and describes them as the "earliest huiguan."[12] Even those who propose a direct link do, however, recognize the essential difference between *jundi* and native-place lodges. *Jundi* were government-owned and -operated facilities, financed and maintained through officially coordinated efforts of regional administrative governments at the prefectural and provincial levels. Zhu Guozhen 朱國楨 (1557–1632) noted this distinction during the

---

9. Li Qiao, *Zhongguo hangye shen chongbai*, 313.
10. See, e.g., Beijing tushuguan, Jinshi zu, ed., *Beijing tushuguan cang lidai taben huibian* (hereafter cited as *BJTSGC*), 91: 141, "Jiaxing liuyi guan ji."
11. (*Chongxiu*) *Shexian huiguan lu.*
12. Wu Zhezheng, "Huiguan," 84.

Ming period (1368–1644): "During the Han, prefectures, states, and fiefdoms respectively established *di* in the capital; the Tang had *jinzouyuan*, and the Song had *chaojiyuan*. This dynasty [the Ming] lacks them and has only privately established huiguan."[13] Ho Ping-ti added to this discussion by pointing out that *jundi* and huiguan differed not only in the nature of the ownership but also in the nature of some of their activities as well.[14] For example, there is no indication that *jundi* provided mortuary-related services for their respective sojourning communities or that they conducted ritual activities associated with the native region; in contrast, these were integral functions of huiguan. *Jundi* operated more as offices to handle the official business of their respective administrative regions, rather than regional lodging houses and clubs, as they have sometimes been depicted.

Interestingly the *jundi* of the Han and subsequent eras prior to the fifteenth century shared fundamental characteristics with the officially established liaison offices, known as capital offices (*zhujing banshichu* 駐京班事處) or capital liaison offices (*zhujing lianluochu* 駐京聯絡處), found in present-day Beijing. It is no coincidence that this type of liaison institution emerged in Beijing during the 1950s as the native-place lodges were being disbanded by state decree. Like the ancient *jundi*, the modern offices are directly operated by the local government of the region they represent and are thus not corporately owned. The contemporary offices also lack the cultural and ritual spaces associated with huiguan, such as opera stages and altars devoted to local heroes and deities. In some respects, it is these contemporary offices that should be seen as continuing the *di* of ancient times. The late imperial huiguan were voluntary associations, whereas both the *di* that preceded them and the liaison offices that replaced them are more directly tied to civil administration. This indicates the vitality of social networks that existed between state and family during the late imperial period and suggests surprising continuity between the patterns of a more ancient China and the contemporary socialist one. The contemporary liaison

---

13. Zhu Guozhen, *Tong chui xiao pin*, "Ya yu fang wu" section; cited in He Bingdi, *Zhongguo huiguan shilun*, 12–13.

14. He Bingdi, *Zhongguo huiguan shilun*, 11–13.

offices of Beijing share one intriguing characteristic with native-place lodges, namely, the great number of them established in Beijing. In recent years, regional and local governments have rushed to establish this sort of tie to the capital; by the year 2000 there were 53 liaison offices representing higher-level regions such as provinces, special economic zones, and other territories directly under the administration of the central government and 597 offices representing lower-level areas.[15]

Finally, one other government-operated institution that also housed visitors to the capital, although functionally less similar to huiguan than the institutions mentioned above, deserves brief consideration. *Huitongguan* 會同館, or state guesthouses, were found in China's ancient imperial capitals and continued to operate in Beijing during the Yuan (1276–1368) and subsequent dynasties to house tribute missions, foreign diplomatic delegations, and trade missions from other nations. They were established and operated by the imperial government (in contrast to the *jundi*, which were operated by regional governments). Known in earlier times as "halls for barbarians of the four quarters" (*siyi guan* 四夷館), by the thirteenth and fourteenth centuries and thereafter they were known as *huitongguan*.[16] *Huitongguan* were, in theory, gracious expressions of the court's generous hospitality to visiting guests from afar, but in practice, at least during the Ming and Qing periods, they functioned equally as holding quarters for foreign guests. When not engaged in scheduled audiences at court, the foreign dignitaries were forbidden to wander unsupervised from the property, although some trade inevitably developed in the immediate area around the facilities.

Huitongguan-type facilities were generally associated with foreigners, but ethnic Han officials were lodged in those located in the

---

15. *Shijie ribao*, Apr. 15, 2000, Section A, 9.

16. For an informative discussion of this institution during the Mongol period, see Serruys, *Sino-Mongol Relations During the Ming, II: The Tribute System and Diplomatic Missions (1400–1600)*. L. C. Arlington and William Lewisohn (*In Search of Old Peking*, 5) translate *siyi guan* as the "Four Barbarians' Hostel" in reference to the vassal kingdoms of Annam, Burma, Korea, and Mongolia. I prefer the broader translation, since from early on these institutions were employed to host a wide variety of visiting foreign dignitaries; Matteo Ricci, for example, was housed there for a period during his stay in Beijing.

northern capitals during some periods of non-Chinese dynastic rule. The *Luoyang qielan ji* 洛陽伽藍記 by Fan Xiangyong 范祥雍, for example, an account of the author's observations in and around the Northern Wei (386–534) capital of Luoyang, includes a description of what were then called the *siyi guan*. Among them was a residence, the Jinling guan 金陵館, set aside for officials from China's lower Yangzi region who had submitted to the regime.[17] *Huitongguan* operated in Beijing during the century and a half of Mongol rule that preceded the period in which huiguan were founded. So-journers from China proper were never housed in them, however.

Since *huitongguan* served a very different clientele than did *jundi* and huiguan, there is little cause to consider them in relation to native-place lodges. But there is a possible etymological link between the terms *huitongguan* and huiguan. *Huitong* 會同 and *hui* 會 share the sense of meeting, although *huitong* is used more narrowly for persons of high rank. Since the terms are essentially identical semantically and since both refer to institutions designed to serve and house visitors to the capital, it is not unimaginable that the former suggested the latter. On the other hand, the terms may simply represent convergent terminological developments, and their similarity should certainly not be presumed to suggest any institutional connection between *huitongguan* and huiguan.

The Disputed Origins of Native-Place Lodges

Until relatively recently, it was generally supposed that the first native-place lodges in Beijing were established during the sixteenth century. This long-held belief was reflected, if not originally suggested, in a widely read late Ming work, the *Di jing jing wu lüe* 帝京景物略, which maintained: "[As for the] . . . establishment of huiguan in the capital. In ancient times, they did not yet exist. They began during the Jiajing [1522–67] and the Longqing reign periods [1567–73]."[18] The *Di jing jing wu lüe* account is echoed in numerous later statements on this subject, including stele inscriptions com-

---

17. Fan Xiangyong, *Luoyang qielan ji*, 160. I am grateful to Pauline Lin for bringing this passage to my attention.
18. Liu Tong and Yu Yizheng, *Di jing jing wu lüe*, 180–81.

missioned by late Qing and Republican period huiguan themselves. The notion is still occasionally repeated in Chinese-language literature on the subject. We now know, however, that the first native-place lodges were established well before that time.

Early in the fifteenth century, during the Yongle reign period (1403–24), Yu Mou 俞謀, an assistant in the Imperial Board of Works, donated his private residential compound to serve visitors and sojourners from his hometown while in the capital. Yu was a native of the Yangzi port city of Wuhu, in Anhui province.[19] He had just retired from his post and was preparing to return to his native place, when he signed over his property to his compatriots. With this gift, Yu established the Wuhu huiguan 蕪湖會館, and although he remained a historically unremarkable figure in other respects, successive generations of Wuhu gentry kept the memory of this act alive. Five hundred years later, the early twentieth-century edition of the Wuhu district gazetteer printed an account of Yu's largess and the subsequent fortunes of the huiguan he had bequeathed.[20] Yu's gift proved impressively long-lasting, for the lodge remained in operation even then.

Ho Ping-ti, in his classic study of Chinese native-place lodges, *Zhongguo huiguan shilun,* first pointed out the significance of the Wuhu gazetteer account, insofar as it demonstrates that huiguan were established early in the fifteenth century.[21] More recently, Han

---

19. During the Ming, Wuhu was under the jurisdiction of the Nanjing or Nan-Zhili area, administered directly by the court (Anhui province was a Qing creation). Unless otherwise specified, provincial designations given in this study refer to the provinces as they existed in the Qing period. This occasionally results in anachronistic designations, but it is the simplest way to provide readily understood geographical context to the numerous local places discussed.

20. *Wuhu xian zhi* (1919), 13.1–2, 48.6.

21. He Bingdi, *Zhongguo huiguan shilun,* 13–14. The detail and the consistency of the Wuhu district gazetteer seem to confirm its historical veracity. The gazetteer contains two separate relevant accounts. In a biographical section on Yu Mou (*Wuhu xian zhi,* 48.6), Yu's initial appointment to a post in Nanjing in 1403 and his subsequent transfer to a post in Beijing are recorded. The original transfer of ownership, which established the Wuhu huiguan, and a later legal dispute regarding ownership between the family of the original seller and the lodge are discussed. A lengthier account (ibid., 13.1–2) briefly records the founding and sketches the vicissitudes it weathered during its five-hundred-year history.

Dacheng, the Beijing-based historian of Ming China, has shown that Yu Mou's largess was matched by similar undertakings around the same time.[22] At least two other native-place lodges were also established in Beijing during the Yongle reign period. One was the (Jiangxi) Fuliang huiguan 浮梁會館, which was founded by a government clerk. Fuliang, a relatively peripheral and administratively unimportant district, may at first glance seem an unlikely sponsor of such an early lodge, but the foundation may reflect links between bureaucrats in Fuliang and the great porcelain production facilities in Jingdezhen, which is located in that district. The other identifiable Yongle-period lodge was the (Guangdong) Yuedong huiguan 粵東會館, established by a small group of fellow-provincial officials.[23]

Chinese who traveled abroad were as enthusiastic as their counterparts within the country in their adoption of the native-place lodge as a valued and useful institution. Native-place lodges thus became a pervasive feature of Chinese communities outside China, especially in Southeast Asia and Chinese communities in the Americas.[24] It is therefore all the more notable that the first Beijing huiguan were, indeed, the first Chinese huiguan established anywhere. As best as we can presently determine, the earliest native-place lodges founded elsewhere were established about one hundred years after the lodges in Beijing. The (Fujian, Putian) Wenxian

---

22. Han Dacheng, *Mingdai chengshi yanjiu*, 407.

23. Han Dacheng (ibid., 407) cites an 1868 stele inscription, "Chongxiu Guangdong jiu yiyuan ji" (Record of the refurbishing of the old Guangdong graveyard), held by the National History Museum of China to substantiate the Yuedong huiguan founding. I was unable to obtain a copy of that text; however, another stele inscription, "Chongxiu Yuedong jiu guan beiji" (Tablet inscription recording the refurbishment of the old Yuedong huiguan) of 1897, confirms the Yongle founding. The latter inscription is photostatically reproduced in *BJTSGC*, 87: 190.

24. Among the growing body of literature on this subject, see, e.g., Crissman, "The Segmentary Structure of Urban Overseas Chinese Communities"; for Taiwan, see Zhou Zongxian, *Xue nong yu shui de huiguan*; for Singapore, see Freedman, "Immigrants and Associations"; and Lin Xiaojuan, ed., *Xinjiapo huiguan shukan mulu huibian*; and Ng Wing Chung, "Urban Chinese Social Organization: Some Unexplored Aspects in Huiguan Development in Singapore, 1900–1941"; for Brunei, see Rao Shangdong, *Wenlai Huazu huiguan shilun*; on huiguan in American Chinatowns, see Armentrout-Ma, "Urban Chinese on the Sinitic Frontier."

huiguan 文獻會館 and the (Guangdong) Chaozhou huiguan 潮州會館, both founded in Nanjing during the Jiajing reign, are the first known native-place lodges outside Beijing.[25]

Proving that an institution existed by a certain date is one thing; demonstrating that it did not exist before then is more problematic. In contrast to the tradition within Chinese scholarship of the late Ming emergence of huiguan, at one time several influential Western scholars maintained that the institution predates the Yongle period. This notion can be traced in part to a misunderstanding inadvertently passed along from scholar to scholar. Writing in 1886, in what must be the first article about huiguan in a Western language, D. J. MacGowan stated: "Early in the Ming era a Kiangsu Guild (Yen-ling Weikuan [i.e., Yanling huiguan]) flourished at Peking."[26] This statement subsequently informed the work of other influential scholars, including Hosea Ballou Morse, who cited MacGowan in a passage on the establishment of huiguan in the early Ming and then parenthetically provided the year of the Ming founding.[27] Morse's inclusion of the date of the dynastic founding unintentionally confused the issue for some later scholars. Pierre Maybon, mistaking the year the dynasty began for the date the lodge was founded, cited Morse as the basis for his statement that a Jiangsu huiguan had been established in Beijing in 1368.[28] Max Weber, clearly building on a mistaken reading of MacGowan and Morse (he cited both), similarly stated that "hwei-kwan guilds of officials and merchants who derived from other provinces . . . had definitely emerged by the 14th . . . century."[29] However, the lodge MacGowan referred to as the "Yen-ling Weikuan" was certainly the Jinling huiguan 金陵會館, which represented sojourners from Nanjing (see Appendix). MacGowan was correct in attributing to it a Ming-period origin, but no definite date of establishment can be determined. (This lodge

---

25. Lü Zuoxie, "Nanjing huiguan xiao zhi," *Nanjing shi zhi*, 1984, no. 5; cited in Wang Rigen, "Ming-Qing shidai huiguan de yanbian," 50.

26. MacGowan, "Chinese Guilds or Chambers of Commerce and Trade Unions," 135.

27. See Morse, *The Gilds of China* (1909 ed.), 36; (1967 ed.), 42.

28. Maybon, *Essai sur les associations en Chine*, 56.

29. Weber, *The Religion of China*, 17.

appears not to have survived the Ming-Qing transition. No record of it exists from the Qing period.)[30] Without specific evidence that it was founded before the Yongle period, we must consider the suggestion that it was unlikely.

Recent, more popular Chinese-language accounts of huiguan refer to a (Jiangxi) Nanchang huiguan 南昌會館 founded during the Hongwu period (1368–98).[31] This claim can be traced to a governmental report summarizing a survey of Beijing huiguan undertaken by the Civil Administration Bureau of the Beijing Municipal Government in 1949.[32] The report was based on information supplied by representatives of the lodges at that time. However, this claim, too, can be confidently dismissed. The local gazetteer for that county provides a detailed description of the Nanchang huiguan in Beijing.[33] From that source, we know that two Nanchang huiguan were founded in Beijing during the Ming, but during the Longqing-Wanli periods (1567–1620), two centuries after the Hongwu period ended. The detail of the gazetteer account (and lack of it in the 1949 account) leaves little doubt that the claim to an earlier founding is wrong.

Some scholars have claimed the earliest huiguan greatly preceded the first decades of the Ming dynasty. Several Asian scholars earlier in the twentieth century suggested that some merchant organizations established well before the Ming essentially operated as huiguan, although not under that name. That huiguan had merchant origins was an understandable conjecture since most Chinese native-place lodges outside Beijing served in many ways as merchant/handicraft guilds. Ming and Qing merchant/handicraft huiguan often dominated certain trades, known in Chinese as *hang*. These scholars argued that the characteristics of late imperial *hang* organizations could be projected back to the *hang* known only through terse references in much earlier texts. Katō Shigeshi went so far as to suggest that huiguan existed as early as the Tang (618–907)

---

30. Han Dacheng, *Mingdai chengshi yanjiu*, 406.
31. See, e.g., Hu Chunhuan and Bai Hequn, *Beijing de huiguan*, 4.
32. Beijing shi renmin zhengfu, Minzhengju, "1949 nian Beijing huiguan qingkuang diaocha baogao."
33. *Nanchang xian zhi* (1870).

and Song (960–1278) periods (although he later reversed himself).[34] As more work was done, however, it become clear that little evidence supports the premise that these earlier forms were as organized as later, fully formed merchant/handicraft huiguan. True, in later times the term *hang* was applied to organized and self-regulating trades, which frequently did possess corporately owned guildhalls, but as used in earlier periods *hang* does not indicate anything more structured than the widespread pattern of marketing certain types of commodities exclusively along particular lanes of a city or market area. Peter J. Golas has argued convincingly that the institutional links between the earlier and the later forms remain tenuous and that the merchant/handicraft organizations of Ming and Qing China originated no earlier than the mid-Ming period.[35]

As we have seen, all available evidence suggests that merchant/handicraft huiguan were inspired by the native-place lodges first established by scholar-officials. Because of the structuring of traditional China's mercantile economy above the local level along native-place lines, it is not surprising that the merchants would have been quick to adopt this institutional innovation of officials in the capital. In fact, no pre-Ming text, whether stone monument inscription, literary reference, or government proclamation, has come to light that refers to huiguan. Other evidence is the near-total absence of later claims to pre-Yongle origins by the lodges themselves. This is especially notable given a seemingly universal tendency for traditional organizations to bolster their prestige and legitimacy through spurious declarations of ancient beginnings. Lineages, for example, have been known to trace their ancestry to figures of Chinese mythical antiquity.

We may note a comparable example of claims to ancient origins in the *compagnnage*, or journeymen's associations, of France. These appeared at roughly the same time as Yongle-period huiguan, but they claimed to have been founded at various dates ranging from the thirteenth century back to the construction of the Temple of Solo-

---

34. Kato, "On the Hang or the Associations of Merchants in China." For a similar view, see Quan Hansheng, *Zhongguo hanghui zhidu shi*, esp. 3–4, 92–99.
35. Golas, "Early Qing Guilds," 555.

mon in biblical times.[36] Some Chinese merchant/handicraft huiguan
asserted their legitimacy with references to the antiquity of measures
undertaken to regulate their trades, but none of them claimed such
early institutional origins.[37] Besides the claim made in 1949 regarding
the Nanchang huiguan mentioned above, I am aware of only one
claim to pre-Yongle establishment made by a representative of a
Beijing lodge and that, too, is demonstrably spurious. The second
claim was made in a response to a questionnaire distributed to caretakers of hundreds of huiguan during the 1930s by a Yenching university student working on her senior thesis. The respondent
claimed that the (Anhui) Guichi huiguan 貴池會館 was established
during the Hongwu period.[38] No evidence of such an early founding
was given. The earliest textual reference to the Guichi huiguan
known to me is found in a 1788 guide to Beijing.[39] Lack of other
supporting evidence, the pattern of demonstrably incorrect establishment dates for other sites found in this thesis, and the relatively
inhospitable conditions in Beijing during the Hongwu period all
combine to persuasively suggest that the respondent was mistaken.

The most eloquent arguments against the idea that the earliest
native-place lodges were merchant/handicraft lodges predating the
Yongle era are the accounts of the origin of the institution given by
many merchant/handicraft lodges. Many such texts openly profess
the idea that these lodges were inspired by those set up earlier by officials in the capital. A typical example, the "Bylaws of the Ningbo
Guild at Wenzhou," translated by D. J. MacGowan in 1886, states:
"Huiguan were first established [in the capital] by mandarins among
compatriots or fellow provincials. . . . Subsequently, merchants
founded guilds like those of the mandarins."[40] The evidence that the
first Chinese native-place lodges were established by scholar-officials
in Beijing during the Yongle period is thus strong; the next question
to be addressed is why Beijing and why the Yongle period.

---

36. Sewell, *Work and Revolution in France*, 47.
37. MacGowan, "Chinese Guilds or Chambers of Commerce and Trade Unions," 133.
38. Zhang Xiaoxin, "Beiping huiguan diaocha."
39. Wu Changyuan, *Chen yuan shi lüe*, 9.26.
40. MacGowan, "Chinese Guilds or Chambers of Commerce and Trade Unions," 135.

Why Huiguan Emerged When and Where They Did

The Chinese economy went through a great commercial boom and period of economic growth during the late fifteenth and early sixteenth centuries, but the Yongle period was far less exuberant. The Yongle period may seem, therefore, a somewhat unlikely time for an unprecedented institutional development such as the emergence of huiguan. Yet even though the Yongle period was not marked by extraordinary economic growth, it was a period of fundamental political and administrative transformation, and it is this that accounts for the emergence of huiguan at that time.

The Yongle emperor's decision to move the national capital from Nanjing to Beijing substantially transformed the city and, in so doing, created conditions conducive to such an institutional innovation.[41] In the late fourteenth century, the disturbances created by the dynastic transition from the Yuan to the Ming and the designation of Nanjing as the capital by the first Ming emperor left Beijing "desolate and grown over with weeds and brambles . . . deserted."[42] Although Beijing was not formally designated the imperial capital until 1421, the decision to move the capital was made in 1403. The decision was accompanied by massive construction in the city proper and of the transportation infrastructure leading to it. These projects greatly stimulated the local economy and elevated the national importance of the city.

A major influx of population from other regions of China occurred during this time. Shanxi and the Jiangsu/Zhejiang areas were the primary sources of new residents, but sojourners from all parts of China gathered in the new capital.[43] The sudden upsurge in migration to the Beijing area was in part a consequence of measures

---

41. For a detailed examination of Ming urban developments, see Han Dacheng, *Mingdai chengshi yanjiu*. For discussion of Ming Beijing, see Cao Zixi et al., eds., *Beijing tongshi*, vol. 6. See also Geiss, "Peking Under the Ming," esp. chap. 2, "The Making of an Imperial Capital: Peking in the Fifteenth Century," 51–106; and Hok-Lam Chan, "The Chien-wen, Yung-lo, Hung-hsi, and Hsüan-te reigns," esp. 37–44.

42. Geiss, "Peking Under the Ming," 11.

43. Cao Zixi et al., eds., *Beijing tongshi*, 6: 52–53.

taken by the Yongle regime. The government exempted newly tilled land from taxation, for example.[44] And when all else failed, the new emperor ordered the forced relocation and settlement in Beijing of tens of thousands of people from other regions of China during the first years of his rule.[45]

The new migrants most closely associated with the establishing of huiguan, however, were not farmers or prosperous families but officials and bureaucrats from the lower Yangzi region and the southeast, who came to staff the many positions within the imperial government. The number of staff and officials needed in the new capital may be assumed to have been commensurate with the number of bureaucrats of all ranks in Nanjing before the transfer of capitals. F. W. Mote has estimated that the size of the overall imperial bureaucracy resident in and around Nanjing at the end of the fourteenth century consisted of "no fewer than 5,000 of the ranked civil and military officials and 10,000 of the subofficials."[46] Certainly most of these found themselves in Beijing following the transfer of capitals. This shift was reflected in a sudden, massive reduction of the population of Nanjing.[47] It was no accident that the relocation of large numbers of southern Chinese, with their strong tradition of corporate organization, led to the birth of the native-place lodge.

The Distribution of Native-Place Lodges Across China

As we have seen, the native-place lodge was a well-established urban institution by the late Ming period.[48] Sojourners across China continued to construct new huiguan throughout most of the Qing, and the numbers of lodges increased until the destruction wrought by

---

44. Ibid.
45. Li Guoxiang et al., eds., *Ming shilu leizuan: Beijing shiliao juan,* 18–19.
46. Mote, "The Transformation of Nanking," 139.
47. Ibid., 150.
48. Works on huiguan in specific cities (other than Beijing, which is discussed in subsequent chapters) also have general implications; see, e.g., Negishi Tadashi, *Shanhai no girudo*; Rowe, *Hankow: Conflict and Community*; and the work of Bryna Goodman on the native-place organizations of Shanghai, including "New Culture, Old Habits," "The Native-Place and the City," and *Native Place, City, and Nation.*

the mid-nineteenth-century rebellions resulted in the devastation of many cities and the consequent abandonment of many lodges. Some of those lodges were never restored, but most did eventually reopen. In addition, many new lodges were established during the 1870s and after. All indications are that the total number of native-place lodges in China reached new heights by the turn of the twentieth century. It is impossible to track with any degree of precision exactly how many huiguan were founded in China around that time. But we can get a rough sense of how many native-place lodges existed, who built them, and where they were located during the late nineteenth and early twentieth centuries. This knowledge gives us insight into patterns of sojourning during this period, and, so far as this study is concerned, it illuminates the ways Beijing huiguan were or were not unusual.

Ho Ping-ti initiated the effort to get some sense of the numbers of native-place lodges in China. Ho consulted over 3,000 local gazetteers produced in a wide array of Chinese counties and prefectures during the nineteenth and early twentieth centuries in order to track references to native-place lodges. As a result of his efforts, Ho was able to identify, in a pathbreaking achievement, some 800 huiguan located in cities other than Beijing.[49]

I have found that the *Shina shōbetsu zenshi* 支那省別全誌 both confirms and significantly adds to Ho's findings.[50] The eighteen volumes of this rich Japanese work compile information gathered by researchers in the field in the first decades of the twentieth century. It reveals the existence of a good number of lodges not recorded in the gazetteers on which Ho relied. When we combine Ho's findings with those of the *Shina shōbetsu zenshi*, we find that native-place lodges had been established in over 300 different Chinese cities and towns. The places that served as hosts to native-place lodges ranged the full gamut of urban types, from provincial capitals with relatively little commercial activity (e.g., Wuchang) to commercial centers administratively ranked only as townships (Hankou

---

49. Ho Ping-ti refers to having "browsed" this number of gazetteers; see He Bingdi, *Zhongguo huiguan shilun*, 69; and idem, "The Geographic Distribution of Hui-Kuan," 37–99, 125.

50. Tōa Dōbunkai, *Shina shōbetsu zenshi*.

and Foshan); in some areas, especially Sichuan, even smaller, commercially less important towns boasted huiguan. Huiguan had been
established in great numbers as well. By the most conservative estimate, there were more than 2,000 native-place lodges, *not including* those located in Beijing.[51] Huiguan clearly had become as
common a feature of the Chinese urban setting as city walls and
ceremonial arches.

Although native-place lodges were established in cities and towns
across China, they were not evenly distributed. To take one dramatic difference as an example, there were well over five hundred
lodges in Sichuan by the late nineteenth century, but in the province
of Jilin we have evidence of only one (see Fig. 2.1).[52] It is possible
that there were several more, or even dozens of huiguan in Jilin, but
an undeniable pattern remains. The greatest numbers of native-place
lodges were established in the provinces along the Yangzi River, and
the northern provinces in general tend to have had significantly
fewer huiguan.

Ho Ping-ti has suggested that the simpler, more crudely produced
local gazetteers from the northern provinces might distort the record and exaggerate the differences. But the *Shina shōbetsu zenshi*
figures were derived from data collected in the field, not documentary evidence, and are thus immune to such bias. Even allowing for
some possible distortion, it is clear the practice of establishing
native-place lodges was *far* more common in Sichuan than in Jilin (if
not necessarily at a 500:1 ratio). This underlying pattern is confirmed by the sweeping geographic area represented by the single
recorded Jilin lodge, which represented natives from the five provinces of Zhili, Shandong, Henan, Shanxi, and Shaanxi.

---

51. Scholars have tended to underestimate the number of huiguan established in
China outside Beijing. L. Eve Armentrout-Ma ("Fellow-Regional Associations in
the Ch'ing Dynasty," 308), for instance, estimates over 800 lodges. James Cole
("Competition and Cooperation") also cites that figure.

52. For a list of the native-place lodges established in cities other than Beijing, see
Belsky, "Beijing Scholar-Official Native Place Lodges," Appendix One, 285–340; see
also ibid., 5–6, for further discussion of the significance of these findings. The figure
of 500 is a conservative count that ignores many multiple lodges established in one
particular place by the sojourners of the same area. If all multiple lodges for which
we have records were included, the figure for Sichuan would top 800.

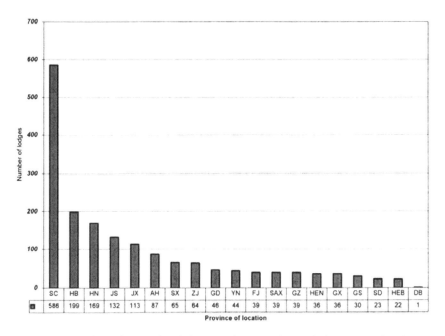

Fig. 2.1 Numbers of native-place lodges outside Beijing during the late Qing and early Republican periods, by provincial location of lodges (SOURCES: He Bingdi, *Zhongguo huiguan shilun*; Tōa dōbunkai, *Shina shōbetsu zenshi*).

Key

AH: Anhui	GS: Gansu	JX: Jiangxi
DB: Dongbei	GZ: Guizhou	SAX: Shaanxi
(NE provinces)	HB: Hubei	SC: Sichuan
FJ: Fujian	HEB: Hebei	SD: Shandong
FT: Fengtian	HEN: Henan	SX: Shanxi
GD: Guangdong	HN: Hunan	YN: Yunnan
GX: Guangxi	JS: Jiangsu	ZJ: Zhejiang

The five provinces represented by the Jilin lodge covered an extraordinarily broad sweep of territory, but this was not unique. Lodges in Xiangtan in Hunan and Zhenjiang in Jiangsu represented the same five provinces as the lodge in Jilin. Nor was this even the largest territory represented by a single lodge. A lodge in Guilin in Guangxi served the "seven northern provinces" (I have not determined which seven), and a lodge in the town of Weiyuan in Sichuan, the "Six-Province" huiguan, is said to have served merchants from eight different provinces! The existence of lodges called on to serve such a great swath of territory indicates that those who hailed from those areas were not otherwise well served. Had more lodges been established in Jilin or these other places, it would have been unnecessary for a single lodge to represent such a vast area.

The extraordinary number of native-place lodges in Sichuan is something of an anomaly. It reflects the widespread establishment of native-place lodges by the many rural migrants to the province (as opposed to the merchant sojourners more commonly associated with huiguan). The substantially different clientele of these lodges, both in terms of class and in terms of their relationship to the local area (migrant rather than sojourner), does mean that these huiguan differed in form and function from those typically found elsewhere. Thus the Sichuan figures are not representative of huiguan patterns elsewhere and need to be treated cautiously.

Even if we disregard the lodges in Sichuan, the pattern of significant regional diversity remains. Far more lodges were found in the provinces of the central Yangzi region than elsewhere. Next to Sichuan, Hubei hosted the greatest number of huiguan (199), followed by Hunan, Jiangsu, and Jiangxi; Anhui, with 87 huiguan, trailed somewhat further behind. Numbers for the other provinces ranged from 65 in Shanxi to 22 in Zhili (not including Beijing).

In addition to variations in the spatial distribution of huiguan, there were also differences in the frequency with which sojourners from different provinces established lodges. Figure 2.2 provides a breakdown of the numbers of lodges established by men of different provincial origins. Since I am interested here in the relative tendency of sojourners from different areas to participate in the establishment and operation of a lodge, whether it served them exclusively or not, I have counted only those lodges for which an area of representation could be confidently determined. In those cases where one lodge served two or more provinces, I have credited each province with one lodge; a lodge that served both Hubei and Hunan people, for example, is counted as one lodge for Hubei and one for Hunan.

The figure clearly shows that sojourners from the mid-Yangzi provinces of Jiangxi, Hubei, and Hunan were most likely to establish huiguan. Men from other southern provinces, such as Fujian,

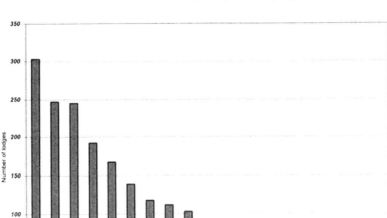

Fig. 2.2   Numbers of native-place lodges outside Beijing during the late Qing and early Republican periods, by provincial origin of sojourners; for the key to province abbreviations,
see Fig. 2.1, p. 37 (SOURCES: He Bingdi, *Zhongguo huiguan shilun*; Tōa dōbunkai, *Shina shōbetsu
zenshi*).

Guangdong, Anhui, and Zhejiang, were also enthusiastic founders.
Lodges were far less frequently established by those hailing from
northern provinces such as Shandong, Zhili, or Gansu and the
provinces of the northeast (Dongbei), or from peripheral southern
provinces such as Yunnan or Guangxi.

What accounts for the dramatically different rates at which the
sojourners of different provinces established native-place lodges?
There is no single, clear-cut answer. My sense is that two separate
factors might be at work. One is that men of the lower Yangzi and
the southeastern provinces may have engaged in domestic sojourning in greater numbers than did those from other areas. It
would be difficult, perhaps impossible, to estimate the relative
numbers of sojourners from different regions in late imperial China.
It certainly lies beyond the scope of this study to attempt such a feat,

but it is easy to imagine a range of factors (access to water routes, the destruction wreaked by the Taiping Rebellion and its suppression, relatively greater economic development in the region as a whole, the existence of native-place networks established by fellow landsmen who had earlier struck out from the local area, and so on) that might have resulted in larger numbers of sojourners from Jiangxi and Hunan than from Gansu and Guizhou "abroad" in China. But it is likely that cultural variation was also a significant factor. It seems probable, for instance, that those from regions in which corporate lineage formation was a more developed custom would have found the corporate native-place lodge a more comfortable and "natural" social institution. I think it is likely that the tendency of sojourners to establish native-place lodges also loosely corresponds to differing rates of corporate lineage formation in their native places.

One interesting variation in the pattern dividing the northern and southern provinces is the relative proclivity of Shanxi, and to a somewhat lesser extent Shaanxi, sojourners to establish huiguan. Although the pattern of northern people founding fewer huiguan than southern people is still valid, it would be a much starker pattern were it not for the relatively large number of men from these two northern provinces to establish lodges. The Shanxi case is especially interesting because men from within that province founded over 80 percent of the huiguan in Shanxi. The sojourners of Shanxi, or at least those that built native-place lodges, came mostly from other parts of Shanxi. No other province exhibits anything like that pattern; outside Shanxi less than 20 percent of the lodges in any given province tended to have been founded by sojourners from within that province. Guangdong ranks second to Shanxi in this regard, with almost 40 percent of the lodges in that province established by Guangdong natives but in a number of provinces, such as Guangxi, Henan, Fengtian, and Zhili, none of the known lodges was established by local provincials. Although this does not answer the deeper question of why Shanxi people stood out among northerners in their lodge-building habits, it is clear that the relatively great number of lodges they established reflected (and perhaps significantly contributed to) the prominence of Shanxi merchants throughout China.

THREE

The Particular Characteristics

of Beijing Scholar-Official

Native-Place Lodges

The Extraordinary Number of
Native-Place Lodges in Beijing

One of the most notable special characteristics of Beijing huiguan is that there had long been so many of them. Before the fall of the Ming dynasty in the mid-seventeenth century, no fewer than 70 huiguan had been established in the capital (see Appendix). Given the paucity of records, it is probable that the actual figure was significantly greater. This is an extraordinary number of lodges for such an early period. No other location at that time came close to hosting so many lodges; indeed, similar numbers of huiguan would not be established in the great commercial centers of the lower

Yangzi, such as Suzhou, Wuhan, and Shanghai, until several centuries later.[1] This unparalleled early proliferation of lodges notwithstanding, the number of huiguan in Beijing continued to expand many times over during the course of the Qing period.

The transition from Ming to Qing rule in the mid-seventeenth century ushered in a period of stalled growth and even a brief reduction in numbers of Beijing huiguan, due in large measure to direct state intervention. When in 1648 the Manchu regent Dorgon banned ethnic Chinese from residing in the Inner City, the result was the loss of many huiguan properties.[2] However, the institution recovered relatively rapidly. Comprehensive information for the early Qing is sparse, but extant stele inscriptions and other texts attest to numerous huiguan foundings through the Kangxi (1662–1722) and Yongzheng (1723–35) periods (see Table 3.1 for a list of lodges founded during the early Qing period to 1735.

During the Qianlong period (1736–95) the number of foundings in Beijing increased greatly. The first comprehensive accounting of huiguan is found in the rich eighteenth-century source on Beijing, the *Chen yuan shi lüe* (Sketches of the imperial enclosure). Table 3.2 lists the 174 native-place lodges in Beijing recorded in that work. As remarkable as this figure is, the *Chen yuan shi lüe* did not record all the lodges that existed in Beijing at that time. In Table 3.3, I list additional huiguan established by the end of the eighteenth century whose existence we can trace through other sources. The combined total indicates that at least 220 native-place lodges had been established in the capital before the turn of the nineteenth century. What accounts for this exceptional proliferation of lodges? Surely, the

---

1. For Suzhou, see Lü Zuoxie, "Ming-Qing shi Suzhou de huiguan he gongsuo." Lu lists 48 institutions organized along obvious native-place lines and 82 *gongsuo*, many of which may well have had some degree of native-place structure. The best attempt to identify individual and merchant associations in Shanghai is Xu Dingxin, "Shanghai gongshang tuanti de jindaihua," 512–13, 518–22. The figures for Beijing are discussed in more detail below. For other cities, see Belsky, "Beijing Scholar-Official Native-Place Lodges," Appendix One.

2. *Qing shilu*, 40:465, edict dated Oct. 5, 1648. For a contemporary account of the loss of property as a result of this edict from the point of view of the native-place associations, see Guo Chunshu, *Bing lu riji*, 15b. For the effect of this edict on the location of lodges, see Chapter 4.

demographic and economic growth of the period, coupled with relative social and political stability, contributed to the unprecedented flourishing of this institution, but it is equally clear that nowhere else in the empire had the institution of native-place lodges developed to this extent. By the late Qianlong period, the development of lodges as a medium of interaction between locality and the imperial center had matured to the point that localities around the empire recognized the value of establishing a lodge in the capital. As Fig. 3.1 shows, not all regions established lodges in equal numbers. Jiangxi and the other provinces of the lower Yangzi and China's southeast, as well as Shanxi and Shaanxi, established the most lodges, whereas the more peripheral provinces such as Guizhou and Yunnan and the northern provinces established far fewer.

The number of huiguan in Beijing continued to increase up to the late nineteenth and early twentieth centuries. Some idea of the unsurpassed number of huiguan operating in the capital at that time may be obtained through a brief survey of several comprehensive Beijing guidebooks and gazetteers. In the mid-1880s the earliest editions of the *Jing shi fang xiang zhi* 京師坊巷志 (Gazetteer of the wards and lanes of the capital), compiled by the cashiered imperial censor Zhu Yixin 朱一新 (1846–94) and Miao Quansun 繆荃孫 (1844–1919), gave the names and locations of some 396 huiguan, 53 of which were said to have been abandoned by that time (leaving a total of 343 extant).[3] A similar number was recorded two decades later. The 1907 edition of the Beijing reference book *Xinzeng dumen jilüe* (A newly augmented, brief account of the capital) listed a total of 385 native-place lodges (see Table 3.4).[4] A 1917 edition of the *Jing shi fang xiang zhi* upped the total to 417 huiguan, of which it claimed 51 had been abandoned (leaving 366 extant).[5] And Sidney Gamble's

---

3. Zhu Yixin and Miao Quansun, *Jing shi fang xiang zhi gao*; and idem, "Jing shi zhi: fang xiang" in *Guangxu Shuntian fu zhi* (Guangxu edition of the Shuntian prefecture gazetteer); with minor variations the two lists are the same. See also the third chapter of He Bingdi, *Zhongguo huiguan shilun*, 23–36, which is given over almost entirely to a list of Beijing huiguan recorded in various early versions of this work.

4. Yang Jingting, ed., *Xinzeng dumen jilüe*, rev. and aug. Xu Yongnian et al.

5. Zhu Yixin and Miao Quansun, *Jing shi fang xiang zhi* (1918).

Table 3.1
Documented Native-Place Lodge Foundings in Beijing During the
Early Qing (Shunzhi through Yongzheng periods)

Lodge	Location	Established
Shunzhi period (1644–61)		
(Henan) Zhongzhou laoguan	Luomashi dajie	SZ 14 (1657)
(Shanxi) Wenxi huiguan	Ganlüshi hutong	SZ period
(Shanxi) Quwo huiguan	Luomashi dajie	SZ 4 (1647)
Kangxi period (1662–1722)		
(Fujian) Anxi huiguan	Ban zhang hutong	KX 54 (1715)
(Fujian) Jianning huiguan	Nan liu xiang	before KX 4 (1665)
(Guangdong) Chaozhou xiguan	Haibo sijie	KX 5 (1666)
*(Guangdong) Xiancheng huiguan	Wangpi hutong	KX 51 (1712)
(Jiangsu) Jiangning huiguan	Nanbanjie hutong	early KX
(Jiangsu) Kunxin huiguan	Xiao Shatuyuan	KX period
*(Jiangsu) Yuanning dongguan	Changxiang xiasantiao hutong	KX 22 (1683)
(Shaanxi) Huazhou huiguan	Nan liu xiang	by KX 48 (1709)
(Shaanxi) Pucheng huiguan	Tielaoguan miao	KX 10 (1671)
(Shanxi) Sanjin dongguan	Luomashi dajie	KX 6 (1667)
*(Zhejiang) Quan-Zhe huiguan	Xiaxie jie	by KX period
(Zhejiang) Xiaoshan huiguan	Xihe yan	by KX period
(Zhejiang) Zhe Shao xiang ci	Xi Zhushi kou dajie	KX 19 (1680)
*(Zhejiang) Zhengyi ci	Xihe yan	KX 6 (1667)
Yongzheng period (1723–35)		
(Fujian) Zhangzhou huiguan	Meishi jie	YZ 4 (1726)
(Gansu) Liangzhou huiguan	Da wailang ying	YZ period
(Jiangsu) Yuanning huiguan	Lanmian hutong	YZ 5 (1727)
(Jiangxi) Nanchang huiguan	Xuanwumen wai dajie	YZ 2 (1724)
(Shaanxi) Yulin huiguan	Qian qing chang	by YZ period
*(Shanxi) Foushan huiguan	Yao'er hutong	YZ 7 (1729)
*(Shanxi) Hedong huiguan	Guang'anmen dajie	YZ 5 (1727)
*(Shanxi) Jinyi huiguan	Xiao Jiangjia hutong	YZ 10 (1732)
(Shanxi) Yicheng huiguan	Hufang qiao	YZ 10 (1732)
(Zhejiang) Wenzhou laoguan	Bingjiao hutong	YZ period

* Indicates a lodge that served a primarily merchant/trade clientele.
NOTE: Li Zhi et al., eds., *Beijing shi Xuanwu qu diming zhi*, 465, gives the Ming Tianqi period (1621–27) as the date of the founding of the Huazhou huiguan. However, no source is cited. A claim of Ming-period origins is also found in the official registration submitted by the lodge to the municipal government in 1947, but it is noted that no extant proof of the claim existed at

that time; see "1947 nian gesheng huiguan zong dengji biao," in Beijing shi dang'anguan, ed., *Beijing huiguan dang'an shiliao*, 1044. The stele cited below establishes the existence of the lodge by the Kangxi period, but it does not discuss the huiguan's origins.
SOURCES: Wenxi: Li Zhi et al., eds., *Beijing shi Xuanwu qu diming zhi*, 476; Quwo: *BJTSGC*, 71: 163; Anxi: *Minzhong huiguan zhi*, "Anxi huiguan," 1; Jianning: *Minzhong huiguan zhi*, "Jianning huiguan," 1a–9a; Chaozhou: *Lüping Chaozhou tongxiang lu*, n.p.; Xiancheng: *BJTSGC*, 83: 1; Li Hua, ed. and comp., *Ming-Qing yilai Beijing gongshang huiguan beike xuanbian*, 15–16; Jiangning: *BJTSGC*, 84: 149; Kunxin: Li Zhi et al., eds., *Beijing shi Xuanwu qu diming zhi*, 479; Yuanning: "Jian Yuanning huiguan ji," in Niida, *Pekin kōshō girudo*, 857–58; see also *BJTSGC*, 68: 58; Sanjin: *BJTSGC*, 62: 85; Huazhou: *BJTSGC*, 66: 135; Pucheng: Li Zhi et al., eds., *Beijing shi Xuanwu qu diming zhi*, 474; Quan-Zhe: *BJTSGC*, 68: 133; Xiaoshan: Li Zhi et al., eds., *Beijing shi Xuanwu qu diming zhi*, 476; Zhe Shao xiang ci: "Chongxiu Zhe Shao xiang ci huiguan beiji (1713), in Beijing shi dang'anguan, ed., *Beijing huiguan dang'an shiliao*, 1317–18; Zheng Yi ci: "Chongxiu Zheng Yi ci beiji," in Li Hua, ed. and comp., *Ming-Qing yilai Beijing gongshang huiguan beike xuanbian*, 11–12; Zhangzhou: *Longyan xian zhi* (1920), 6.16b–18; Liangzhou: Li Zhi et al., eds., *Beijing shi Xuanwu qu diming zhi*, 471; Yuanning: *BJTSGC*, 68: 58; see also *BJTSGC*, 77: 59, 77: 52, and 77: 59; Nanchang: Wang Shiren et al., *Xuannan hongxue tuzhi*, 153; Yulin: Li Zhi et al., eds., *Beijing shi Xuanwu qu diming zhi*, 465; Foushan: *BJTSGC*, 72: 129; confirmed in *BJTSGC*, 91: 61; Hedong: *BJTSGC*, 71: 174; Li Hua, ed. and comp., *Ming-Qing yilai Beijing gongshang huiguan beike xuanbian*, 46–50; Jinyi: *BJTSGC*, 79: 160, 93:75; see also Li Hua, ed. and comp., *Ming-Qing yilai Beijing gongshang huiguan beike xuanbian*, 19–30; Yicheng: *BJTSGC*, 93: 75; Wenzhou: Li Zhi et al., eds., *Beijing shi Xuanwu qu diming zhi*, 462–63; Hu Chunhuan and Bai Hequn, *Beijing de huiguan*, 276.

Peking: A Social Survey, published in 1921, provided a count of 413 huiguan (see Table 3.5).[6] These sources testify to the extraordinary number of native-place lodges in Beijing in the late nineteenth and early twentieth centuries. There are obvious discrepancies between the sources, and it is simply not possible to resolve all the contradictions, not the least because the available primary source materials are incomplete and conflicting. Prosperous huiguan left ample documentation of their existence in printed gazetteers, stele inscriptions, contemporary accounts, and other such texts. For these associations there is a wealth of information. But documentation on the majority of the huiguan is sparse, and too often, little or nothing remains.[7]

Even government attempts to determine the number of lodges in Beijing fell well short of perfect coverage. A government-sponsored

---

6. Gamble, *Peking: A Social Survey*, 232–33.

7. At the very least, all lodges would have generated land deeds recording the purchase of property, which would have been filed at the district yamen. Unfortunately no repository of Beijing land deeds still exists. Copies of deeds are preserved in the records of certain lodges. For more detail, see Chapter 5.

Table 3.2
Native-Place Lodges in Beijing Recorded in *Chen yuan shi lüe* (1788)

Province	Provincial	Prefectural	Sub-prefectural (*zhou/xian*)	Sub-total
Zhili	2	2	0	4
Shandong	2	2	0	4
Shanxi	3	3	14	20
Henan	2	0	0	2
Jiangsu	0	4	7	11
Anhui	0	1	14	15
Zhejiang	2	3	11	16
Jiangxi	1	10	26	37
Hunan	0	6	2	8
Hubei	1	2	8	11
Shaanxi	1	3	12	16
Guangdong	1	9	2	12
Guangxi	2	0	0	2
Sichuan	1	0	0	1
Guizhou	3	0	0	3
Yunnan	2	0	0	2
Fujian	0	4	5	9
Fengtian	1	0	0	1
TOTAL	24	49	101	174

NOTE: Observant readers will discern minor discrepancies between the tally presented here and the table presented by Naquin of lodges, which is also based on *Chen yuan shi lüe*. Naquin calculates different provincial subtotals in some cases and derives an overall total of 181 lodges. The difference in overall totals results largely from Naquin's inclusion of eleven "miscellaneous lodges" with no native-place orientation. I have included only lodges organized according to native-place ties. The marginally different provincial subtallies provided by Naquin and myself no doubt derive from Wu's listing of the lodges by name only, which leaves it to later scholars to assign provincial status. Since the minor discrepancies between Naquin's calculation and my own are inconsequential, I leave it to others to reconcile the difference.
SOURCE: Wu Changyuan, *Chen yuan shi lüe*, see esp. 581–83 (9.26a–27a), and 678–80 (10.45b–46b).

Table 3.3
Eighteenth-Century Huiguan in Beijing Not Recorded in *Chen yuan shi lüe*

Anhui

Shexian huiguan: on Xuanwumenwai dajie; established 1741. An earlier site was located near Caishikou during the Ming dynasty. In 1560, the lodge moved to a site west of Qianmen. The 1741 date represents the establishment of the lodge on Xuanwumenwai dajie.

Yixian huiguan: on Nan banjie hutong; established 1794.

Fujian

Longyan huiguan: on Shitou hutong; established 1772.

Puyang huiguan: on Chongxing si hutong; established during the Ming period.

Quanjun huiguan: on Housun gongyuan; established 1744.

Tongan yiguan: on Banzhang hutong; established 1757.

Yan-Shao huiguan: on Yingzi hutong; established 1739.

Zhangzhou dongguan: on Bingjiao hutong; established during the Ming.

Zhangzhou xiguan: on Meishi jie; established 1726.

Guangdong

Chaozhou nanguan: on Shengjiang hutong; established 1740.

Chaozhou xiguan: on Haibo sijie; established 1666.

Shaozhou huiguan: on Da Jiangjia hutong; established ca. 1768.

Xiancheng huiguan: on Wangpi hutong; established 1712.

Henan

Zhongzhou xiang ci: on Shang xiejie; established during the Ming Wanli period (1573–1619).

Hubei

Tianmen huiguan: on Xuanwumenwai dajie; established during the Qianlong period.

Hunan

Changde huiguan: on Gao miao; established during the Ming Wanli period (1573–1619).

Jiangsu

Jiangning huiguan: on Nan banjie hutong; established during the early Kangxi period. Originally established as the Shang-Jiang huiguan serving the cities of Shangyuan and Jiangning. In 1877 the name was changed to Jiangning junguan to reflect representation of all of Jiangning prefecture.

Kunxin huiguan: on Xiao shatuyuan; established during the Kangxi period.

Jiangxi

Fuzhou xinguan: on Xianglu ying toutiao hutong; established 1784.

Ji'an erzhong ci: on Chaoshou hutong; established 1576.

Table 3.3, *cont.*

Jiangxi, *cont.*

Nanchang dongguan: on Changxiang shang sitiao hutong; established during the Ming Longqing–Wanli periods (1567–1619).

Poyang huiguan: on Weiran hutong; established 1777.

Tiezhu gong: on Damo chang; established during the Ming Jiajing period (1522–66).

Xincheng xiguan: also known as Lichuan huiguan and Lichuan xinguan; on Chunshu toutiao hutong; established 1780.

Xinjian dongguan: on Changxiang xia toutiao hutong; established during the Ming.

Yongxin huiguan: on Jiaochang toutiao hutong; established during the Qianlong period.

Shaanxi

Guanzhong nanguan; on Baoan sijie; established by the Qianlong period.

Jingyang xinguan: on Jiaochang wutiao hutong; established during the Qianlong period.

Sanyuan xinguan: on Jiaochang toutiao hutong; established 1781.

Yulin huiguan: on Qianqing chang; established by the Yongzheng period.

Shandong

Ji'nan huiguan: on Lanmian hutong; established before the Qianlong period in another location and relocated during the Qianlong period.

Shanxi

Shanxi huiguan: also known as the Shanyou huiguan; on Mingyin sijie; established 1772.

Wenxi huiguan: on Ganlüshi; established during the Shunzhi period.

Taiping huiguan: on Nantangzi hutong; established 1739.

Linxiang huiguan: on Xiaoshi dajie; established in the Ming.

Linfen xiguan: on Dashalanr; established in the Ming (*Chen yuan shi lüe* lists a Linfen huiguan on Damochang, also established during the Ming, but multiple sources indicate that these are actually two sites).

Quwo huiguan: on Luomashi dajie; established 1647.

Pingyao huiguan: also known as the Yanliao huiguan; on Bei Lucaoyuan; established during the Ming.

Xiangling huiguan: on Shejia hutong; founded during the late Ming, as a site for banquets and to lodge examination candidates and scholars and officials. During the dynastic transition was briefly abandoned and occupied by others; reclaimed in 1646. The site then went through a long period of decline exacerbated by an earthquake in 1679, which left it half in ruins. The site was refurbished in 1685 and refurbished again during the Xianfeng / early Tongzhi periods.

Xijin huiguan: established in 1766. A somewhat unusual example, it was trade-related and located outside the city walls in the northwestern district of Haidian; it appears to be more of a cemetery than a lodge.

Sichuan

Tongchuan huiguan: on Bei banjie hutong; established during the Qianlong period.

Zhejiang

Jiaxing huiguan: on Nanheng jie; established during the Qianlong period. Also known as the Jiaxing liuyi guan; many sources list the two names as separate *huiguan*, but stele inscriptions and the like indicate that there was only one lodge.

Wenzhou laoguan: on Bingjiao hutong; established during the Yongzheng period.

Xiaoshan huiguan: on Xihe yan; established during the Kangxi period.

Yuyao xiang ci: on Houtie chang; established during the Ming Jiajing period (1522–66).

Zhengyi ci: also known as Yinhao huiguan; established by Shaoxing bankers in 1667.

Zhe-Yan huiguan: also known as Yanzhou huiguan; on Nanwulao hutong; established by 1795.

SOURCES: Changde: *Changde fu zhi* (1813), 8.24–25; Chaozhou nanguan: *Lüping Chaozhou tongxiang lu*; Chaozhou xiguan: *Lüping Chaozhou tongxiang lu*; Fuzhou: *BJTSGC*, 77: 112; Guanzhong: Li Hua, ed. and comp., *Ming-Qing yilai Beijing gongshang huiguan beike xuanbian*, lists it as having been founded during the Ming period and cites four stele inscriptions (but does not provide texts); Li Zhi et al., eds., *Beijing shi Xuanwu qu diming zhi*, 466–67, claims this site was not established until 1761; Ji'an erzhong: *Ji'an fu zhi* (1870), 49.3–4b; the Ming-period founding is confirmed in *Jiangxi huiguan jilüe*, 51a–b; Jiangning: *BJTSGC*, 84.149; Jiaxing: *BJTSGC*, 91.141 (Shen Defu, *Wanli yehuo bian*, 24.608–9, records the establishment of a Jiaxing huiguan during the Ming Wanli period but does not give a location); Ji'nan: Li Zhi et al., eds., *Beijing shi Xuanwu qu diming zhi*, 464; Jingyang: Li Zhi et al., eds., *Beijing shi Xuanwu qu diming zhi*, 474; Kunxin: Li Zhi et al., eds., *Beijing shi Xuanwu qu diming zhi*, 479; Linfen: Li Hua, ed. and comp., *Ming-Qing yilai Beijing gongshang huiguan beike xuanbian*, "Qianyan," 2; 106–7; Linxiang: "Chongxiu Linxiang huiguan luocheng ji," in Niida, *Pekin kōshō girudo*, 2: 176–77; see also Li Hua, ed. and comp., *Ming-Qing yilai Beijing gongshang huiguan beike xuanbian*, "Qianyan," 2; Longyan: Li Zhi et al., eds., *Beijing shi Xuanwu qu diming zhi*, 460–61; *Minzhong huiguan zhi*, "Longyan huiguan," 3a, confirms QL founding; Nanchang: *Nanchang xian zhi* (1870), 2.7–10b; Pingyao: Li Hua, ed. and comp., *Ming-Qing yilai Beijing gongshang huiguan beike xuanbian*, "Qianyan," p. 2; Poyang: *Poyang xian zhi* (1824), 8.8b–9; Puyang: *Minzhong huiguan zhi*, "Puyang huiguan," 1a–9; Quanjun: *Beiping Fujian Quanjun huiguan zhi*, 1; Quwo: *BJTSGC*, 71: 163; Li Hua, ed. and comp., *Ming-Qing yilai Beijing gongshang huiguan beike xuanbian*, "Qianyan," p. 2; Shanxi: *BJTSGC*, 73: 72; Sanyuan: *BJTSGC*, 74: 95; Shaozhou: *BJTSGC*, 83: 137; Shexian: Terada, Takanobu, "Guanyu Beijing Shexian huiguan"; *Shexian huiguan lu*; Niida, *Pekin kōshō girudo*, 6: 1165–75; Taiping: *BJTSGC*, 72: 78; Tianmen: Li Zhi et al., eds., *Beijing shi Xuanwu qu diming zhi*, 464; Tiezhu gong: Zhu Yixin et al., *Jing shi fang xiang zhi* (*JSFXZ*), 8.2; Zhu Yixin et al., *Jing shi fang xiang zhi gao* (*JSFXZG*), 208; Tongan: *Beiping Fujian Quanjun huiguan zhi*, 1 (the *Tongan xian zhi* [1928], 40.9b–10, includes two stele inscription texts written by the founder Chen Lusheng; they record that the lodge was originally founded during the Ming period. After 1648 the lodge moved to a site outside the Chongwen Gate. Eventually that site was also lost. The founding of a new site was proposed in 1736, but establishment was not accomplished until Chen donated a residential compound in 1746); Tongchuan: Li Zhi et al., eds., *Beijing shi Xuanwu qu diming zhi*, 476 (this dating is based on this site's having been the private residence of the famous scholar Meng Shao [*jinshi*

(SOURCES for Table 3.3, *cont.*)
1760]. Meng was a native of Zhongjiang county in Tongchuan prefecture, and it is a fair assumption that he transferred the property to the lodge, perhaps at retirement, which was a common pattern); Wenxi: Li Zhi et al., eds., *Beijing shi Xuanwu qu diming zhi*, 476; Wenzhou: Li Zhi et al., eds., *Beijing shi Xuanwu qu diming zhi*, 462–63; Hu Chunhuan and Bai Hequn, *Beijing de huiguan*, 276; Xiancheng: *BJTSGC*, 83: 1; Li Hua, ed. and comp., *Ming-Qing yilai Beijing gongshang huiguan beike xuanbian*, 15–16; Xiangling: *Xiangling xian zhi* (1881), 24(b).11b–14a, 24(c).23b–24; Xiaoshan: Li Zhi et al., eds., *Beijing shi Xuanwu qu diming zhi*, 476; Xijin: *BJTSGC*, 72: 158; Xincheng: *Xincheng xian zhi* (1871), 2.8a–10a; Xinjian: *Xinjian xian zhi* (1871), 18.7b–12a; Yanshao: Li Hua, ed. and comp., *Ming-Qing yilai Beijing gongshang huiguan beike xuanbian*, "Qianyan," p. 5; Yixian: *Yixian zhi* (1870),. 15.84–85; *Huizhou fu zhi* (1827), 3.88; Yongxin: *Yongxin lüjing tongxianghui kan*, 3 (according to Li Zhi et al., eds., *Beijing shi Xuanwu qu diming zhi*, 458–59, this site was sold in 1867 and property on Bingma ci purchased the next year); Yulin: Li Zhi et al., eds., *Beijing shi Xuanwu qu diming zhi*, 465; Yuyao: *JSFXZ*, 10.18b; *JSFXZG*, 253 (these sources note that a stele from KX 60 (1721) recording the original establishment date existed on the premises in the last decades of the nineteenth century); Zhangzhou dongguan: *Minzhong huiguan zhi*, "Zhangzhou huiguan," p. 1; Zhangzhou xiguan; *Longyan xian zhi*, 6.16b–18; Zheng Yi: "Chongxiu Zheng Yi ci beiji," in Li Hua, ed. and comp., *Ming-Qing yilai Beijing gongshang huiguan beike xuanbian*, 11–12; Zheyan: Li Zhi et al., eds., *Beijing shi Xuanwu qu diming zhi*, 456; Zhongzhou xiang ci: Li Zhi et al., eds., *Beijing shi Xuanwu qu diming zhi*, 453.

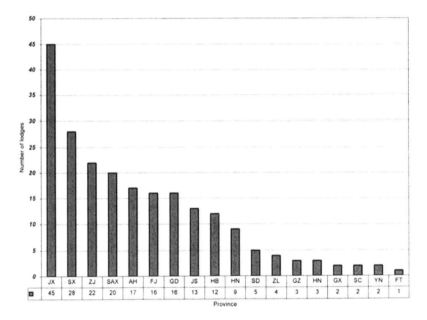

Fig. 3.1 Native-place lodges in Beijing at the end of the eighteenth century; for the key to province abbreviations, see Fig. 2.1, p. 37 (sources: Wu Changyuan, *Chen yuan shi lüe*; and sources listed in Tables 3.1 and 3.3).

Table 3.4
Native-Place Lodges in Beijing During the Last Years of the
Qing Period According to the *Xinceng dumen jilüe* (1907)

Province	Provincial	Prefectural	Sub-prefectural (*zhou*/*xian*)	Sub-total
Zhili	2	4	6	12
Shandong	1	3	3	7
Shanxi	6	5	24	35
Henan	4	3	5	12
Jiangsu	3	3	20	26
Anhui	2	4	27	33
Zhejiang	2	11	19	32
Jiangxi	4	19	43	66
Hunan	4	4	9	17
Hubei	2	7	17	26
Shaanxi	5	5	18	28
Guangdong	4	14	15	33
Guangxi	6	2	0	8
Sichuan	7	2	3	12
Guizhou	7	0	0	7
Yunnan	5	1	3	9
Fujian	2	7	13	22
TOTAL (plus 6 trade guilds)	66	94	225	385

SOURCE: Yang Jingting, *Xinceng dumen jilüe* (note that a document dated to 1911 entitled "Dumen huiguan" by the same author and cataloged independently in the Beijing Academy of Sciences (Kexue yuan) Library, contains minor variations).

Table 3.5
Native-Place Lodges in Beijing During the 1910s
According to Sydney Gamble (1921)

Province	Number	Province	Number
Anhui	39	Jiangsu	27
Fujian	24	Shaanxi and	
Guangxi	7	Gansu	26
Guangdong	36	Shanxi	34
Guizhou	7	Shandong	7
Henan	14	Sichuan	15
Hunan	23	Yunnan	9
Hubei	26	Zhejiang	38
Jiangxi	69	Zhihli	12
TOTAL			413

SOURCE: Gamble, *Peking: A Social Survey*, 232–33.

survey of Beijing huiguan was undertaken by the Census Section of the Civil Control Office of the Ministry of Civil Administration in the last years of the Qing dynasty.[8] Unfortunately, only a portion of the survey, the part covering the western half of the Outer City, remains extant. Luckily the western half of the Outer City was where most of the huiguan were located, but even though several hundred huiguan are recorded in the Ministry of Civil Administration account, numerous examples of well-documented scholar-gentry huiguan are absent from that source.

Another document bearing on the question of the number of huiguan in Beijing during this period, cited by both James Cole and G. William Skinner, was procured in Beijing by the Japanese scholar Niida Noboru. Although this document, which is held at the Institute of Oriental Culture (Tōyō bunka kenkyūjo) at Tokyo

8. See Minzhengbu, Minzhici, Hujike, *Minzhengbu guanyu diaocha jing waicheng huiguan, pu hu, miaoyu de biaoce* (the document is undated but must have been produced between 1906, when the Minzhengbu was established, and 1911). Following my use of the document in the Number One Historical Archive of China, the survey was reprinted in *Lishi dang'an* 1995, no. 2: 59–65. It has also been reprinted under the title "Qingmo Beijing waicheng xunjing youting huiguan diaocha biao," in Beijing shi dang'anguan, ed., *Beijing huiguan dang'an shiliao*, 798–818.

University,[9] is not dated, Cole conclusively demonstrates that it must have been compiled between 1911 and 1944, the year Niida purchased it. Further textual evidence indicates, somewhat less conclusively, that it was most probably composed before the Nationalist transfer of the capital to Nanjing in 1928.[10] Both Cole and Skinner describe the text as listing 598 huiguan and other associations organized along native-place lines, such as compatriot shrines.

The Oriental Institute list is further evidence of the multitude of native-place lodges that existed during the Republican period. However, it bears pointing out that the figure of 598 refers to the number of entries. The majority of the entries deal with native-place-type associations, but other kinds of associations are listed as well, including academic, charitable, and political associations, most of which were not organized along native-place lines. The document does record an impressive 442 entries under the section heading "Huiguan, *tongxiang hui*, and compatriot shrines, etc."[11] An additional thirteen huiguan are listed as trade associations, although many of these (such as the Yanliao [dyestuffs] huiguan 顏料會館,

---

9. See Cole, *Shaohsing*, 78, 197n17; and Skinner, "Introduction: Urban Social Structure," 539.

10. All references to Beijing in association titles found in this document use that as the place-name, rather then "Beiping," the name given the city from 1927 until 1949. Other association names reflect earlier usages as well: for example, the (Guangdong) Xiangshan huiguan 香山會館 is still listed under that name rather than as Zhongshan huiguan 中山會館. (The name of the district was changed from Xiangshan to Zhongshan after the death of Sun Yatsen [Sun Zhongshan] and the name of the lodge changed accordingly.)

11. The document is entitled "Zai Beijing huiguan mulu." I am grateful to Adam Schneider for obtaining a copy of this document for me. The question of how many associations with native-place ties are included in this list is more complicated than one might suppose. For example, some of the entries list two or more sites. If we include these 38 sites, the figure for native-place and trade associations comes to 493. Note that this figure includes the separate entries for some associations, such as the Association of Students from the Six Municipalities of Zunyi Studying in Beijing and Tianjin (Zunyi liuyi liuxue jingjin tongxue hui 遵義六邑留學京津同學會), that were headquartered within the corresponding huiguan of their relevant administrative district, in this case the Guizhou huiguan. Thus, not all these associations were corporate or propertied. The figure given above is adjusted to exclude properties listed twice (e.g., the two [Jiangxi] Xincheng huiguan 新城會館 sites, which were listed again under the alternative name Lichuan huiguan 黎川會館, and so on).

which was also known as the [Shanxi] Pingyao huiguan 平遙會館)
were based on native-place principles. However, even by a generous
definition, only a handful of the remaining 140 associations may be
considered to have had native-place ties. The majority, the American Red Cross and the Beijing Esperanto Society are just two examples, did not and thus should not be considered in the overall
count of native-place organizations. A more detailed analysis of this
document is provided in the notes to this chapter.

The State of Beijing Native-Place Lodges in 1949

As is discussed in Chapter 11, the Republican period (1911–49), especially the period following the establishment of the national capital
in Nanjing in 1927, was a period of decline for the native-place lodges
of Beijing. Although the native-place communities in Beijing fell on
hard times, however, the lodge properties for the most part remained intact. On November 15, 1949, less than a year after Beijing
was peacefully surrendered to communist troops and little more
than a month after Mao Zedong proclaimed the founding of the
People's Republic, the Civil Administration Bureau of the Beijing
Municipal Government submitted a report entitled "Work Report
on a Survey of Huiguan" ("Huiguan diaocha gongzuo baogao" 會館
調查工作報告).[12] Based on responses to questionnaires distributed
and collected by government representatives, this remarkable survey provides a detailed picture of huiguan on the eve of their demise.
Reminiscent of the 1909 survey carried out by the Ministry of Civil
Administration under the late Qing government, this investigation
set out to gather even more information, including data on property
holdings, demographics, and administrative structures of huiguan,
in unprecedented detail. During the five centuries native-place
lodges existed, no other single survey ever systematically gathered
such a wealth of information about the lodges.

---

12. Beijing shi renmin zhengfu, Minzheng ju, "Huiguan diaocha baogao"; reprinted as "1949 nian Beijing huiguan qingkuang diaocha baogao"; and in Beijing shi
dang'anguan, ed., *Beijing huiguan dang'an shiliao*, 1066–76.

Table 3.6
Number of Native-Place Lodges in Beijing According to the
Civil Administration Bureau Report (1949)

Province	Provincial	Prefectural	County	Total huiguan (*huiguan chu*)	Property sites (*fangchan chu*)
Hebei	4	4	4	12	15
Shandong	2	1	0	3	7
Shanxi	4	13	21	38	50
Henan	7	9	2	18	25
Jiangsu	1	12	12	25	54
Anhui	1	9	19	29	89
Zhejiang	3	11	10	24	77
Jiangxi	1	23	32	56	86
Hunan	1	9	11	21	46
Hubei	1	9	26	36	40
Shaanxi	2	7	15	24	30
Guangdong	2	11	23	36	74
Guangxi	3	4	0	7	12
Sichuan	7	4	1	12	25
Guizhou	7	0	0	7	8
Yunnan	3	0	0	3	13
Fujian	1	9	12	22	38
Gansu	5	0	0	5	6
Fengtian	1	0	0	1	6
Jilin	2	0	0	2	3
Suiyuan	2	0	0	2	2
Taiwan	1	0	0	1	1
Xinjiang	1	0	0	1	1
Huguang	1	0	0	1	1
TOTAL	63	135	188	386	709

SOURCE: Beijing shi renmin zhengfu, Minzhengju, "1949 nian Beijing huiguan qingkuang diaocha baogao."

The report confirms that huiguan properties had not disappeared during the years of occupation and civil war. It recorded a total of 386 native-place lodges (plus five strictly trade huiguan not organized along native-place principles, which are omitted from the following discussion). In total, these lodges occupied 709 different sites and owned an additional 88 cemeteries. The breakdown of sites by administrative region is given in Table 3.6.

The Civil Administration Bureau Survey

Valuable as the findings of the Civil Administration Bureau survey are, they need to be treated critically. The questionnaires used to gather these data were filled out by huiguan representatives, and the findings as a whole are obviously no better than the information reported by the informants. Although the authority of the government encouraged accurate reporting, plenty of evidence indicates problems in the data. In some cases, vaguely worded questions may have given rise to confusion, in other cases the respondents may have not had access to complete information, and in still other cases, a conscious effort to underreport property holdings may have been at work.

The Jiangxi lodges illustrate how difficult it is to calculate the accuracy of the survey figures. Three years after the Civil Administration survey was submitted, the property committee of the Jiangxi huiguan published a public notice in the *Beijing ribao* 北京 日報, the leading local newspaper, listing the sites for which it no longer had proper property contracts; 67 huiguan compound sites (with addresses) were included.[13] The Civil Administration survey, by contrast, records only 56 Jiangxi huiguan sites, but 86 property sites (for the distinction between the two categories, see below). Thus even though the huiguan sites listed in the *Beijing ribao* notice may not be sufficiently documented, the list is larger than the one in the survey (though less than the recorded number of property sites).

How do we account for such discrepancies? For one thing, it is not immediately clear how huiguan sites (*huiguan chu* 會館處) differed from property sites (*fangchan chu* 房產處), and there may have been some confusion about this among the informants. For example, the survey records 86 Jiangxi huiguan property sites, a figure close to the 85 Jiangxi huiguan sites I found in a number of different sources. This suggests that the "property sites" recorded in the survey correspond to separate huiguan compound sites but not to other properties owned by the lodges, such as rentals used by lodges to generate income. This leaves the meaning of "huiguan site" unclear, although we may speculate that the administration of some

---

13. See *Beijing ribao*, 1952.11.12, 3.

properties had been consolidated by 1949 and that the lower number recorded in the survey represented the number of independent huiguan administrative bodies at that time. For example, five provincial-level Jiangxi huiguan sites are listed in the *Beijing ribao* notice, but only one is recorded in the survey. This might reflect the administration of all provincial-level huiguan properties by a single body (whereas each of the various prefectural- and county-level huiguan would have had its own administrative body, some of which would also have administered multiple sites).

Although this explanation appears to explain the Jiangxi numbers, it does not work for all the provinces. For example, the survey records 29 Anhui huiguan sites and 89 property sites. The figure for huiguan sites is unexpectedly low. I have found 44 Anhui sites, and the late Qing *Jing shi fang xiang zhi* records 34 sites. The relatively low number might be explained by administrative consolidation of some sites, but the figure of 89 property sites appears unaccountably high, unless it is assumed that some informants included rental properties in their calculations.

The authors of the report themselves recognized that some of the findings were problematical. They pointed out that not all huiguan listed cemetery holdings and emphasized that only 47 of the huiguan provided information on movable property (*dongchan*), a category that included furniture, equipment, savings accounts, and so on. As we have seen, the claim of one huiguan that it was found in the Hongwu period is demonstrably false.[14] Nevertheless, the value of the survey should not be underestimated. It provides an unparalleled look at the state of huiguan at that time, and because the late Republican period was largely a period of stagnation in terms of establishment of native-place lodges, we can assume it generally reflects the amount and extent of huiguan property holdings in Beijing in the early Republican period as well.

In the course of researching this study, I have consulted an extensive range of late nineteenth- and early twentieth-century sources, including gazetteers, stele inscriptions, government reports, and huiguan records. I have found a total of 532 separate Beijing native-place lodge sites for the late nineteenth and early twentieth centu-

---

14. See note 32 to Chapter 2, p. 30.

ries. The extraordinary number of scholar-official huiguan might be considered little more than historical trivia, if the lodges had not been overwhelmingly concentrated in one section of the city. As I argue in subsequent chapters, the sheer number of lodges packed together in relatively close spatial proximity helped to transform the urban ecology of the capital and created an environment that facilitated inter-lodge interaction, which in turn affected both the construction of identity among lodge clientele and associational and political activities. But in order to appreciate the impact the lodges had on the Beijing social environment, it is first necessary to appreciate the ways in which the Beijing lodges were unusual in kind, not just in number.

Huiguan Types

Huiguan of all sorts shared a number of common attributes. Fundamentally, huiguan promoted cooperation among, facilitated the interests of, and alleviated the problems faced by people who identified themselves with localities in the provinces. Among their many functions, huiguan typically promoted social networking among compatriots, provided meeting places, offered banqueting facilities to celebrate festive occasions, and maintained altars to local deities and notable local personages so that the ritual ties to the native place might be observed and reinforced.

Scholars have long recognized that despite such commonalities, different Chinese native-place organizations tended to cater to different sets of sojourning communities, and in doing so, the lodges took on certain distinguishing characteristics. These differences were not always formally declared, and they allowed for a great deal of flexibility in practice, but they are systematic enough to allow for the categorization of the lodges into types. This typing of lodges is not new. Late imperial sources often distinguished between scholar-official lodges and merchant lodges, as was shown in the previous chapter in the discussion of the institutional origins of huiguan. The author of the seminal work on Chinese huiguan, Ho Ping-ti, suggested there were three principal sorts of lodges: those that catered to scholars and officials, those that catered to merchants and tradesman (i.e., producers of handicrafts), and those, unique to the upper Yangzi watershed, established by peasant immigrants to that region.[15] L. Eve Armentrout-Ma took this classification scheme one step further and proposed four types: literati, merchant, trade, and resettlement.[16]

For this study, only the distinction between scholar-official and merchant/handicraft lodges is relevant. The resettlement huiguan of the upper Yangzi were a regional phenomenon; this form did not spread beyond that area, and those particular lodges did not interact with the lodges of Beijing and thus do not figure in this study. As for merchant huiguan and handicraft huiguan, although Armentrout-Ma's division may help in addressing certain questions, most scholars have not seen the need to consider them separately. Since the distinction does not contribute to the main concerns of this study, the two are treated as essentially one group here.

Generally speaking, most huiguan in late imperial China outside Beijing catered primarily to merchants, their employees, and/or those engaged in handicraft production. Thus, most Chinese huiguan were essentially merchant/handicraft huiguan. That native-place and trade interests so often converged is attributable to the remarkable degree to which China's late imperial economy was structured along native-place lines. In any given city, men from a particular native place tended to dominate if not monopolize particular trades (although which native-place group dominated which line might vary from place to place). Thus Chinese native-place lodges tended to serve as the locus for trade-related activities, and management of trade affairs, pursuit of common trade interests, and so on were typically handled through the lodges. It is for this reason that Chinese huiguan have frequently been considered primarily economic organizations, and both Western and Japanese scholars have customarily referred to them as "guilds."

In contrast, one of the most distinctive characteristics of native-place lodges in Beijing is that the great majority of them did not fit the mold that predominated elsewhere. Most Beijing huiguan were not merchant/handicraft huiguan but scholar-official lodges, established by and maintained on behalf of government officials, expec-

---

15. Ho, "The Geographic Distribution of Hui-Kuan," 120–22.
16. Armentrout-Ma, "Fellow-Regional Associations in the Ch'ing Dynasty."

tant officials, examination candidates, and other members of China's national political elite. Li Hua, China's pre-eminent scholar of merchant/handicraft huiguan, estimates that the commercial huiguan represented no more than 14 percent of all Beijing lodges; the rest catered to scholar-officials.[17]

Anyone who has dealt with Chinese social institutions knows that they are flexible in practice. There was not in all cases a hard and fast distinction between the types of lodge. It would be wrong to assume that merchant/handicraft lodges excluded scholar-officials from their premises and their activities; they did not. If, for example, a sojourning community in a provincial town was fortunate enough to have a fellow provincial appointed to the area as a local official, it made sense for the lodge to welcome him, invite the official to take part in social and ritual activities, and otherwise maintain and nurture the ties that existed between them. These lodges were also open to scholars and officials who might be traveling through the area. In Beijing, scholar-officials occasionally attended operas and other events held on the premises of merchant/handicraft huiguan; the same no doubt was true in reverse. It is also true that some lodges had more of a mixed character than others, and some evolved over time from one type to another. But essential differences remained, and because I argue in later chapters that scholar-official huiguan and the native-place ties that animated them served as a crucial nexus in an evolving scholar-official identity in Beijing, the distinction deserves examination.

Not all scholars who have discussed Beijing huiguan have seen fit to recognize the difference between scholar-official and merchant/handicraft lodges. In some cases, this appears to be the result of a misunderstanding; for example, in John King Fairbank's final book, *China: A New History*, he referred to all the Beijing lodges in the latter part of the nineteenth century as "native-place guilds catering to merchants."[18] In other cases, a more knowing rejection of the distinction seems to be at work. In her recent magisterial study of temples and city life in Beijing, Susan Naquin decided that distin-

---

17. Li Hua, ed. and comp., *Ming-Qing yilai Beijing gongshang huiguan beike xuan bian*, 20.

18. Fairbank, *China: A New History*, 160.

guishing between scholar-official and merchant/handicraft lodges was not necessary for the purposes of her study, but in justifying her decision to "lump all huiguan together," she also expressed doubt of the demarcation.[19]

Although this study will go further in teasing out the historical significance of the scholar-official lodges in the capital, it breaks no new ground by simply recognizing that they were somewhat different from the usual huiguan. Chinese references to huiguan in Beijing have long distinguished between scholar-official and merchant lodges and have consistently noted that the former predominated in Beijing. Non-Chinese scholars who have addressed Beijing huiguan have made similar observations, although consideration of these differences has not always been drawn in the form of a strict typology. Writing in 1909, H. B. Morse shied away from drawing clear lines of distinction between scholar-official and merchant/handicraft lodges and instead depicted the difference as more one of degree than of type: "In the [provincial] clubs in Peking the official element naturally predominates; in those in the provinces the greater number are merchants."[20]

Sidney Gamble drew a more marked distinction in his classic work, *Peking: A Social Survey*. He devoted the great bulk of the chapter "Commercial Life" to a discussion of merchant/handicraft "gilds."[21] What he acknowledged were the far more numerous "provincial gild halls" (i.e., scholar-official huiguan) received only a brief description tucked away in a chapter entitled "Recreation." According to Gamble:

The Provincial Gild Halls are among the social gathering places in Peking. These halls, and there are 413 of them, all but six of which are in the South City, were built during the Manchu Dynasty so that the natives of the different provinces and districts who came to Peking for the literary examinations might have some place to live or at least meet their fellow provincials.[22]

---

19. Naquin, *Peking*, 601n136.
20. Morse, *The Gilds of China*, 37.
21. Gamble, *Peking: A Social Survey*, 161–202.
22. Ibid., 232–33.

He then described their uses as clubhouses following the abolition of the examination system. The defining of scholar-official lodges as social rather than commercial organizations was somewhat amplified by John Stewart Burgess in *The Gilds of Peking*, in which he distinguished between "Provincial Guilds (social)," that is, scholar-official huiguan, and "Provincial Guilds (economic)," or merchant/handicraft huiguan.[23] Later scholars such as Niida Noboru and Li Hua followed Gamble and Burgess both in distinguishing between scholar-official huiguan and merchant/handicraft huiguan and in finding the latter of far greater interest.[24] It is striking, given the amount that has been written about Beijing huiguan over the years, that so little attention was devoted to the scholar-official lodges.

Historical Trends in the Clientele of Beijing Huiguan

According to Ho Ping-ti, during the Ming period there were two types of native-place lodge: one served as exclusive clubs for officials in the central government; the other catered to all compatriots—officials, merchants, government bureaucrats, and examination candidates.[25] During the Qing period, one of the primary functions of huiguan was the provision of temporary lodging to examination candidates, but Ho argued that neither of the Ming types was concerned primarily with providing this service. Ho's provisional characterization of the clientele of huiguan during the Ming period still stands, but we still do not have enough evidence to determine the social mix of clientele at that time conclusively. Ho's contention that the focus on providing lodging for examination candidates did

---

23. Burgess, *The Guilds of Peking*, 17–18.

24. Other works on the merchant/handicraft huiguan of Beijing include Katō Shigeshi, "Shindai ni okeru Pekin no shōnin kaikan ni tsuite"; Niida Noboru, "The Industrial and Commercial Guilds of Peking"; idem, *Pekin kōshō girudo shiryō shū*; and Li Hua, ed. and comp., *Ming-Qing yilai Beijing gongshang huiguan beike xuan bian*. Two popular books on Beijing *huiguan*, both entitled *Beijing de huiguan*, were published in the 1990s. One was by Tang Jincheng and the other by Hu Chunhuan and Bai Hequn. Of the two, the second, written by a husband-and-wife team, is more reliable. Both works distinguish between scholar-official huiguan and merchant/handicraft huiguan.

25. He Bingdi, *Zhongguo huiguan shilun*, "English Abstract," 2.

not develop until the early Qing is challenged, however, by a passage in the late Ming *Di jing jing wu lüe*, which clearly distinguishes between huiguan in the inner city and those in the southern city based on differences in those who used their services. According to that work, gentry (*shen* 紳) operated those in the inner city, and the huiguan located in the southern city existed primarily to provide lodging for examination candidates.[26]

If the exact nature of the clientele is somewhat unclear, it is nevertheless apparent that the majority of Beijing huiguan during the Ming period did not exclusively or even primarily cater to sojourning merchants. Each of the three huiguan known to have been established during the Yongle period, for instance, was founded by, and apparently for, government officials and bureaucrats. Although the evidence is sketchy, this pattern appears to have held true for most of the Beijing lodges throughout the Ming period. This does not mean that all Ming-period Beijing huiguan served scholars and officials alone, however. A few Ming-period huiguan had clear links with trade. Among the seven identifiable Shanxi lodges established before 1644, for example, four served primarily merchants. This reflects the relatively dominant position of Shanxi tradesmen in the capital during the late imperial period.[27] Two other lodges established during the Ming also appear to have served primarily merchants: one representing Shaanxi and another Yinxian 鄞縣 (Ningbo) in Zhejiang.

The provision of temporary lodging was a far more prominent feature of scholar-official huiguan than it was of other types of lodges. Indeed, whereas many merchant huiguan would not accommodate short-term residents, it was among the most important functions of the majority of Beijing scholar-official lodges. Beijing's position atop the bureaucratic central-place hierarchy of Chinese cities ensured a constant and pervasive presence, to a much greater degree than was true elsewhere, of large numbers of scholar-official sojourners. This neatly confirms William Rowe's observation that we should expect a greater "socioeconomic dominance by non-

---

26. Liu Tong et al., *Di jing jing wu lüe*, 180.
27. See Peng Chang, "The Distribution and Relative Strength of the Provincial Merchant Groups in China, 1842–1911."

locals ... in cities ranked higher in the hierarchy of central place in China," because of "a greater orientation of the city to ... [a] broader geographic scale."[28]

Proper administration of the empire required tens of thousands of officials, bureaucrats, and clerks drawn from across the realm. This sojourner-staffed metropolitan bureaucracy was composed of officials who tended to be posted in the capital for long periods of time, often for their entire professional careers; other non-merchant sojourners in the city usually came for shorter stays. Provincial officials, for example, periodically arrived for imperial audiences or on other business, and expectant officials came to wait for appointments to government posts.

By the seventeenth century, much of the demand for huiguan accommodations came from examination candidates. Twice every three years, Beijing was subject to great influxes of candidates, for the capital was host to both the metropolitan examination (*huishi* 會試) and the Shuntian prefectural examination. At the metropolitan examination, candidates with the provincial-level *juren* 舉人 degree vied for the coveted *jinshi* 進士 degree, which was the qualification for most imperial administrative posts. The Shuntian prefectural examination was a provincial-level examination (*xiangshi* 鄉試), similar to the examinations held in provincial capitals across the empire every three years, but it was unique in that it was not restricted to those from a specific province or region. Instead, it was open to candidates hailing from all regions of the empire who had purchased the first degree or otherwise obtained permission to sit this examination. Moreover, the ratio of those awarded the *juren* degree to the number of participants was significantly higher at the Shuntian prefectural examination than it was elsewhere, and therefore candidates had a distinct incentive to make the trip to the capital.[29] This added to the pressure to find lodging for the candidates.

---

28. Rowe, "Introduction," 10.

29. See Chang Chongli, *The Chinese Gentry*, 22. Chang gives regional quotas of degrees awarded according to rank and region of native-place registration and comparison quotas for *xiangshi* in the provinces; see ibid., 167–68n9.

The demand for lodging stimulated the formulation of regulations stipulating who could reside in a particular huiguan, and these regulations serve as one of our best sources on the nature of the clientele of native-place lodges in Beijing. The earliest extant copy of lodge regulations explicitly setting out who may reside on lodge premises is that of the Jiangxi huiguan, which dates to 1678. Merchants are clearly excluded from residence. Residency privileges in that lodge were limited to serving officials, expectant officials, examination candidates, and students of the Imperial Academy (Guozijian).[30] In a clear indication of the consideration given to examination candidates, the regulations state that since "poor but honest" men were found in greatest numbers among those taking the highest examination, if no rooms in the lodge were available, then non-candidate residents were to be moved in order to make room. If that was not possible, then the examination candidates were to receive a stipend, paid from the income from lodge rents, to pay for lodgings elsewhere.[31]

Beginning in the late eighteenth century, lodge regulations often openly spelled out the sorts of person to be denied residency. Specified undesirables varied somewhat from lodge to lodge (merchants frequently made the list), but it was common to exclude all but elite scholars and officials. The 1741 regulations of the (Anhui) Shexian huiguan 歙縣會館 (a huiguan Ho Ping-ti cites as an example of a Ming-period mixed scholar/merchant lodge) stated that the lodge had specifically been founded to benefit examination candidates. To allow sojourning merchants to live in the Shexian lodge, it proclaimed, or even to let them store their merchandise there would be counter to the original purpose of the lodge.[32] The Daoguang-era (1821–51) rules of the Jiangxi huiguan forbade the coming and going of the servants of officials and travelers of different backgrounds and occupations (*zaxiang youshou* 雜鄉游手).[33] The late nineteenth-century rules of the (Hunan) Baoqing huiguan 寶慶會館 excluded

30. *Zijian* 子監 here refers to student of the Imperial Academy (*jiansheng* 監生). *Jiansheng* was a purchased title, roughly corresponding to the *shengyuan* 生員 degree.

31. *Jiangxi huiguan jilüe*. These rules date to 1678.

32. (*Chongxiu*) *Shexian huiguan zhi*, vol. 1, "Xulu houji," 13.

33. *Jiangxi huiguan jilüe*, These rules date to 1848.

those coming to the capital to pursue court cases, merchants, and all disreputable characters (*wulai* 無賴).[34] The (Zhejiang) Shan-Gui yiguan 山會邑館, which represented Shaoxing, refused admittance to, among others, "candidates for the [low-ranking degree of] *tongsheng* 童生 [junior student], 'would be private secretaries,' 'those employed at the Boards' (i.e., Central Board Clerks), medical doctors, fortune tellers, 'vaudeville performers' (*zaji ren* 雜技人), scribes hired by candidates for the *juren* or *jinshi* degrees to copy poetry or prose . . . and candidates for the military *jinshi* degree and military functionaries."[35]

A somewhat more complicated problem was whether to allow family members of residents to stay in the huiguan as well. The responses to this question differed. Some lodges forbade the practice. During the Qianlong period, the (Anhui) Jingxian huiguan 經縣會館, for example, explicitly prohibited the lodging of family members.[36] This was true of many other lodges as well, but others were more flexible. The (Hunan) Changjun huiguan 長郡會館 regulations of 1778 prohibited "excessive" residence by family members, but if metropolitan officials, officials waiting for vacancies, and expectant officials found themselves unable to rent accommodations outside, then some "deviation from principle" could be considered and their families might be allowed to stay temporarily.[37] Some lodges, such as the Baoqing huiguan, forbade families to occupy some, but not all, of the lodge facilities and clearly specified which areas were off-limits to family members.[38]

Two fundamental issues were involved in this question. One was a matter of space, and the other a fear families might occupy rooms intended for examination candidates. For this reason, special limitations were often placed on the use of the facilities during the examination years. During these times, candidates were given priority over those staying with families and even in many instances single officials and expectant officials.

----

34. *Jingdu Baoqing guan zhi* (1887).
35. Translation from Cole, *Shaohsing*, 84–85; original text in *Shaoxing xianguan jilüe*, 6–7b.
36. *Beiping Jingxian huiguan lu*, 6b.
37. *Jingshi Changsha junguan zhi*.
38. *Jingdu Baoqing guan zhi* (1887); see also *Jiangxi huiguan jilüe*.

The other issue involved the presence of women within the lodges. As a general rule in late imperial times, native-place lodges were men's preserves. Given the social/political order of the day, there was no question of women meeting the residency qualifications on their own. Regulations tended to forbid even the casual presence of women, and many regulations prohibited prostitutes in the lodge. Even if such behavior was not explicitly prohibited, we may suppose that it was deemed unacceptable.

The exclusively male nature of the native-place lodge must have contributed to their image as a respectable type of association. However, as the flexibility of the rules regarding families shows, in practice huiguan grounds were not as strictly free of women as might be supposed. Even in those cases where women were not allowed to live on huiguan premises, they were not completely barred from visiting. During the Qing, women were allowed to attend some opera performances in the lodges. In 1868, the powerful late Qing official Weng Tonghe 翁同龢 (1830–1904) recorded in his diary that on two successive days his mother, accompanied by other women, had witnessed opera performances in the (Anhui) Xiuning huiguan 休寧會館. Women were not permitted to mingle freely among the crowd of men in the audience, however. When Weng hosted an opera party to celebrate his mother's birthday, he held it in the Anhui huiguan. A special area was set aside for the women, and curtains hung around the women's area achieved the appropriate gender separation.[39]

Even explicit residency rules were sometimes bent. A law case from the late Qing, for example, reveals that at least one official who stayed in the (Guangdong) Xiangshan lodge 香山會館 on his way home had secured rooms there to put up three of his young servant women. One of them was abducted, and this led to charges being brought against a cook at the lodge. This is all that alerts us to the fact that women were ever in residence there. In the end, the regulations must be seen more as statements of the ideal and less as reflections of actual conditions.[40]

---

39. Weng Tonghe, *Weng Tonghe riji paiyin ben*, 1868.6 (TZ 7.*run*4.16), 432.5, 538.
40. Number One Archive, Xingbu #01134.

Perceptions of the Beijing
Scholar-Official Huiguan

One of the interesting consequences of the different nature of Beijing scholar-official huiguan and merchant huiguan (and further evidence that the distinction between them is real) is the different treatment of the two sorts of lodges in local gazetteers, an important source of our knowledge about them. This markedly different coverage casts light on how local communities viewed this institution. Perhaps the most striking contrast is the degree to which the Beijing huiguan are recorded. Traditional local gazetteers devote relatively little space to native-place organizations generally, yet a number of gazetteers provide substantial information on their locality's Beijing huiguan.

Ho Ping-ti once observed that the "majority of local histories [i.e., gazetteers] usually overlook records on huiguan."[41] Despite this, as we saw in the previous chapter, Ho relied on gazetteer accounts to achieve some systematic sense of native-place lodges in cities other than Beijing during the late nineteenth and early twentieth centuries.[42] Thus, even though only a minority of gazetteers contain records of huiguan, taken together those records allowed Ho to discover the general patterns. In regard to the huiguan of Beijing, however, Ho commented: "In general, local gazetteers do not mention huiguan built in Beijing by that locality."[43] This explains Ho's use of the *Jing shi fang xiang zhi* as the main source—indeed almost the only source—for the part of his study devoted to lodges in Beijing.[44] But Ho's assessment of the coverage of Beijing huiguan by gazetteers is not accurate. In fact, gazetteers of regions with scholar-official lodges in Beijing often did mention those lodges. This is especially true of post–Taiping Rebellion local gazetteers. Indeed, in these later gazetteers not only are the Beijing huiguan

---

41. Ho, "Geographic Distribution of Hui-kuan," 121.
42. Ho refers to having "browsed" this number of gazetteers, see He Bingdi, *Zhongguo huiguan shilun*, 69; and Ho, "Geographic Distribution of Hui-kuan," 125.
43. He Bingdi, *Zhongguo huiguan shilun*, 35.
44. Ibid., 37–99. There were many editions of Zhu and Miao's *Jing shi fang xiang zhigao*. The 1983 edition cited in the bibliography is the more readily available.

frequently mentioned, but their coverage tends to be markedly more detailed than that of lodges located elsewhere. Gazetteers make only terse mention, if any, of huiguan established by locals in places other than Beijing. Often the entire reference to such a lodge consists of its name and perhaps the street on which it was located. References to scholar-official huiguan, on the other hand, often include property diagrams, the texts of stele inscriptions, records on their establishment, and detailed information on notable events (earthquake damage, refurbishings, and so on).

There are other differences in local gazetteer accounts. For instance, references in a local gazetteer to non-scholar-official huiguan usually concern the huiguan in the region covered by the gazetteer, not huiguan organized by local men sojourning elsewhere. Thus, the gazetteers record activities in the local area of sojourners from other places or, more specifically, the structures that housed those activities. A check of Ho's findings confirms this pattern. Every gazetteer cited by Ho in his identification of the 800 non-Beijing huiguan deals with the area in which the organization was located. References to Beijing scholar-official huiguan, on the contrary, are found in gazetteers covering the areas the huiguan represented. The native-place lodges built by men from Wuhu in Anhui province illustrate this phenomenon. Information on the Wuhu huiguan located in Zhongxiang, Hubei, is found in the Zhongxiang gazetteer.[45] The gazetteer of Wuhu itself refers only to merchant huiguan founded in Wuhu by non-locals, but it gives a detailed account of the scholar-official lodge founded by men from Wuhu in Beijing.[46]

Only after the fall of the empire did this pattern began to change somewhat, at least as far as gazetteer reference to merchant huiguan founded by landsmen in cities other than Beijing is concerned. Some gazetteers compiled after the founding of the Republic do provide material on such lodges.[47] To the best of my knowledge, there is no similar reference in any earlier gazetteer. The reason for this change is unclear and ultimately lies beyond the scope of this study. One

---

45. He Bingdi, *Zhongguo huiguan shilun*, 71; *Zhongxiang xian zhi* (1867), 5.34b–35.
46. *Wuhu xian zhi* (1919), 13.1–5.
47. See, e.g., *Jing xian zhi* (1914), 10.32a–36b; *Huaining xian zhi* (1915), 4.35; *Nanling xian zhi* (1924), *juan* 9b; and *Tong'an xian zhi* (1928), 41.10.

may speculate, however, that it reflects an emerging redefinition of regional identities in a new national context, as well as a more open incorporation of merchants and tradesmen into the body politic.

Another difference in gazetteers' treatment of huiguan is the way the two types of lodges were categorized. As a rule, it is difficult to locate discussions of either type of lodge in gazetteers. Tables of contents rarely identify the sections dealing with huiguan. As Ho Ping-ti noted, "Huiguan materials within gazetteers are hidden away in the sections on shrines, temples, and so on."[48] Beijing scholar-official huiguan seldom appear in tables of contents; nor do references to them appear in the sections on shrines and temples. Some gazetteers include material on them under such miscellaneous rubrics as "structures" or within the biographies of notable local persons.[49] Valuable information on them may also be found in transcriptions of stele inscriptions in sections devoted to "literary pieces."[50] The information also turns up under "miscellaneous records."[51] However, material on the Beijing huiguan is most often included in categories indicative of a more public or official status. Accounts of Beijing huiguan are often found appended to such sections as "public institutions" or "public bureaus," "civil-service examination halls," and "schools" and "academies."[52] An additional challenge for the researcher is that the information may be found in sections devoted to biographical accounts or stele inscriptions.

---

48. He Bingdi, *Zhongguo huiguan shilun*, 68.

49. *Nanchang xian zhi* (1870), 2.7–11b. See also *Wuhu xian zhi* (1919), *juan* 13. This section also contains a reference to huiguan in Wuhu founded by non-locals there.

50. For transcriptions of Beijing huiguan stele inscriptions in local gazetteers, see *Xiuning xian zhi* (1815), 22.45–46; *Nanxiong zhili zhou zhi* (1819), 20.37b–39; *Ji'an fu zhi* (1870), 47.60–61, 47.71–72, 49.3–4; *Xiangling xian zhi* (1881), 24(b).11b–14, 24(c).22b–23; *Wuyuan xian zhi* (1883), 59.21–22; and *Jianning xian zhi* (1919), 23.13. Other types of huiguan texts can also be found in literary sections; for example, the *Shidai beizhi huibian* (5.4b–5) includes the foreword to a no longer extant huiguan gazetteer.

51. See, e.g., *Tong'an xian zhi* (1928), 40.9b–10.

52. For examples of listings in public institutions sections, see *Poyang xian zhi* (1824), 8.7b–9; *Huaining xian zhi* (1825), 10.17; *Xuancheng xian zhi* (1888), 9.6b; and *Nanhai xian zhi* (1910), 1.10b–14b. For listings appended to sections devoted to examination sheds, see *Dongguan xian zhi* (1921), 17.17b; for listings under schools, *Huizhou fu zhi* (1827), 3.88; and *Wuyuan xian zhi* (1883), 10.31–33; for listings under academies, see *Yixian zhi* (1870), 10.5b.

What does the coverage of huiguan in local gazetteers tell us? The far more complete and detailed information on the scholar-official huiguan no doubt betrays the interests of the compilers, who were more directly served by the Beijing huiguan than they were by such organizations elsewhere. But there is reason to think that the differential coverage reflects more than the mere recording by scholar-officials of "their" huiguan and the ignoring of merchant and other huiguan. After all, officials patronized and were served by non-scholar-official huiguan in other cities. Rather, I believe, the difference is attributable to the fact that scholar-official huiguan became, especially in the nineteenth century, increasingly seen as more public or quasi-official in character than other lodges and as outposts of the locality in the capital.

As noted above, it was not unusual for local gazetteers to include information on Beijing huiguan under, or appended to, such categories as schools or examination halls. This reflects the notion that a primary function of huiguan in the capital was to provide local candidates at the Shuntian and metropolitan examinations with lodging. This function is by far the most frequently stressed reason for establishing huiguan given in the hundreds of stelae commemorating such foundings. The institutional connection between local academic institutions and Beijing huiguan sometimes included ongoing financial support from the locality. For example, a yearly sum of 160 taels of silver drawn from the proceeds of a charitable estate established to fund educational enterprises in the Guangdong district of Panyu was earmarked for the Panyu huiguan 番禺會館 in Beijing. Additional sums were available to pay the expenses of examination candidates attending the metropolitan examinations.[53] Such community funds to defray the expenses of examination candidates were expressions of the public interest in their success.[54] This was also reflected in the most common term for examination candidates, "public chariots" (*gongche* 公車), a term derived from

---

53. *Panyu xian zhi* (1871), 6.30. A similar practice in nearby Nanhai district for use by the Nanhai huiguan is recorded in Liu Boji, *Guangdong shuyuan zhidu*, 333.

54. Ho Ping-ti provides a good overview of this "community chest" system in *The Ladder of Success in Imperial China*, 203–9. Ho's brief account of Beijing huiguan provided in this book (which predates his later, thorough study of Chinese huiguan) is given in this context of community-generated educational aids.

the age-old practice of providing public transportation for the scholars making their way to the capital to take the examination.[55]

Clearly, perceptions of the Beijing scholar-official huiguan and other regional organizations differed significantly. The various categories under which materials on the Beijing huiguan were incorporated into gazetteers point to some uncertainty, or at least a lack of consensus, regarding the exact nature of this institution, but the range of sections—from public bureaus to schools—indicates that (unlike other huiguan, which were most frequently grouped with temples) the Beijing huiguan tended to be thought of as official or quasi-official institutions. The dramatic increase in the inclusion of information on Beijing huiguan following the Taiping Rebellion is also telling. It might be argued that the increase simply reflects the tendency of gazetteers after the mid-nineteenth century to be more detailed generally. Nevertheless, it is my sense that the shift toward providing more information about Beijing huiguan greatly exceeds any overall trend toward greater comprehensiveness on other matters within gazetteers. Instead, I believe the trend reflects a growing appreciation among the compilers of gazetteers, and thus among scholar-officials more widely, of the important role the lodges played in linking localities and the capital, at a time when that relationship was being fundamentally redefined. As we will see in later chapters, Beijing native-place lodges assumed new roles in articulating and mediating the interests of locality and state during the late nineteenth century; hence, it is no surprise that local communities became more aware of and sought to give more emphasis to the lodges in the gazetteers.

The implications of the difference between scholar-official huiguan and other native-place lodges are far-ranging. As the gazetteer

---

55. See Yang Liansheng, "Keju shidai de fukao lüfei wenti," for a general discussion of public financial support for the travel expenses of examination candidates. The term *gongche* was widely used in late imperial texts. Scholars disagree about the proper pronunciation of the term, with some (including an anonymous reviewer of this work) insisting that the proper pronunciation is *gongju*. I have long been aware of the alternative pronunciation, but an informal canvassing of Chinese scholars has revealed no consensus on this point, and I follow the pronunciation given in two authoritative Chinese dictionaries, the *Hanyu da cidian* and *Cihai*.

coverage suggests, one of the most important was the unique role Beijing scholar-official huiguan played in mediating interactions between the locality and governmental agencies in the capital, a point explored in later chapters. Essentially, whereas other types of native-place lodges were understood as serving primarily the interests of the various communities of local people sojourning elsewhere, Beijing scholar-official lodges came increasingly to be perceived as representing the home community itself and serving as quasi-official outposts of the community in the capital.

FOUR

Huiguan in Space

This chapter and the next examine the spatial characteristics of native-place lodges. This chapter focuses on "huiguan in space" and studies the evolution of lodge placement within the city over time and describes how the concentration of huiguan in one ward affected scholar-official identities. My central argument in this section is that the spatial arrangement of the lodges both affected and reflected scholar-official identification with the *imperium* (by which I mean not so much the empire as mapped as the manifest imperial power represented by the union of court and governing elite composed of scholar-officials). This chapter deals with "macrospatial" issues. The next chapter turns to a consideration of "microspatial" issues, and the focus shifts from "huiguan in space" to "huiguan as space"; that is, it examines not where the lodges were located but how lodge property was spatially arranged and what the physical arrangement of huiguan can tell us about the nature of scholar-official identity.[1]

---

1. The "in space/as space" dichotomy was suggested by Henri Lefebre's neo-Marxist critique of traditional spatial analysis, especially as presented in Mark Gottdiener, *The Social Production of Urban Space*, 123–32. My use of the "as space" concept departs significantly from Lefebre's, however. His concept was developed in conjunction with his critique of the modern capitalist city and is principally

Beijing's late imperial form took shape during the early Ming dynasty, when the decision was made to rebuild the Yuan dynasty city known as Khanbalig (the khan's city) to the Mongols and Dadu (great capital) to the Chinese.[2] The Ming rulers shifted the city slightly to the south and somewhat reduced its size, but they kept many of the essential features of the earlier capital. Indeed, the east and west walls of Ming Beijing were largely constructed on the Yuan foundations. The north wall of the Ming city was built approximately one and two-thirds miles south of the earlier wall, and the new south wall was constructed approximately a third of a mile south of the previous fortification. Work on the city wall was essentially completed in 1420, although the construction of the gate towers was not finished until 1437. Once the macrostructural configuration of walls, imperial temples, streets, and waterways was completed in the early Ming period, Beijing's physical form remained fundamentally unchanged until an additional city wall was built on the south side of the city in 1552–53.[3] China's capital became, with that addition, a city of two discrete, though contiguous, walled enclosures, commonly referred to thereafter as the Inner (*nei*) and Outer (*wai*) Cities. The newly enclosed Outer City extended approximately two and a half miles further south of the Inner City, and approximately a third of a mile further to the west and east on each side.[4] Access between the two "cities" was restricted to three gates located along the southern wall of the Inner City, which divided the two areas. From west to east, these were named the

---

concerned with understanding urban space as a factor of bourgeois production. For my use of the term, see below.

2. Uradyn Bulag (pers. comm.) informs me that the proper transcription of the Mongolian name of the city should be Hagan [Khan] Balagasu.

3. Cao Zixi et al., eds., *Beijing tongshi*, 6: 71–73. The entire project was not completed until 1564, with the construction of bricked gates. The original plan had called for the complete enclosure of the Inner City on all four sides, but insufficient resources prevented this.

4. The Inner City was somewhat larger than the Outer City. The total land area of the Inner City was 35.5 sq. km; the Outer City occupied 26.5 sq. km (Chen Chengxiang, *Beijing de dushi fazhan*, 24).

Xuanwu 宣武 (proclaiming martiality); Zhengyang 正陽 (primary cardinal); and Chongwen 崇文 (revering civility) gates.[5]

The area enclosed by the new Outer City wall included the large Altar of Heaven and Altar of Agriculture complexes, reserved for imperial ritual, and bustling business districts. Beyond erecting a wall around the Outer City, the state made little attempt to remake the area within. The most important elements of imperial city planning were roads. The north–south Central Axis connected the central gates in the southern walls of the Inner and Outer Cities. The principal avenues leading into the city from the other gates were also laid out along general (if not uniform) north–south and east–west axes, but the original twisting lanes, haphazard street layout, and irregular intersections of the Outer City were otherwise left essentially untouched. This contrasted sharply with the orderly grid-like arrangement of streets imposed on the Inner City. Apparently, China's rulers deemed the extension of such regularity into the Outer City unnecessary, satisfied that the stricter order imposed on the Inner City sufficiently symbolized imperial rule.

With the final addition of the Outer City wall in the sixteenth century, Beijing's major physical features remained set for the rest of the late imperial period. The Manchu administration of the succeeding Qing dynasty by and large adopted the walls and intramural urban structures of the Ming capital, with only minor adjustments. Physically, Beijing was little affected by the 260 years of Qing rule. Although the Qing court developed the Summer Palace complexes to the northwest of the walled city and constructed two imperial tomb complexes further out from the capital, they left intramural Beijing much as they found it.[6]

---

5. Translation of gate names based on (though slightly altered) Geiss, "Peking Under the Ming," 24.

6. Even maintenance of form takes work, and the Qing rulers repaired and restored a number of major structures; see Dai Yi, *Qianlong di ji qi shidai*, 433–98. Dai Yi's work shows that although major new constructions were undertaken outside the city wall, construction within the wall was largely limited to reconstructing existing structures and the addition of a small number of symbolic structures, such as the White Pagoda and the transformation of a former princely palace into the Yonghegong, a major Tibetan/Mongolian Buddhist temple that symbolically represented and diplomatically consolidated Manchu ties with the newly incorporated Inner Asian portions of the empire.

Although the major physical structures of Beijing remained impressively constant over time, the same cannot be said of its social space. Indeed, the social configuration of Beijing was fundamentally transformed during the seventeenth and eighteenth centuries. This transformation was produced both as a consequence of administrative fiat and as the result of a more spontaneous process whereby scholar-officials and merchants gravitated toward different wards of the city. To better understand the significance of this transformation and to locate my work within its scholarly context, I begin by briefly reviewing previous scholarship on Chinese urban social structure in general and the patterning of Beijing's social space in particular.

Skinner's Binuclear Model of Chinese Urban Ecology

In a characteristically thought-provoking essay, G. William Skinner proposed an influential set of hypotheses regarding the configuration of urban social space in China.[7] Previously scholars had argued that traditional Chinese cities exhibited little demographic or socioeconomic spatial differentiation. The areas within Chinese city walls were believed to exhibit only minor variations in population density and little in the way of residential neighborhoods, business districts, or wards distinguished by the relative wealth of their inhabitants.[8] Skinner disputed this vision by arguing that the demographic character of late imperial cities varied significantly from ward to ward. Indeed, Skinner proposed a model of Chinese "urban ecology" in which two spatially discrete "nuclei" shaped urban social space. One nucleus was associated with merchants; the other

---

7. Unless otherwise noted, the following discussion is based on Skinner, "Introduction: Urban Social Structure," particularly the "Urban Ecology" section of this essay, 527–38. My own thinking regarding the social structure of Beijing is deeply indebted to Skinner's discussion of this topic, although my understanding runs counter to his in several fundamental respects.

8. These works are discussed in more detail in Skinner's rebuttal to them; they include C. K. Yang, "Some Thoughts on the Study of Chinese Urban Communities"; and Fitzgerald, *China: A Short Cultural History.*

with the "gentry."[9] Each served as the center of socioeconomic activity and of residence for its respective group.

Both nuclei were characterized by occupational homogeneity but personal-wealth heterogeneity.[10] The scholar-official nucleus consisted of both wealthy officials and poorer examination candidates; the merchant nucleus acted as the residential and business center for merchants and tradesmen at all levels. Yet because each served as host to a relatively elite group, Skinner not only refuted early notions of an undifferentiated urban social space in China but also contradicted a consensus among comparative urban sociologists that "in premodern cities social class is inversely related to distance from the center."[11] Instead of an "elites toward the center" pattern, the Skinnerian model suggests a general principle of nucleus location in which scholar-official nuclei were positioned close to the principal imperial institutions associated with that class (state-sponsored academies, civil-service examination grounds, Confucian temples, and so on). The merchant nucleus or business district, on the other hand, tended to gravitate toward one or several adjacent city gates, on the fringes of the city and away from the geographic center in response to economies of transportation costs.[12]

Skinner tangentially referred to a number of Chinese cities in his essay, but to illustrate his model he took Beijing as his principal case study. He identified a long strip to the south of the wall dividing the Inner and Outer Cities, just outside the Xuanwu, Zhengyang, and Chongwen gates, as the site of the Beijing merchant nucleus. The scholar-official nucleus he located in the eastern third of the Inner City, between the imperial school-temple complex consisting of the Imperial Academy (Guozijian) and the Confucian Temple (Wen

---

9. Skinner did not explicitly define his use of the word "gentry"—a term whose meaning in the late imperial Chinese context has been disputed—but he evidently conceived of the group as composed exclusively of scholar-officials.

10. The term "occupational homogeneity" is mine not Skinner's. It is intended to suggest that these two groups were defined by their different livelihoods. For example, examination candidates and successful officials may have differed greatly in personal wealth, but they shared a commitment to making their livelihood in government service.

11. Skinner, "Introduction: Urban Social Structure," 528.

12. Ibid.

miao 文廟) in the north and the imperial examination grounds in the south.[13] Skinner did not address the historical origins of the proposed nuclei, but his presumption of the relative immutability of social structure is clear. In making his case, he used evidence from the eighteenth century and early twentieth century almost interchangeably and explicitly maintained that Beijing's binucleated pattern existed "in the 1910's as in the 1750's."[14]

Skinner's essay was cogently argued and theoretically innovative. My own research shows that Skinner correctly delineated the spatial segregation of merchant and scholar-official areas at least during the last century and a half of imperial rule. However, Skinner's model of social space has two major shortcomings insofar as it applies to Beijing. First, the implied steady-state model of late imperial urban ecology masks the considerable transformation of social space that occurred during this period. Second, although nuclei much as he describes did exist in Beijing during the Qing period, the location of the scholar-official nucleus was in an entirely different part of the city. Below, I review the historical origins of these nuclei, examine the historical dynamic that led to the placement of the two centers, and provide a preliminary analysis of the scholar-official nucleus, which has received relatively little scholarly attention.

Social Space in Beijing During the Ming Period

A binucleated division between scholar-officials and merchants did not characterize the configuration of social space in Beijing during the Ming period. Before 1644, social distinctions were spatially expressed primarily along lines of wealth, not occupation. In other words, during the Ming, the eastern third of the Inner City was better characterized as a center, although not necessarily the center, of the wealthy rather than of scholar-officials.[15] This somewhat overlapping but by no means equivalent social group included

---

13. Ibid., 533.

14. Ibid., 529.

15. The terms "Inner City" and "Outer City" are, for the sake of convenience, used here to refer to these areas throughout the Ming period, although their use is admittedly anachronistically applied to the period preceding the mid-sixteenth century.

wealthy eunuchs and merchants but excluded poorer scholars, officials, and others less well off.

During the Ming period, the eastern third of the Inner City was
best known for expensive and luxurious retail markets. For example, the Lantern Market was located to the east of the Forbidden
City. It ran for blocks in several directions around Lantern Market
Intersection (Deng shi kou 燈市口), which is still known by that
name today. The market was held from the eighth to the eighteenth
day of the first month of each year, around the time of the Lantern
Festival (Yuanxiao 元宵). It was a seat of bustling commerce
and extravagant worldly entertainments.[16] Despite a proscription
against high-ranking officials frequenting the market, it is obvious
from later poetic descriptions that officials attended in great numbers, as did eunuchs and other members of the prosperous elite.[17]
During the course of the Ming, the Lantern Market gradually became a periodic general market held three times a month, at which a
whole host of luxury objects were sold.[18] Yamen clerks, scholars,
soldiers, and commoners visited the market, but only the truly
wealthy could afford the high-priced rented rooms with entertainment and the expensive conspicuous-consumables the fair had to
offer. The Imperial Market was another high-priced market located
just to the west of Lantern Market Intersection. It was held three
times a month inside the eastern gate of the Imperial City. It, too,
sold expensive items for connoisseurs and givers of elaborate gifts.[19]

Other Ming period markets located within the eastern third of
the Inner City are reflected in street names, which have been retained to this day. These include the Goldfish Market on Goldfish

------

16. For an excellent contemporary description of the market, see Liu Tong and
Yu Yizheng, *Di jing jing wu lüe*, 57–63. For another account, see Wu Changyuan,
Chen yuan shi lüe, 5.29–30. For a colorful description, see Geiss, "Peking Under the
Ming," 202–3.

17. For more on the proscription of participation by officials in the market, see
Liu Tong and Yu Yizheng, *Di jing jing wu lüe*, 58. The subsequent poems included
there provide numerous descriptions of officials enjoying the festivities, nevertheless.

18. Han Dacheng, "Mingdai de Beijing," see esp. 127.

19. Geiss, "Peking Under the Ming," 77.

Lane (Jinyu hutong 金魚胡同) and the Pasteboard Market located on Pasteboard Lane (Biaobei hutong 裱褙胡同). The latter market catered to a Ming-period custom of papering "the walls and ceilings of palaces and the mansions of the wealthy with the pictures of dragons, phoenixes, lions, tigers, or other designs, such as flowers, leaves, and insects."[20] The market also produced paper items intended for funerals and other rituals.

The prominence of luxury markets by itself would not have precluded the eastern third of the Inner City from serving as a center of scholar-official activity, but the fact that the area did not is demonstrated by a number of other factors, including scant evidence of the numerous "academies, bookstores, stationery shops, and used-book stands" that Skinner's model leads us to expect. A book market was held in front of the examination hall around the examination period. This market opened somewhat to the north of that area in the days following the New Year, but the three primary book markets in Beijing during the Ming were located on the fringes of that area or in other parts of the city: one was just south of the Zhengyang Gate; one lay in the south-central part of the Inner City; and the third was located further west in the Inner City.[21] The only other commercial activity in this part of the city specifically associated with scholar-officials during the late traditional period was found in a street located on the southeast corner of the examination hall compound. Carp Lane (Liyu hutong 鯉魚胡同) was the traditional route used by examination candidates to and from the examination hall. Carp Lane, which retains that name to this day, is said to have been named after a canal boat company that catered to examination candidates. The traditional association of the carp with

---

20. Arlington and Lewisohn, *In Search of Old Peking*, 159.
21. Cao Zixi et al., eds., *Beijing tongshi*, 6: 97. Ma Jiannong locates the three most "bustling" Ming-period markets somewhat differently: (1) in the area to the north of the Zhengyang Gate and south of the southern gate of the Imperial City; (2) in the Lantern Market area; and (3) near the Temple to the City God, in the western part of the Inner City (Ma Jiannong, "Beijing shu si fazhan shi kaolüe," see esp. 110). Ma cites primary sources that suggest books were one of many things sold at these markets. Ma also quotes an account of books purchased outside the Imperial Academy in 1497. Ma suggests that the record may refer to a bookshop established there at that time (ibid., 110).

examination candidates is reflected in such phrases as "a carp becomes a dragon" (*li hua long* 鯉化龍) and "a carp leaps the dragon's
gate" (*liyu tiao longmen* 鯉魚跳龍門), which referred to success in
the civil examinations.[22] I have been unable to determine when this
service was first offered, nor do I know when this lane first acquired
this name, but I have found no reference to the name dated before
the late nineteenth century. It seems quite possible that this service
originated in the Qing period; yet even if it existed earlier than that,
that fact by itself falls short of confirming a scholar-official nucleus
in this area.

The apparent dearth of activities specifically related to scholar-
officials in the eastern third of the Inner City argues against the
presence of a scholar-official nucleus in that area during the Ming.
Likewise, the locations of markets across the city call into question
the existence of a concentrated zone of commercial activity and
merchant residence in the area south of the three gates of the
southern Inner City wall at that time. Of the three major markets of
Ming-period Beijing, only one, the market to the south of the
Chongwen Gate, was entirely located in the Outer City.[23] Another
market was located on Drum Tower Avenue (Gulou dajie 鼓樓
大街) in the north-central area of the Inner City. The third major
market was located near and mainly to the north of the Zhengyang
Gate.[24] The area to the east of that market, in what would become
the well-known Legation Quarter of the late nineteenth and early
twentieth centuries, was the site of the specialized buying, selling,
and trading of foreign and domestic products that accompanied the
large tribute mission delegations quartered in that area. It was the
site of the capital's principal rice market, reflected in the earlier
name for the major east–west lane of the district, Riverine Rice Lane
(Jiangmi xiang 江米巷), later and to this day known as Intermin-
gling of Peoples Lane (Jiaomin xiang 交民巷).[25] Other important

---

22. Arlington and Lewisohn, *In Search of Old Peking*, 155. On the scholarly
connotations of the carp, see *Mathews' Chinese-English Dictionary*, entry #3866, 565.

23. Han Dacheng, "Mingdai de Beijing," 126–27.

24. Geiss, "Peking Under the Ming," 76–77.

25. The present name of this lane is derived from the original, more prosaic
name. This reflects a pattern observable over the past two centuries or so, whereby
Beijing place-names shifted from coarser appellations to more refined homophones

markets were located near the Temple to the City God in the western part of the Inner City and just outside the Desheng Gate 德勝門, the northwestern gate of the Inner City.

A final means of testing for the existence of concentrated and segregated scholar-official and merchant nuclei in Ming Beijing is by tracing the distribution of native-place lodges. As noted in Chapter 3, the 70 known huiguan established by sojourners in Beijing by the end of the Ming period far exceeded the numbers established in any other city at that time. If the Ming-period lodges served a less rigidly segregated clientele than did the Qing-period lodges, it is clear that they nevertheless served a relatively elite group of sojourners distinguished by wealth, learning, or official appointment. We may therefore expect that the location of the lodges would correspond roughly to the locations of the scholar-official and merchant nuclei, if they existed. However, the known distribution of Ming-period lodges does not indicate such concentrations. I have been able to determine the sites (either exact or approximate, e.g., Inner City/ Outer City) for 58 (82 percent) of the identified Ming huiguan. Of these, only thirteen (22 percent) were located in the Inner City; of those I have been able to locate five precisely. Only two were located in the eastern third of the Inner City. One, the (Jiangxi-Ji'an) Huaizhong huiguan 懷中會館, was located beside the Shuntian Prefectural Academy and on the same lane as the Imperial Academy and the Confucian Temple. The other, the Yunnan huiguan 雲南會館, was located somewhere in the vicinity of the Chaoyang Gate 朝陽門 in the eastern city wall. The other Inner City lodges were located either in the central third or the western third of the Inner City.

To the degree that the pattern of Ming-period huiguan location reflects spatial segregation based on social distinctions, it suggests that such distinctions were drawn more in accordance with socio-economic status than by occupation. Some anecdotal evidence indicates that lodges serving the wealthiest and the most powerful tended to gravitate toward the Inner City, whereas the less well off

---

or near-homophones. Thus, for example, Ox Blood (Niu xue 牛血) Lane in the southwest section of the Outer City became Overseas Study (Liu xue 留學) Lane. For more on this pattern, see Niu Ruchen, "Hutong mingcheng de yahua."

found themselves relegated to the Outer City. A late Ming account of the sites of Beijing, for example, reflects such a spatial separation within the ranks of scholar-officials: "Officials (*shen*) lodge in the Inner City huiguan, whereas the huiguan of the Outer City put up metropolitan examination candidates, provincial graduates, and scholars."[26] Another reference to huiguan from this period also describes divisions between the well-to-do and those less fortunate, rather than by occupation. An early seventeenth-century writer informs us that the lodge representing his native place "had been constructed in a lofty and splendid style, but had been taken over for the most part by prosperous sojourners from our native-place. Petty officials and scholars could not take shelter there."[27] Such evidence, taken together with the concentration of luxury markets in the Inner City, might loosely support the notion, mentioned above, of an early-modern residential pattern in which elites gravitated toward the geographical center of premodern cities. But if such a tendency existed, it was by no means universal. We can, for example, identify a number of spacious courtyard-style domiciles built by prominent scholar-officials in the western section of the Outer City during the Ming.[28]

It is clear from this evidence that Ming-period Beijing had not yet developed separate nuclei of scholar-officials and merchants. The eastern third of the Inner City was neither home to a marked concentration of socioeconomic activity associated with scholar-officials nor the site of any significant number of native-place lodges. There is no indication of an exclusive convergence of scholar-officials in any other single area. By the same token, no merchant nucleus existed in the Outer City during the Ming. Merchant activity was diffusely scattered across both the Inner and the Outer City. The origins of scholar-official and merchant nuclei in Beijing must postdate the mid-seventeenth-century transition from the Ming to Qing periods.

------

26. Liu Tong and Yu Yizheng, *Di jing jing wu lüe*, 180–81.

27. Shen Defu, *Wanli yehuo bian*, cited in He Bingdi, *Zhongguo huiguan shi-lun*, 17.

28. A rich source on the residences of former officials is found in the lane by lane descriptions of Zhu Yixin and Miao Quansun, *Jing shi fang xiang zhi*.

Urban Ecology During the
Ming-Qing Transition

The social space of Beijing was dramatically reshaped following the transition to Qing rule. To some degree this transformation resulted directly from state intervention in local society, but more sponta-neous or at least non-state-directed developments also played im-portant roles. In terms of the impact on the urban structure of Bei-jing, the single most consequential decision made by the new regime was to keep the capital in Beijing. Had the Qing government des-ignated another city as its capital, the impact on the spatial compo-sition of Beijing would have been great. Nevertheless, the early Qing years brought a tumultuous social restructuring. One major source of change was the decision on the part of the imperial regent, Dorgon, to impose a form of urban ethnic segregation. On October 5, 1648, four years after the Manchu consolidation of power in Bei-jing, Dorgon issued an edict forbidding ethnic Chinese from living or lodging in the Inner City:

Even though relocation [of the Chinese populace] will entail momentary suffering, Manchus and Han will [thus] each [live] in peace, without mu-tual annoyance. [This will] actually be for [their] eternal convenience. With the exception of Han people who have offered their services to the eight banners and who will not be relocated, all Han officials, merchants, and commoners, and so on will be moved to the South City to reside permanently.[29]

Ethnic Han owners of property within the Inner City were given the option of disassembling their structures and relocating them for reconstruction elsewhere or selling their property outright for the fixed price of four ounces of silver per column space of building. Because of the ethnic separation brought about by the edict of 1648, the Inner City and Outer City came to be known in Western ac-counts thereafter as the "Tartar City" and the "Chinese City," re-spectively.

---

29. *Qing shilu*, 40: 465, edict dated Oct. 5, 1648, cited in Wakeman, *The Great Enterprise*, 1: 147–48. The translation is based on Wakeman's, although it has been slightly altered. For an account of the loss of property as a result of this edict from the point of view of the native-place associations, see Guo Chunyu, *Bing lu riji*, 15b.

The removal of all ethnic Han from residence within the Inner City recast the social space of the capital city. Markets and other retail establishments located within the Inner City were removed to the Outer City, as were native-place lodges. The sharp contrast between the largely non-merchant character of the Inner City and the economically bustling Outer City characteristic of the Qing period did not arise until after the proclamation of this edict. Likewise, it was only after the proclamation that the spatially identifiable differentiation between scholar-official and merchant nuclei began to emerge. The area extending south from the Zheng-yang Gate to the northern edge of the Altar of Heaven and from there east roughly to the Chongwen Gate and beyond became a zone of increasingly concentrated merchant activity. By the mid-eighteenth century, this section of the Outer City had developed the attributes one should expect from the merchant nucleus described by Skinner, as the area filled with shops, markets, pawnshops, banks, and merchant guildhalls. The commercial character of the district remained its principal feature through the end of the imperial period and after.

As the area south of the Zhengyang and Chongwen gates developed into a merchant nucleus, so, too, did the area lying to the west of that district correspondingly emerge as an urban "community of scholars."[30] Soon after the 1648 edict, the area south of the Xuanwu Gate, a ward popularly referred to as the Xuannan 宣南 area, increasingly served as the locus of scholar-official activity and residence. Increasing numbers of prominent intellectual and bureaucratic figures purchased residences in the Xuannan ward beginning around the year 1650 and continuing through the next several decades.[31] Scholar-official native-place lodges also increasingly established themselves in this area. Roughly 70 percent of the 172 huiguan listed in a late eighteenth-century street gazetteer of Beijing were located in the Xuannan area (see Fig. 4.1).

---

30. The term *shixiang* 士鄉 (community of scholars) to describe the scholar-gentry nucleus in Beijing during the Qing period was suggested by Wu Jianyong, "Qing qianqi jingshi Xuannan shixiang." Wu and He Xiaolin have since more thoroughly developed the concept in their *Xuannan shixiang*.
31. Cao Zixi et al., eds., *Beijing tongshi*, 7: 274–86.

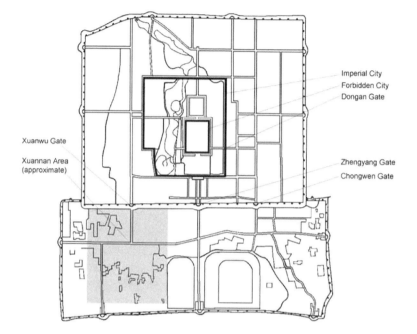

Imperial City
Forbidden City
Dongan Gate

Xuanwu Gate

Xuannan Area
(approximate)

Zhengyang Gate

Chongwen Gate

Fig. 4.1   The Xuannan area of Beijing

The scholar-official and merchant spheres became increasingly defined in the eighteenth century, and the distinction between them became further consolidated thereafter. The scholar-official nucleus was not only marked by its many luxurious literati residential quarters and its concentration of scholar-official huiguan. During the Qing, book markets and other scholar-related business activities also became fixtures of the Xuannan area. For example, the former site of the imperial roof tile kiln site, the Liuli chang 琉璃廠, located in the eastern portion of the Xuannan area, was transformed into the famous retail center for cultural products such as books, antiques, and paintings during the eighteenth century.[32] Restaurants and teahouses catering specifically to literati clientele also began to proliferate.

---

32. Hou Junxia and Wang Ruiqi, "Beijing Liuli chang wenhua jie ji," 350–51.

Why the scholar-official nucleus emerged where it did is less immediately apparent. Although the 1648 edict enforced residence in the Outer City, in some ways it would have made more sense for scholars and officials to gather on the eastern side. Residence there would have put the scholars in close proximity to such official institutions as the examination grounds and the Imperial College, to which Skinner argued they should have been drawn. The inconvenience created by the distance from the west side of the Outer City to those attractions was exacerbated by the difficulty of transportation within Beijing. Even the principal Inner City streets were not paved until the early twentieth century.[33] Needless to say, the streets of the Outer City were in a worse state. Throughout the Qing period, official neglect left the streets of the capital deeply rutted and hard to traverse. A popular local couplet humorously described Beijing street conditions:

> When the wind is calm, there is three feet of dirt.
> When the rain falls, the whole street is all mud.[34]

Clearly the Xuannan ward was not chosen for its convenience to the official literati institutions located in the eastern part of the Inner City.

The eastern side of the Outer City would appear to have had greater formal appeal as well as greater convenience. The names of city gates typically reflected the areas they presided over; for example, the gate through which the army ceremoniously passed on its way to campaigns was called the Desheng (achieve victory) Gate. One of the eastern gates was named the Chaoyang (facing the sun) Gate, and so on. If residential patterns followed the proclaimed character of each area, one would expect the scholars to have converged around the eastern Chongwen (revering civility) Gate rather than the Xuanwu (proclaiming martiality) Gate. Indeed, the most prominent official activity associated with the Xuannan area was hardly one that brought civil distinction to the district: criminals scheduled for capital punishment were transported from the Board of Punishments through the Xuanwu Gate and out to the state

---

33. Chen Zongfan, ed., *Yandu congkao*, 163.
34. Ibid.

execution ground, which stood at Vegetable Market Intersection (Caishi kou 菜市口) in the very heart of the Xuannan area.[35]

One popular explanation of why scholar-officials settled in the Xuannan area is that, as the southernmost ward of the city, it was closest to the road that brought travelers in from the North China plain via the Marco Polo Bridge (Lugou qiao 盧溝橋). That road was so closely associated with scholar-official travel into the city that daybreak as seen from the bridge was considered one of the celebrated "eight sights" of the capital, which all learned visitors to Beijing hoped to see. Because the bridge was considered one full day's journey from the city, travelers tried to pace their trips so that they would spend the final night near the bridge. That way they could awake the next day in time to see the dawn and arrive in the city before nightfall. But the proximity of the Xuannan district to this land route as an explanation for the congregation of scholar-officials there is unconvincing for a number of reasons, including the fact that in later years travel from the southern provinces was more frequently undertaken by way of the Grand Canal or by sea. Either route brought the traveler into the city from the east rather than the southwest.

It seems more likely that scholar-officials were drawn to the area partly for historical rather than strictly geographical reasons. As I mentioned above, some prominent scholar-officials had built extensive residential compounds in the Xuannan area by the late Ming period. This trend continued through the latter half of the seventeenth century.[36] Apparently the relative emptiness of the area was among the features that attracted those who sought to build spacious quarters, some of which contained sizable gardens with considerable reputations. Over time the presence of some scholar-officials attracted others to that area. Indeed, during the eighteenth

---

35. The location of the execution ground in the heart of the scholar-official residential district was not only a mark of symbolic odium but also a practical nuisance. The public procession of the condemned and the crowds of curious onlookers attracted to the spectacle of beheadings greatly disrupted transportation. See Kang Youwei, "Chronological Autobiography of K'ang Yu-wei," 46–47.

36. Wu Jianyong, "Qing qianqi jingshi Xuannan shixiang." See also Wu Jianyong and He Xiaolin, *Xuannan shixiang*.

century more and more native-place lodges were established on sites that had once served as the private residences of scholar-officials, both because those sites lent themselves to huiguan purposes and because a good number of officials donated their Beijing residences to their fellow provincials when they returned to their home regions upon retiring from office.[37] With the increase in the number of scholar-officials came the restaurants, bookstores, and other services that catered to the scholarly elite. Once a critical mass of scholars and officials emerged in the Xuannan area, others increasingly came. Thus to some degree, China's learned and powerful scholar-officials served as their own center of social gravity and pulled others of their type closer to them.

Clearly a push factor was at work in the creation of Xuannan as a scholar-official nucleus as well. Xuannan's distinctive scholarly cast was no doubt tied to the fact that the merchants of the city were attracted to the central and eastern sections of the Outer City. These parts of the Outer City afforded those engaged in commerce maximum convenience and economy. The Grand Canal served as the primary conduit for goods transported to Beijing in later imperial times. Tongzhou, the department seat just to the east of the capital, served as the northern terminus of the canal. Goods from there entered the Outer City through its eastern gate. Operating commercial enterprises on the northern side of the central and eastern sections of the Outer City provided convenient access both to the Inner City and to the source of supplies.

Even after the full emergence of the two nuclei in the eighteenth century, the merchant and scholar-official districts were never entirely distinct. Some merchant establishments that did not cater specifically to scholar-official interests existed within the Xuannan ward, and some scholars resided and socialized, at least temporarily, in the area to the south and east of the Zhengyang Gate. But the general character of the two areas became increasingly distinct over

---

37. See ibid. for a discussion of the connection between the early private compounds and the rise in the popularity of Xuannan for scholar-officials. For a partial list of Xuannan temples, parks, and well-known scholar-officials formerly resident in the district, see the impressively detailed Wang Shiren et al., eds., *Xuannan hong-xue tuzhi*, 26.

time. This development can be traced, among other ways, through stele inscriptions documenting huiguan foundings. A 1728 stele inscription from a native-place lodge established by sojourners from Nanjing, for example, describes the process that led to the increasing domination of a lodge located in what became the merchant nucleus.

Our native-place predecessors established a huiguan in the capital in order to accommodate later generations of examination candidates. . . . Since the Ming, even though small prefectures and districts produce few who have been selected for office, a great many contended to build them, yet Jinling [i.e., Nanjing] lacked one. Then in the twenty-second year of the Kangxi reign [1682], Luo Dali gathered together the strength of the community and established a huiguan to the east of Zhengyang Gate on behalf of scholars and officials. Over the years merchants began to congregate there, until there was no longer enough room to put up candidates at examination time.[38]

The text notes that through the efforts of a recently accredited graduate of the imperial examinations a plot of abandoned residential property belonging to a compatriot merchant located in the Xuannan district was obtained, and a separate huiguan for candidates and officials was established. That the two Nanjing huiguan retained their separate characters is confirmed in another stele inscription from 1805: "Originally there were established two huiguan sites, one in the east and one in the west. The western huiguan is a site for lodging examination candidates; the eastern huiguan is a site for the satin trade to offer sacrifices to the gods and to deliberate affairs."[39]

Other huiguan texts from the early eighteenth century also reveal an emerging tendency to maintain spatial separation between scholar-official and merchant huiguan. A stele erected to commemorate the establishment of a huiguan for merchants from Guangzhou in 1712 also indicates a growing separation of literati from merchants within sojourning communities from the same area:

---

38. Beijing tushuguan, Jinshi zu, *Beijing tushuguan cang Zhongguo lidai taben huibian*, vol. 68, "Yuanning xinguan bei," 58.

39. Li Hua, ed. and comp., *Ming-Qing yilai Beijing gongshang huiguan beike xuanbian*, 90.

Why is our lodge called the Xiancheng [huiguan] 仙城會館? The old lodge in the western part of the city is exclusively owned by scholar-officials (*shidafu* 士大夫). It is the Guangzhou [huiguan]. This new lodge is located in the central section of the city. It belongs to sojourning merchants. In order to distinguish it, it is not called the Guangzhou [huiguan]. It is called Xiancheng as this also is [a name for] Guangzhou.[40]

These sentiments clearly contrast with the tendency during the Ming period for wealthy officials and merchants to meet on common ground within huiguan. Thus scholar-officials clearly were increasingly drawn (and pushed) into one area of the city. It is all the more noteworthy therefore that even though the institutions that attracted scholar-officials to the area and kept them in the area were native-place lodges, the Xuannan ward itself was not noticeably segregated into separate native-place blocks or neighborhoods.

The Absence of Regional Subdivisions in the Xuannan Area

In late nineteenth-century Shanghai, residential and architectural patterns marked specific areas of the city dominated by sojourners from particular areas, such as Guangdong, Ningbo, Fujian, and Jiangxi.[41] A similar phenomenon developed in Beijing during the 1990s with the emergence of pockets of relatively homogeneous subethnic communities popularly tagged "Zhejiang Village," "Anhui Village," "Xinjiang Village," and so on.[42] In late imperial Beijing, however, there was little spatial demarcation of regional groups. This is not to say that the social space of the city as a whole was marked by an absolute homogeneity of regional groups. Some neighborhoods became gathering places for certain non-Han peo-

---

40. For a photostatic reproduction of "Xiancheng huiguan bei," see Beijing tushuguan, Jinshi zu, *Beijing tushuguan cang Zhongguo lidai taben huibian*, 67: 40. A printed version can be found in Li Hua, ed. and comp., *Ming-Qing yilai Beijing gongshang huiguan beike xuanbian*, 15–16, under the title "Chuangjian Huangpi hutong Xiancheng huiguan ji." Another version, with some textual variations, is found in Niida Noboru, *Pekin kōshō girudo*, 5: 973–75.

41. See Goodman, *Native Place*, 16–17.

42. For a sophisticated and compelling analysis of this, see Zhang, *Strangers in The City*.

ples. The area around the Tibetan-Mongolian Buddhist temple, the Yonghegong 雍和宫, in the northeast ward of the Inner City, for example, became known for the "hostelries and caravansaries (*hsia-ch'u* or *tien*), where, especially at the New Year or at other religious festivals, Mongols from Urga, Kiahkta, and Kobdo, Buryats from the Baikal lake, Kamucks from the Volga river, Manchus from Tsitsikhar, Tanguts from the Kuku-nor, Tibetans from Lhasa, and occasionally even [. . . Gurkhas] from Nepal, bustled and jostled."[43] Likewise, the area surrounding the mosque on Ox Street (Niu jie 牛街) in the southwestern ward of the Outer City had been known for its Moslem residents since before the founding of the Ming dynasty.[44] Of course, the forced relocation of Han residences to the southern city in the early years of the Qing is another example of the organization of social space along regional/ethnic lines.

What is rarely seen in Beijing of this period is the spatial demarcation of ethnic-Han regional groups. In the Xuannan area, there was a slight tendency for regional groups to try to locate their lodges near lodges already established by those from the same region. It is not unusual to find references in huiguan-produced texts to a decision to buy a particular property partly because of its proximity to an existing lodge or lodges serving those from the same general area, but no significant pockets of spatially defined native-place communities developed among scholar-officials or other classes. Throughout the Xuannan area, the lodges of different provinces were intermingled in no perceivable pattern; there were no neighborhoods dominated by the sojourners of one region or another.

The pattern of lodge location reflects the fact that social interaction within the Xuannan ward was by no means limited to contacts among those with native-place ties. The diaries of later literati figures such as the powerful late nineteenth-century official Weng Tonghe and the early twentieth-century author Lu Xun 鲁迅 (1881–1936) are revealing in this respect. Both Weng and Lu lived in the Xuannan area for years. Weng lived in a private residence on Nan-heng jie 南横街 within the Xuannan ward, but he maintained

---

43. Lessing, *Yung-Ho-Kung*, 2.
44. Naquin, *Peking*, 213.

close contact with the lodge representing his native city of Changshu (Jiangsu). Lu lived for seven years in the Shan-Gui xian guan otherwise known as the Shaoxing yiguan 紹興邑館 on Nanbanjie hutong 南半截胡同. Although separated in time, social status, and political rank, both Weng and Lu were meticulous keepers of diaries, and both record a life richly packed with social contact. Weng records over a hundred visits to a wide range of huiguan representing other regions, and Lu's diary, too, is replete with references to visits to other huiguan. Both diarists reveal patterns of constant, frequent social interactions with other members of their class, most of it within the Xuannan area and much of it on huiguan grounds. But interaction was not especially limited to native-place compatriots. Rather, the hundreds of huiguan packed into one section of the city helped create a spatially defined social sphere of scholar-official values and interests. Although operating along lines of native place–based particularistic ties, scholar-gentry huiguan did not channel or limit scholar-official interaction along regional lines. On the contrary, huiguan provided all scholars having the proper credentials with access to a cosmopolitan world of literati from around the empire.

In important ways, the Xuannan "community of scholars" operated in ways diametrically opposed to the regional "villages" of recent years. As Li Zhang has argued, the villages are composed of and represent marginalized populations of laboring and petty-entrepreneurial migrants; the spatial coalescing of these groups reinforces regional bonds and regional identities.[45] The Xuannan area, on the other hand, after it became the scholar-official nucleus in Beijing in the eighteenth century, served to bring scholar-official elites of different regions together and helped to forge a sense of imperium that would greatly facilitate and inform the emergence of a concept of a "national" China in the late nineteenth century.

---

45. Li Zhang, *Strangers in The City*.

The Extent of Space
Occupied by Native-Place Lodges

The huiguan occupied a surprising amount of space in Beijing. Exactly how much can be estimated only crudely, but it is worth trying, since the amount of space in the city controlled by native-place lodges is one more indicator of the degree to which the capital was shaped by this form of local/center interaction. In fact, property belonging to native-place lodges constituted a significant portion of the total real property area in Beijing. The amount of property owned by huiguan peaked in the late nineteenth and early twentieth centuries, but the trend toward extensive purchases of real estate by native-place lodges began much earlier. According to contemporary accounts, vigorous acquisition of property by huiguan dramatically affected property values as early as the latter part of the eighteenth century. A dramatic rise in the purchase prices of all buildings and land in the Outer City over a period of several decades around that time was directly attributed to the competition among sojourners to establish huiguan.[46]

Not all huiguan property was used to lodge compatriots. As mentioned in the previous chapter, operation of cemeteries was another important huiguan function. The location of huiguan cemeteries was also marked by a distinct macrospatial pattern. In addition to the scholar-official nucleus in the Xuannan area on the west side of the Outer City, and the merchant/trade nucleus in the area to the south of the Zhengyang Gate and extending further east from there, a third area of the Outer City was largely given over to these native-place cemeteries. This area was located in a wide swath running inside the western, southern, and eastern edges of the Outer City, just inside the city walls.[47] This explains the reformer/philosopher Tan Sitong's 譚嗣同 (1865–98) otherwise cryptic remark that "the Southern City had few people and many ghosts" (*cheng nan shao ren er duo gui*). Native-place cemeteries were not the only cemeteries in Beijing; the government operated graveyards for paupers, and prosperous lineages maintained cemeteries outside the

---

46. Wang Qishu, *Shui cao qing xia lu,* cited in Wu Zhezheng, "Huiguan," 85.
47. Tan Sitong, "Cheng nan si jiu ming bing xu" in idem, *Tan Sitong quanji,* 23.

city walls, but huiguan clearly operated the most extensive cemetery facilities in the capital. Maps printed well into the Republican period still clearly mark the native-place cemeteries along this urban-fringe area, and it was not until the 1950s, when the graves were removed under government direction, that that area began to be more vigorously dedicated to other purposes.

How much area was occupied by lodge compounds and cemeteries? The total area is not easily approximated, but the 1949 survey conducted by the Civil Administration Bureau, discussed in the previous chapter, can give us a good idea of the impressive extent of holdings. This report, as its own authors admit, significantly understated actual holdings. Nevertheless, the investigation records a total of 716 main compound and subsidiary compound sites, representing 21,775.5 *jian* in building area (a *jian*, a traditional Chinese measurement of building size based on the area between building columns, is approximately equivalent to a room). An additional 48 native-place charitable cemeteries occupying 855 *mu*, or approximately 130 acres, were also recorded.[48]

How much area do these figures actually represent? Since *jian* vary in size, and since the very nature of this traditional measurement excludes open space, it is difficult to estimate. However, we do have data on building space in *jian* and on acreage in *mu* for the Guangdong huiguan from several years later.[49] According to this later and more detailed report, Guangdong huiguan holdings consisted of 3,002.5 *jian* or 298.853 *mu* (approximately 45.3 acres). Of this amount, 61 *jian* or 152.708 *mu* represented graveyard land and associated buildings.[50] If we subtract the figures for cemeteries from the total (since the *jian* to *mu* ratio of graveyards was uniquely skewed

---

48. Beijing shi renmin zhengfu, Minzhengju, "1949 nian Beijing huiguan qingkuang diaocha baogao," 32–33. Note that the graveyard figure is especially underestimated here: of the 98 huiguan that reported owning graveyards, 63 (64.3 percent) did not report the extent of those holdings. The figure of 716 huiguan sites also appears to exclude strictly rental properties owned by huiguan.

49. Beijing shi Guangdong sheng huiguan caichan guanli weiyuanhui choubei, *Diyi jie weiyuanhui gongzuo baogao* (1951).

50. This figure does not include 3.1 *mu* of land belonging to the Guangdong xin yiyuan graveyard, which was appropriated by the state in November 1951; see ibid., "Beijing shi Guangdong sheng huiguan caichan guanli weiyuanhui choubei hui jieguan fangdi chan tongji biao," n.p.

in favor of *mu*, and because the two types of properties were typically separately reckoned), then the total non-graveyard property owned by Guangdong huiguan in Beijing amounted to 2,941.5 *jian* and 146.145 *mu*. These figures are interesting for a number of reasons. For one thing, they indicate the degree to which the 1949 report may have underestimated total huiguan holdings. The Civil Administration Bureau survey recorded only 2,479.5 *jian* of non-graveyard Guangdong huiguan property (a 15 percent underestimate), and it recorded none of the huiguan's extensive (approximately 23 acres) graveyard property. There is no reason to assume that the Guangdong figures in the 1949 report were unusual in their degree of miscalculation, although some of the other provincial graveyards were included in that report.

The Guangdong provincial huiguan figures also give us an approximate ratio of twenty *jian* per *mu* of compound land that we may cautiously apply to the total for all lodges in Beijing. This ratio yields a rough calculation that the combined total of 22,237.5 *jian* of non-graveyard property reported in the Civil Administration Bureau and Guangdong huiguan reports represents 1,112 *mu*, or 168 acres, occupied by huiguan. Adding the 1,010 *mu* of graveyard property included in the two reports gives a figure of 2,122 *mu* (321.5 acres, or approximately half a square mile) of real estate owned by huiguan, the vast majority of which was located within the Outer City walls. There can be little doubt that this underestimates the land occupied by native-place lodges. In terms of the volume of occupied space alone, there seems little doubt that native-place lodges ranked as the one of most expansive civil institutions of the capital.

In dealing with the spatial aspects of huiguan, not only the extent of lodge property but also the nature of that property has much to tell us. In the next chapter, therefore, the focus turns to an analysis of the characteristic physical features of lodge property.

FIVE

Huiguan as Space

Native-place lodges often consisted of several sites or compounds. The heart of every lodge was the main compound. Although these compounds were not necessarily the most spacious of huiguan holdings (charitable graveyards were often larger), they were, invariably, the centerpiece and social focus of huiguan properties. Some main compounds were much larger and more elaborate than others, but almost all had some form of public area, whether meeting hall or altar, in addition to the residential quarters. Many lodges also managed subsidiary compounds in addition to the main compound. These may have stood immediately adjacent to the main compound or have been located separately in another lane or in another area of the city altogether. The smallest lodge compounds were simple and spartan, consisting of only plain lodging rooms arranged around a single courtyard or two. Such compounds may have offered little beyond meager living quarters and a small altar. In contrast, more elaborate main compounds occupied large portions of city blocks, boasted courtyard after expansive courtyard, and provided a variety of facilities from meeting halls to opera stages (all described in more detail below).

The spaciousness of a compound area depended on a number of factors, including the relative wealth of the lodge to which it belonged. To a certain degree, the scope and architectural features of compounds reflected the administrative level of the region represented by the huiguan. Provincial-level huiguan were more likely to boast opera stages and gardens, whereas district-level huiguan tended to have only living quarters, meeting areas, and altars. There were innumerable exceptions to this pattern, and it cannot be taken as strict principle, but there was a clear general tendency for huiguan representing relatively larger administrative areas to have more ceremonial and social facilities.

Bryna Goodman has suggested that the architectural features of native-place lodges in Shanghai were modeled on or, perhaps more to the point, symbolically reflected the style of government office compounds (*yamen* 衙門).[1] Such a style of represented authority provides a telling contrast with Beijing scholar-official huiguan, which were conspicuously not constructed in the style of *yamen*. To begin with, any attempt to emulate *yamen* architecturally would have been thwarted by the inability of huiguan planners to guarantee the necessary south-to-north layout that marked *yamen* and other official buildings as seats of power.[2] The directional coordinates of lodge layouts could only conform to the characteristics of the irregular-shaped plots of land they occupied within the haphazard jumble of Outer City streets and oddly shaped property units. Some huiguan units faced north; others faced east or west, or any of the other possibilities.

Ordinational coordinates aside, the adoption by scholar-official huiguan of the residential walled courtyard (*siheyuan* 四合院) style of architecture characteristic of Beijing represented an even more telling difference between *yamen* and the lodges. The *siheyuan* style was primarily a residential style. Indeed, a great number of huiguan

---

1. Goodman, *Native Place*, 18–21.

2. It might seem that we could ignore the directional coordinates, but the highly developed directional awareness of Beijing residents is well known even within China. There must be nowhere in the world where the term "receiving directions" can more appropriately be employed. To this day, it is not unusual even within buildings to be given instructions such as "walk down this hall and turn north"!

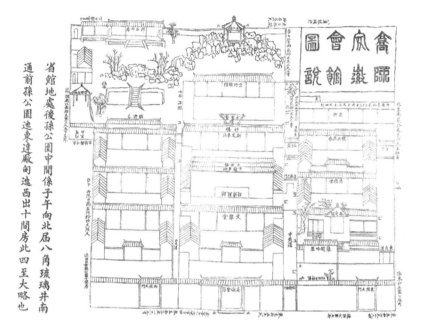

Fig. 5.1   The Anhui huiguan on Hou Sun gongyuan.

began as the residences of important officials and other prominent men before being reconstructed to serve as lodges. Some cases of particular interest include the (Guangdong) Guangzhou huiguan, which occupied the former site of the northern Mustard Seed Garden compound of famed Ming-period playwright and author Li Yu 李漁 (1611–80?), and the (Guangdong) Dongguan huiguan 東莞會館, which was situated within the former residence of the Ming loyalist general Zhang Jiayu 張家玉 (1615–47). The spacious residential compound of the late Ming–early Qing official and author Sun Chengze 孫承澤 (1592–1676) was divided to form the compounds of the (Jiangsu) Xijin huiguan 錫金會館, the (Fujian) Quanjun huiguan 泉郡會館, the (Zhejiang) Taizhou huiguan 台州會館, and the Anhui huiguan 安徽會館 (see Fig. 5.1). Indeed, the lanes on which these lodges were located are still called Qian Sun gongyuan (前孫公園) and Hou Sun gongyuan (後孫公園), in reference to Sun's earlier residence.

Fig. 5.2   Courtyard of a Beijing native-place lodge (SOURCE: this sketch was drawn for the author by He Zhengqiang, who grew up in the (Guangdong) Zhaoqing huiguan on Li Tiegui xiejie).

Architecturally speaking, huiguan sites most resembled the elite residential compounds belonging to the Manchu aristocracy, offi-cials, or other gentry. This style was expressed in, among other features, the low (one-story) style of most buildings, the unfolding procession of semi-discrete courtyards arranged within the com-pound, the expansiveness of contained open areas, and the numer-ous trees and internal gardens (see Fig. 5.2). The significance of this style should not be underestimated. If the *yamen* humbled the visitor and bespoke authority, the *siheyuan* style welcomed the so-journer with a more personable promise of some privacy from the outside world and ordered social harmony within. In an insightful analysis of the significance of this architectural style, Yingjin Zhang comments, "The [*siheyuan*] architectural style seems to predispose residents to close human connections." Zhang tellingly compares the *siheyuan* style, not with *yamen*, but with the buildings of the village.[3] The architecture of huiguan expressed the prominent social status of the scholar-officials they served, but in a way that offered less the authority of power than the bonds of community.

Compound Features

From the street, no particular architectural grandeur identified huiguan, but each compound was marked by a large wooden placard inscribed with the name of the lodge. These placards were customarily carved in the calligraphy of noted compatriots and were occasionally accompanied by eulogistic poetic couplets hung on either side of the main gate. Some huiguan entrances were protected with iron gates (*zha lan* 柵欄), which sealed off the compound from the disorder of the streets when closed at night. Even during the day, little inside the compound would have been visible from the street, since large spirit screens built just within the front entrances kept out stray gazes and bad *fengshui*. Once beyond the spirit screen, and the watchful eyes and possible inquisition of the lodge caretaker (*kanguan* 看館 or *zhangban* 長班), a visitor would have found the compound divided into numerous courtyards. Although the compound would have been similar to a typical residential layout, a number of architectural features specifically characteristic of huiguan would also have been present.

Among the unique features were large meeting halls; banqueting facilities, courtyards lined with small cubicle-like rooms designed to put up one person or at most two, multitiered opera stages with two-story audience areas, and ceremonial space designed around altars. Many huiguan compounds also boasted gardens, kitchens, and even small libraries. Basic design features varied little over the centuries. Unlike Shanghai and Nanjing, where some native-place associations—a Republican-period incarnation of native-place lodges—were established in "modern" Western-style buildings, no similar trend was evident in Beijing (see Fig. 5.3).[4]

---

3. Yingjin Zhang, *The City in Modern Chinese Literature and Film*, 87–88.
4. For Shanghai, see Goodman, *Native Place*, 278–81; for Nanjing, see Fig. 5.3.

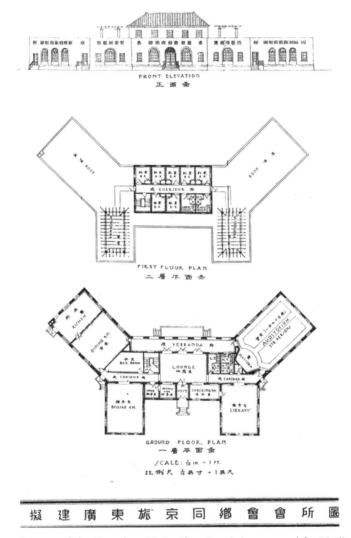

Fig. 5.3   Diagram of the Guangdong Native-Place Association proposed for Nanjing (late Republican period) (SOURCE: diagram from *Guangdong lüjing tongxiang hui gongzuo gaikuang*, 1930).

Note how greatly this design differs from the courtyard style adopted by the native-place lodges of Beijing. Rooms for temporary lodging are still provided on the second floor, although such features as the bar, billiard room, check room, and even the second floor itself were alien to Beijing huiguan. The western style of the building and even the style of the diagram (complete with English as well as Chinese labels) connote a "modern" sensibility, and may also reflect the style of Nanjing's government buildings.

A large meeting hall, typically the most prominent and majestic of the buildings, served as the architectural focus of most huiguan. The hall provided compatriots with a space for meetings to discuss matters of concern to the lodge or to the sojourning community in the capital and events back home. During examination times, the hall also doubled as study space for last-minute preparation by the candidates. From the pillars supporting the hall were hung couplets extolling the superior qualities of the region represented. Wooden placards inscribed with the names of the locality's graduates of the imperial examinations, permanent reminders of the accomplishments of the men from that region, were displayed along the hall's roof beams. The meeting hall was generally located near the main entrance to the compound. It presented to visitors both a practical gathering space and symbolic confirmation of the accomplishments of compatriots over time. The size and placement of the hall also served to separate the more public area of the compound from the residential area to its rear, which was filled with smaller courtyards and guest rooms.

The lion's share of space within lodge compounds was set aside for temporary lodgers with dormitory-style rooms typically set around any number of small courtyards. The rooms were utilitarian and designed along relatively egalitarian lines; there were no first- or second-class rooms, and none was extravagantly larger than the others. As far as residential form was concerned, within the huiguan all compatriots were brothers.

Over the next few pages, I briefly reconstruct living conditions inside huiguan. This is a worthwhile exercise for many reasons. Knowledge of the living arrangements of scholars and officials in the capital adds to our understanding of Beijing's social and cultural life. As I discuss below, the spatial arrangement of the lodges provides insight into the roles they played (and did not play) as transmitters and replicaters of cultural practices and habits. Perhaps even more important, the interior spaces of huiguan compounds, including the residential areas, became the sites of meetings and actions with political overtones in later years. In the following chapters, I show that the public/private nature of these spaces was an important factor shaping the relationship between the lodges and the state.

Lodgers were put up one or two to a room, depending on circumstance and demand. Huiguan regulations often strictly prescribed the number of lodgers to be boarded in each room. The
Nanchang huiguan rules are typical: "As for huiguan rooms, those
that are small [shall accommodate] one person per room, wide and
spacious rooms [shall accommodate] two persons acquainted with
each other."[5] Some huiguan stipulated that lodgers were expected to
live one to a room except during examination periods, when all
boarders were to double up. The (Fujian) Zhangzhou huiguan 漳州
會館 insisted that two to a room was the norm, although the rules
did allow a "departure from principle" (*tongrong* 通融) and individual occupation of rooms at times of low demand.

Huiguan beds consisted of thin padded-cotton mattresses atop
wooden bedsteads. *Kang*, the traditional heated bed of Beijing and
other north China residences, typically depended on coals from the
kitchen for heat, and in huiguan the rooms for lodgers far out-
numbered kitchens and stoves. Sharing a room presumably would,
in some cases, have meant sharing a bed. But the regulations of the
(Hunan) Shanhua huiguan 善化會館 make clear that sharing a bed
was not always expected; they dictate that larger rooms be furnished
with two cots (*ta* 榻), one per lodger.[6]

According to the rules of most huiguan, lodgers were not supposed to occupy more than one room.[7] Yet some evidence suggests
that, in practice, lodges may have been somewhat flexible on this
point. If demand was low, a well-connected guest, or one generous
with his tips to the caretaker, might have been able to arrange to
occupy several rooms. In some lodges, occupying several rooms
might even have been standard practice, at least at times when the
examinations were not being held or demand for huiguan space was
low. The regulations of the (Anhui) Shexian huiguan provide clear

---

5. *Nanchang xian zhi* (1870), 2.9. The regulations of the Shanhua huiguan similarly mandated one lodger per small room and two per large room. They further
stipulated that the person who arrived first was forbidden from arbitrarily
occupying more than his share of the space and relegating the later-arriving tenant
to the fringes of their shared room; see *Shanhua guan zhi* (1888), *juan* 1, "Huiguan
guiyue," 7.

6. *Shanhua guan zhi* (1888), *juan* 1, "Huiguan guiyue," 3.

7. See, e.g., *Minzhong huiguan zhi*, "Zhangzhou huiguan."

evidence that "suites" of two or three rooms were rented out as a set to some lodgers. The huiguan rules of 1805 indicate that there were two sets of housing principles. The first article dictated the rooming policy for examination periods and stated that no individual was to occupy more than one room. However, another article declares that during those years in which no examinations were held, expectant officials, those coming for an imperial audience, and metropolitan officials were permitted to stay in the lodge, and the rent for these lodgers was to be calculated according to the number of *jian* 間 per *fang* 房.[8]

What is meant by this distinction between *jian* and *fang* (which are used synonymously in the modern vernacular to indicate a room)? The map of the (Guangdong) Nanhai huiguan makes the answer readily apparent (see Fig. 5.4). Rooms were divided into sets (*fang*) of two or three rooms (*jian*). A *fang* typically represented one side of an interior courtyard. In practice, some lodgers were allowed to occupy a whole *fang* instead of a single *jian*. The layout of the Shexian huiguan similarly depicts sets of rooms (here labeled *wu*) arranged around courtyards (see Fig. 5.5). Indeed, the number of *jian* per *wu* is noted but not drawn on the diagram; this may reflect a tendency to think of these sets of rooms as single units.

We can point to several examples of lodgers allowed to occupy more than one room. Tan Sitong, the philosopher, reformer, and martyr of the Hundred Days Reforms, occupied three rooms in the (Hunan) Liuyang huiguan 瀏陽會館 in the 1890s. Tan's father had been a leader in the effort to establish the huiguan in 1872, and at one point in 1874–75 Tan's entire family had resided on the premises. Tan dubbed his quarters the Verdant Studio (Mang cang cang zhai 莽蒼蒼齋), and that name was later bestowed on his poetry collection.[9] Interestingly, perhaps the most important reformer of that time, Kang Youwei 康有爲 (1855–1927), also dubbed his quarters

---

8. *Shexian huiguan lu*, "Xinji," 12–13.

9. Tong Xun, "Liuyang huiguan Mang cang cang zhai." This informative article includes a diagram of the Liuyang huiguan indicating the rooms occupied by Tan. Tan's collection of poetry, published the year before his execution, was entitled *Mangcangcang zhai shi*.

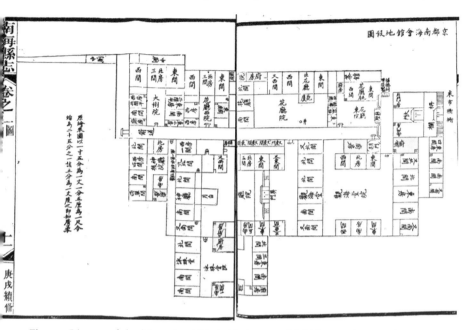

Fig. 5.4 Diagram of the (Guangdong) Nanhai huiguan on Mishi hutong (SOURCE: diagram from the *Nanhai xian zhi*, 1910).

Note the main entrance is on the upper right side. The diagram indicates that there used to be an iron gate in front of the entrance (which no longer exists). The site stands on the west side of the street and entrance is from the east. Upon entry into the compound, the first courtyard on one's right contained a small altar and a ceremonial burner for the burning of paper on which there was writing. Kitchens have been highlighted for emphasis.

in the (Guangdong) Nanhai huiguan 南海會館 with a literary name and later published a collection of his poetry under that name. Kang, too, appears to have occupied a set of rooms on one side of an interior courtyard in that compound, but I have not been able to verify this.[10]

During the Republican period, at least one lodger in the (Zhejiang) Shaoxing xianguan 紹興縣館 (known earlier as the Shan-Gui yiguan) certainly occupied multiple rooms. When Lu Xun first moved into the lodge, he was allotted only a single room, but years

---

10. Kang styled his quarters the Ship on the Wide Seas Studio (Han man fang 汗漫舫). His collected works of poetry were published as the *Han man fang shiji*. See *Beijing Lingnan wenwu zhi*, 51–54; and the informative article by Wei Jingzhao, "Nanhai huiguan chunqiu."

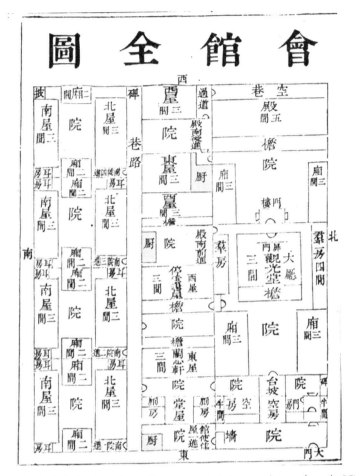

Fig. 5.5   The (Anhui) Shexian lodge on Xuanwumen dajie (SOURCE: diagram from the [*Chong-xu*] *Shexian huiguan lu*, 1834).

Note the main gate is at the bottom right-hand corner. The lodge stood on the west side of the street; thus entrance was from the east. The meeting hall is in the right central part of the diagram. The lodge altar is in the top right-hand corner. Kitchens have been highlighted for emphasis.

later he moved to a set of rooms in a different part of the compound. In fact, as is discussed in the last chapter, Lu moved to new quarters twice. During the last several years of his stay, Lu occupied a set of rooms that formed one side of a private courtyard. Lu's brother, Zhou Zuoren 周作人 (1885–1967), moved into one of the rooms for a period following his return from Japan, and he later described Lu's accommodations in great detail. Indeed, so vividly did Zhou recreate the physical presence of Lu's quarters, and so rare is such a detailed description of the spatial arrangement of huiguan living quarters, that it is worth quoting Zhou's comments at length.

The Replaced Tree Studio consisted of a row of four rooms facing east. The front door was located in the center of the second room. The room to the south, and the two rooms to the north were attached. In the courtyard against the north wall was a small room with a cooking stove inside. It was intended to house a servant. On the east side of the courtyard, abutting the back wall of the lodge shrine and down a narrow alley was a northern-style lavatory, with a "squatting latrine." Because this small toilet stuck out in front, the window of the north room was blocked off from the sunlight and was therefore very dark. When Lu Xun lived there, he did not ordinarily use [the north room]; so he sealed off that door and used only the three southern rooms.

In the middle room was the door. Across from it against the wall stood a drawing table, in front of which stood a round eight-person table at which meals were taken. The table was an extremely old and beat-up thing that probably belonged to the lodge. The room to the south was where Lu Xun lived originally, but when I came to Beijing, he gave it to me and moved into the opposite room. All the rooms were very old-fashioned. The windows were Japanese style and were entirely papered over. There was no glass. In the summer, one could put in a strip of green coarse cloth [used in North China to screen in windows] to make a roll-up window. I found a small pane of glass and inserted it into the window frame myself, so I could see guests coming through the round moon gate [to our courtyard], but Lu Xun never even put green coarse cloth into the window in his room.

In the southwest corner of the southernmost room of the Replaced Tree Studio was a bed; in the southeast corner below the window stood a square desk with drawers; beside that to the north were placed two leather trunks covered with burlap. Against the northern wall stood a bookcase, although it did not hold books. On the top shelf were tea, matches, and various miscellaneous items including some copper cash, and on the bottom shelf were piled old and new newspapers. In front of the bookcase was a rattan lounge, and in front of the desk stood a rattan chair. In front of the bed against the wall were two square stools between which was squeezed a narrow tea table. All this was used for guests. When, between hosts and guests, there were more than four people, the bed was used. At the height of the summer when the weather was hot, occasionally the chairs were moved outside beneath the eaves.[11]

In this passage Zhou referred to two other types of compound space that greatly marked the character of the lodges. These are kitchens and altars, both of which deserve brief consideration.

Space as
Cultural Bulwark: Kitchens

In a fascinating article on the cuisines of China during the Yuan and Ming periods, F. W. Mote argued that huiguan played a significant role in the production and replication of regionally specific cultures during the Ming period and thereafter. Mote's article essentially presented huiguan as outposts of regional cuisine in "alien" territory and thus as institutions engaged in a process of regional cultural reproduction in urban centers throughout the empire:

> Characteristically, the huiguan in Beijing had a staff of employees from the home locality, including cooks. The Suzhou merchant or statesman residing temporarily at the Suzhou huiguan in Beijing, at any of the important centers along the Grand Canal or the Yangtze, or at other important locations, could expect to hear his Suzhou speech and to eat his fine Suzhou soup noodles and pastries for breakfast. Although this is mere conjecture, one might assume that the great expansion of the huiguan institution from mid-Ming times onward contributed much to establishing provincial cuisines in all the major cities.[12]

This is a vision to which I was favorably disposed when I began this study. However, I have found little evidence that huiguan kitchens were organized replicaters of regional culture—a point worth examining in further detail.

As Mote suggested, many of the most prominent huiguan did have large central kitchens, but did lodge kitchens employ compatriot chefs to produce regional food? Weng Tonghe recorded in his diary the dishes presented at several elaborate banquets held in various provincial huiguan, but although he briefly described some

---

11. Zhou Xiashou, *Lu Xun de gu jia*: first paragraph, 406–7; second paragraph, 412; third paragraph, 420.
12. Mote, "Yüan and Ming," 244.

of the more elaborate dishes, he did not mention, and it is not possible to infer with any certainty, whether these dishes were examples of regional cuisine.[13] In fact, repeated entries in his diary make clear that major banquets held in huiguan were prepared under the direction of chefs brought in and employed by the host. Huiguan facilities were booked because they were spacious and because guests could also be entertained with opera performances, but they were not noted as showcases for regional cuisines because the actual direction of the cooking was not left to the employees of the lodge. One example is a New Year's get-together thrown for government officials in 1888, which cost over 700 taels (the Board of Revenue contributed 300 taels, the Imperial Household Department 100 taels, the Head Office of the Customs and Octroi at the Chongwen Gate [Chongwen men shuiwu yamen 崇文門稅務衙門] 100 taels; each guest kicked in 2 taels) and which Weng characterized as lavish. It was held in the Anhui huiguan, but in his diary Weng noted that the head chef was the family chef of one Mr. Lao.[14] At other banquets, Weng often recorded the name of the chef employed to cook the meal, especially when he himself was the host. For example, for a banquet at the Anhui huiguan in 1893, Weng hired his own chef.[15] It seems clear that the major banquets thrown on huiguan premises did not serve the cuisine associated with the region the lodge represented. Instead, the chef hired by the host determined the style of food. But what about the daily fare served within huiguan for the lodgers in residence there? Might that have been prepared in regional cuisine style?

Part of Mote's contention is that all the cooks employed within a huiguan would have hailed from the region represented. One can easily imagine the advantages of hiring only compatriots for such jobs, but there is little evidence to support the notion that huiguan

13. Weng, for instance, describes a fish served at a dinner held at the (Guangdong) Guangzhou merchant huiguan, the Xiancheng huiguan, as "delicious beyond what one tastes in ordinary life," but whether it was cooked in Guangdong style is unknown.

14. Weng Tonghe, *Weng Tonghe riji* (GX 14.1.22), 1526. Mr. Lao was presumably Lao Kaichen, an official in the Board of Punishments, who managed other banquets hosted by Weng as well; see, e.g., ibid. (GX 14.10.08), 1563.

15. Ibid. (GX 19.9.26), 1843.

employees were fellow natives. Can we identify the places of origin of huiguan staff? Although huiguan regulations are quite specific about who qualified to be selected as an administrator, they say nothing about the qualifications required of huiguan employees. The absence of regulations about this may, indeed, reflect an open policy regarding the geographical origins of lodge workers. The only direct evidence on this point that I have come across is found in documents relating to a late nineteenth-century court case involving a cook employed by the (Guangdong) Xiangshan huiguan.[16] The case itself is briefly discussed in Chapter 3, but what is of interest to us here is that the depositions and other documents reveal that the cook was officially registered as a native of nearby Wuqing county (a rural county to the southeast of Beijing), not Xiangshan or any other county in Guangdong province.

This evidence, of course, is merely anecdotal. It is quite possible that the major huiguan kitchens did, in general, employ regional natives and did, in general, prepare regional fare, although, if true, the fact received remarkably little comment from contemporaries. The idea of huiguan as institutionalized bulwarks of regional cuisine is fundamentally challenged by another fact, however. This brings us back to Lu Xun's courtyard and his brother's description of a "small room there with a cooking stove inside." The majority of huiguan appear not to have operated central kitchens. Most scholar-gentry huiguan instead provided smaller kitchens, located at various spots around the residential area, for communal use by lodgers. They did not, however, offer any kind of prepared meal service. If the Suzhou traveler depicted by Mote wanted to enjoy his "fine Suzhou soup noodles and pastries" for breakfast, in most cases he or a servant would have had to prepare them. The 1770 regulations of the (Hebei) Hejian huiguan 河間會館 give specific instructions for the use of such kitchens, noting that each of the six kitchens within the compound was reserved for the use of lodgers in a specific set of rooms. Guests were forbidden to use the kitchens assigned to other areas; they were further forbidden to set up cooking stoves in their own rooms for fear of fire.[17] Although other huiguan regulations tend to

---

16. Number One Historical Archives of China, Xingbu, no. 01134.

17. [*Chongxiu*] *Hejian huiguan ji*, 38.

say less about the use of kitchens, it is evident from the maps of huiguan that many shared this feature of multiple kitchens provided for the individual use of lodgers (consider the eleven kitchens depicted in Fig. 5.4 and the three kitchens depicted in Fig. 5.5).

Huiguan also invariably established altars dedicated to the worship of regional deities of particular significance to scholars and officials. In many huiguan the altar was the second largest building in the compound. Generally speaking, altars were located toward the rear of the main compound. Like meeting halls, and unlike lodging rooms, which were constructed in traditional single-story (*pingfang* 平房) style with brick walls and angled tile roofs, huiguan altars were often built with columns supporting a multi-bracketed roof. At times of great demand for lodging space, there was considerable pressure to open meeting halls and altars to accommodate temporary boarders. Presumably, this did happen from time to time, even though many regulations explicitly forbid even short-term occupation of these public spaces by lodgers.[18] Indeed, the very existence of the regulations implies the occurrence of the proscribed behavior, yet clearly the space represented by altars was valued beyond its potential residential utility. Because the role played by altars in the replication of regional culture and construction of scholar-official identity was tied to the rituals conducted in them, they are discussed in more detail in the next chapter.

Huiguan Stages

The final category of space within the huiguan compound that deserves to be discussed was the area set aside for opera stages. One feature of provincial scholar-official huiguan that was not typical of lodges representing subprovincial regions is that scholar-official lodges representing whole provinces generally set aside a space for an opera stage. Not all provincial-level huiguan boasted stages, but among those with notable stages were the Anhui huiguan, the Hunan xinguan 湖南新館, the Jiangsu huiguan 江蘇會館, the (Guangdong) Yuedong huiguan, the (Yunnan) Zhao gong ci 趙公祠,

---

18. See, e.g., *Minzhong huiguan zhi*, "Fuzhou huiguan."

and the (Hunan and Hubei) Huguang huiguan 湖廣會館. Indeed, the Huguang huiguan has recently been refurbished and opened to the public as a Chinese opera museum, and has become one of the more popular venues for Beijing opera in the city.

Somewhat in contrast to the scholar-official lodge pattern, numerous merchant huiguan, including many representing sub-provincial level regions, boasted stages. Among the merchant huiguan in Beijing with stages were the (Zhejiang, Shaoxing) Zhengyi ci 正乙祠, also known as the Yinhao huiguan 銀號會館, representing Zhejiang native bankers; the (Shanxi, Pingyao, and Jiexiu) Ping-Jie huiguan 平介會館, representing bankers and those involved in the pawn, dyestuffs, and silk trades; the (Shanxi) Taiping huiguan 太平會館, representing all trades and, as of the eighteenth century, scholars and officials as well; the (Fujian, Yanping, and Shaowu) Yan-Shao huiguan 延邵會館, representing paper merchants; the (Shanxi provincial) Hedong huiguan 河東會館, representing all tobacco and other merchants; and the (Shanxi, Pingyang prefecture) Pingyang huiguan 平陽會館, representing all merchants from there. Many of these stages still exist. There is evidence that the stage at the Pingyang huiguan may date to the seventeenth century, which would make it one of the oldest wooden theatrical stages in the world.[19]

The association of opera stages with provincial huiguan reflects the role of these lodges as banqueting facilities and social centers for the highest-ranking officials of the capital. The lodging of examination candidates was a less central function of these facilities, and some even forbade examination candidates and officials below a specified rank from using the premises (a point discussed in more detail in Chapter 9). In some sense, these sites might be thought of as a subcategory of the Beijing scholar-official lodge. Architecturally they tended to contain more public spaces, and the public spaces tended to be more elaborate, including larger gardens and meeting halls. The huiguan mentioned above served as frequent sites for large annual banquets hosted by the boards during the New Year's

---

19. See Li Chang, "Tantan Yangping huiguan juchang." As the title of this article suggests, there has been some confusion about whether this site was the Pingyang or Yangping huiguan. It was, in fact, the Pingyang huiguan.

season on behalf of the officials who worked in them. They also served as sites for elaborate personal parties featuring opera and banquets. Throughout his diary, Weng Tonghe mentioned many examples of both kinds of affairs held at various lodges.

Huiguan in Space and Huiguan as Space

The spatial characteristics of Beijing native-place lodges reveal much about the social history of the capital and the character of this important institution. Consideration of "huiguan in space" facilitates our understanding of Beijing in several ways. During the Ming, huiguan were widely distributed across both the Inner and Outer Cities, and the principal spatial division between lodges existed between those serving a wealthier clientele in the Inner City and those serving poorer examination candidates and official runners located in the Outer City. By the mid-eighteenth century, however, scholar-officials increasingly converged on the Xuannan area of the Outer City. There the learned and the powerful lived, either in huiguan or in their own private residences, in close proximity to one another. With the new concentration of these men came the rise of services such as teahouses, restaurants, and bookstores catering to the scholar-official class. The presence of these services, then, further intensified the attraction of this area to more of this class.

As significant as the overall consolidation of scholar-officials in this ward is the fact that the Xuannan area remained largely undivided by spatial subgroupings of rich or poor or of those with particular regional backgrounds. The social homogeneity represented by this undivided distribution of scholars and officials reflected and facilitated the creation of an elite cosmopolitan community among China's imperial political class. Huiguan were instrumental in creating a space within the city, accessible both to the most powerful and to those aspiring to power, that facilitated and promoted a high level of social interaction among members of this elite. Significantly, native-place ties served as building blocks in the establishment of this cosmopolitan community without generating overt kinds of regional tensions.

Consideration of "huiguan as space" reveals several fundamental aspects of the nature of the native-place lodge as an institution. Some of the implications of the insights gained through this cursory summary of the microspatial aspects of arrangement of lodge space are discussed in the following chapters. For example, the courtyard-style living arrangements of huiguan lodgers had particular consequences in terms of the private/public nature of huiguan life. Activities within huiguan were walled off from, and to a significant extent protected from, the outside world (and the government). At the same time, the close proximity of quarters within the compound prevented complete privacy and ensured that some of what occurred within a huiguan would be known to others, at least to others in the compound. This particular balance of public and private character greatly shaped the social-control function of huiguan and profoundly affected their relationship to the state. These issues are discussed further in Chapter 8.

Perhaps the most important aspect of huiguan as space is the meaning of such space to those who established and used it. Native-place lodges occupied a unique position between the region and the political center of China. On one hand, huiguan essentially recreated native-place space within the capital. For *tongxiang* 同鄉 scholars and officials in Beijing, huiguan served as "virtual *xiang*" or as recreated pockets of regional territory. In some respects, lodges served as "ritual embassies" within which the rituals most closely tied to native place could be effectively performed. Ritually, huiguan space was equivalent to regional space. It is tempting to think of the lodges as "native-place theme parks" where the enjoyment of dialect, culture, and cuisine of one's native place satisfied nostalgic desires for a taste of home, but the ritual efficacy of such space, seen most clearly in respect to the altars and cemeteries, indicates they served as much more than that. At the lodge altar alone could one worship the particular deities of one's region, and where, outside one's native place, but in the soil of the huiguan cemetery could one's bones be buried with the assurance that the proper annual sacrifices to the dead would be effectively performed by compatriots and that one's ghost would never go hungry.

But huiguan space had many meanings, and the role of the lodges as regional space in the capital represents only one side of them. For as much as they served as links from Beijing to the region, they also served as links from the region to the capital. Without undermining the significance of the first function, I believe the second function was considered at least as important, if not more important, than the first by those who established huiguan and made use of them. This explains the close connection between the people of a region and their huiguan in Beijing (reflected in their coverage in the local gazetteer and in the degree of direct financial support from the sponsoring locality). The role of Beijing huiguan as a conduit to the capital region was at least as important as their role as a link back to the region.

Finally, the role of huiguan as cultural space needs to be addressed. This topic may be best approached in conjunction with the closely related question of scholar-official identity. I have already shown that the notion of Beijing huiguan as cultural bastions is flawed, at least insofar as the matter of lodge *cuisine* is concerned. The findings related to matters of cuisine are further confirmed in regard to the performance of operas. On each of the stages listed above, what was performed was Beijing opera, not the particular regional opera of the huiguan where the performance was put on.

Beijing opera, indeed, serves as a fine example of the elite cosmopolitan culture that native-place lodges did so much to promote. A product of multiple regional influences, the Beijing opera style came to be considered the highest expression of the form and was held in high regard by the learned elite from all parts of the empire. If there was a "national" or "elite cosmopolitan" style of opera, it was Beijing opera. As a cultural form, it owed much to its many Manchu patrons, but it serves as well as a superb symbol of the Xuannan community of scholars and officials. As mentioned in the Introduction, there has been a long-standing debate about the relationship between native-place lodges and local identity. Unlike cities such as Chongqing, Hankou, or Shanghai, however, the question of a Beijing identity was an irrelevant one for the men served by Beijing huiguan. The scholars and officials had no interest in becoming Beijing men.[20]

---

20. The question of Beijing identity remains somewhat problematic to this day. In response to my informal querying of Beijing residents over the years as to who qualifies as an authentic Beijinger (*didao de Beijing ren* 地道的北京人), I am in-

The culture of the Xuannan district was not one of handed-down folkways but one of collective self-invention. It was in some respects a consciously created culture that expressed refinement, learning, proximity to power, and connections with China's learned and powerful. For ambitious and aspiring scholars across China, the native-place lodge that represented them in the capital meant much more than affordable lodging during examination periods; it meant access to the world of China's cosmopolitan political elite, and it meant for the lodger some degree of identification with other scholar-officials gathered in the capital and through them the imperium.

---

variably told that that designation belongs to the old Manchu banner families alone. I believe there is a true connection between a culturally defined "Beijing-ness" and a Manchu background. This, as much as anything, explains why the writing of a Manchu author such as Lao She 老舍 (1899–1966) can seem at once so definitively Beijing and at the same time so divorced from the culture of the Xuannan district. On the Manchu domination of and impact on Beijing culture, see Crossley, *Orphan Warriors*, 90.

SIX

Native-Place Rituals

Both voluntary associations and particularistic networks shaped social interaction among scholars and officials in late imperial Beijing. Among the most noteworthy voluntary associations were the literature and poetry societies of the Outer City.[1] Next to the networks based on a shared native-place (*tongxiang*), upon which huiguan were established, the most important of the particularistic networks were those based on relationships forged through the shared experience of passing the same sitting of the civil service examination (*tongnian* 同年). Other bonds based on shared personal qualities (once playfully described by Philip Kuhn as "tong-ties"), which served as honored channels of reciprocity within Chinese society in general, also proved influential among scholars and officials.[2] Yet among all the overlapping and intersecting associations and networks maintained by the scholars and officials in Beijing, only huiguan were established as formally constituted corporate

---

1. These are discussed in terms of their role in early nineteenth-century political factions in James Polachek's fascinating monograph, *The Inner Opium War*.

2. Kuhn, pers. comm. For an insightful anthropological analysis of how such shared bonds are translated into social action in contemporary China, see Mayfair Yang, *Gifts, Favors, and Banquets*.

bodies. Corporateness was far more than an incidental characteristic of native-place lodges. It profoundly affected the nature of the institution and the state's interaction with the lodges. This chapter focuses on the corporate character of huiguan. It begins with a discussion of contemporary definitions of the term and then focuses on specific aspects of the phenomenon.

Defining Corporations

There is little consensus among scholars of China on the question of whether corporations existed in late imperial China. To some degree, the differences in opinion reflect views about the nature of late imperial associations, but the much more significant disagreement arises from the meaning assigned the term "corporation." Some authors apply the term without hesitation to native-place lodges and other traditional Chinese associations. P. Steven Sangren, for example, has argued that corporate organizations were a characteristic feature of traditional Chinese society. In a classic essay Sangren attempts to delineate the "deep cultural" similarities that, he argues, exist between all "traditional Chinese corporations."[3] Other authors have used the term in a more circumspect fashion. William Rowe discusses the "corporate functions" of huiguan and merchant guilds but does so with the caveat that he does not "use the term 'corporate' with any technical strictness."[4] More recently, William Kirby has essentially denied that these traditional associations were corporations at all, although he allows they possessed "certain corporate qualities."[5]

These differences derive from two separate—although not completely unrelated—meanings of "corporation." In common usage, the term is reserved for those associations or groups that enjoy specific sorts of legal rights. In this sense, a corporation is considered to be a "legal individual," and in a key extension of this sense, the law recognizes that members of the corporation bear no or only limited financial liability for the debts and obligations incurred

---

3. Sangren, "Traditional Chinese Corporations."
4. Rowe, *Hankow: Commerce and Society*, 299–300.
5. Kirby, "China Unincorporated."

by the corporation. Defined this way, the term can be applied to traditional associations such as native-place lodges only with difficulty.

Another sense of the term "corporate" is more closely associated with anthropologists and those whose work has been heavily influenced by the anthropological literature. In this sense, a corporate group is one that holds property in common. Maurice Freedman introduced this sense of the term to scholarship on China in his early work on lineages.[6] In an important addendum, Freedman noted that periodic ritual observances associated with the promotion of a common group identity were also necessary corporate attributes. I have adopted this sense of the term and define native-place lodges as corporate because property was held in common and because periodically held rituals were an essential feature of the associations. This chapter examines the ritual aspects of huiguan "corporateness"; the next chapter focuses on the nature of lodge property.

Ritual Activities at Charitable Cemeteries

A great variety of ritual activities served to promote cohesion within huiguan in Beijing. Some of these took place outside the huiguan compound; others were carried out within it. By far the most important of the external rituals were mortuary rites associated with native-place charitable cemeteries. Generally speaking, outside Beijing the operation of charitable cemeteries for deceased compatriots whose families could not afford to have the remains shipped back home was a principal function of many native-place lodges. Being buried far from home fell short of the ideal, but sojourning communities made sure that the graves were well tended; appropriate rituals were performed on holidays, graves were swept, and sacrifices were offered. To this degree at least, the minimum level of postmortem welfare was secured for deceased members of the community. For those who could afford to have their remains shipped back to the home region, mortuaries were operated on the cemetery grounds so that the encoffined corpses of departed com-

---

6. Freedman, *Lineage Organization in Southeastern China*.

patriots could be stored until arrangements had been made for shipment.

Beijing scholar-official huiguan also operated cemeteries, but they appear to have been of less importance to scholars than they were to merchants and tradesmen. Kwang-ching Liu has pointed out that the subscription of funds to establish a graveyard and a mortuary was often the first step in setting up a merchant lodge.[7] However, this rarely occurred among scholar-official huiguan. There were several reasons for this. First, merchant and trade sojourners often essentially immigrated to their new places of residence. It was not at all uncommon for successive generations of "sojourners" to be brought up away from their ancestral home, although ties to their native place were maintained. Such extended stays naturally resulted in greater demand for funeral services. The sojourning experience of scholars and officials in the capital was quite different, however. Examination candidates came for only brief periods, and although many arrived before the examinations began or stayed on to sightsee in the capital or to network among the officials there, few stayed for more than a number of months. Metropolitan officials, unlike their colleagues in provincial posts, who were transferred to a new position every three years or so, were allowed to occupy the same post for decades, and many essentially spent their entire careers in the capital. Still, their stays fell short of permanent relocation, since officials posted to Beijing were required by law to return to their hometowns upon retirement. Although this regulation was no doubt broken regularly, most officials did leave Beijing upon retirement; indeed, as I discuss in Chapter 8, many lodges were established when a retiring official donated his private residence for that purpose. Examination candidates and officials were, in short, much less likely to require the services of a cemetery while in the capital.

In fact, the cemeteries of both scholar-official huiguan and merchant huiguan served a broader cross-section of society than did the lodges themselves. Although we should not discount the role of altruism in the sponsorship of projects by scholar and merchant elites that may not have benefited them directly, we may nevertheless

---

7. Kwang-ching Liu, "Chinese Merchant Guilds."

discern aspects of self-interest. It is easy to see why the provision of such charitable services was more centrally important to those involved in trade, since the availability of cemeteries served as a mechanism of cross-class social cohesion among the communities served by them. Officials in Beijing who sponsored such projects were regarded as upright gentlemen, and their social status within the community was certainly elevated. In general, however, officials had less riding on native-place community cohesion than, say, wholesale operators in a trade organized along native-place lines.

Nevertheless, scholar-officials did sponsor the founding of cemeteries, if less for themselves or overt class interests than out of genuine altruistic belief in the rightness of taking care of one's compatriot community and for the social prestige bestowed on community benefactors. Because of the wider demand for cemetery services, operation of the cemetery often represented the primary institutional channel of interaction between prominent scholar-officials and the greater community of sojourning native-place merchants. The cemetery of the (Anhui) Shexian huiguan is a good example. Founded in 1563 (only three years after the establishment of the first Shexian huiguan) under the direction of officials from Shexian serving in Bei- jing, it was intended: "To charitably assist the burial of all people of our city who lack the means to return [to our native place]. [So that] the dead may thereby obtain the peace of the soil, and the living may avoid a mourning marked by anxiety [literally: 'mourning with perspiration on one's forehead']."[8] And although the cemetery grounds were conspicuously divided into a high-class (*gao ji* 高級) section for those from honorable families (*liang jia* 良家) and a low-class (*di ji* 低級) section for those who were base (*jian zhe* 賤者), the commemorative texts associated with its founding and upkeep explicitly declared all people from the region, regardless of their lot in life, eligible for burial there.[9]

---

8. *Shexian huiguan lu,* 2.2a–b.

9. *Mathews' Chinese–English Dictionary* (entry #3941) defines *liang jia* as "honorable families, whose members have not engaged in trade, business, or any dishonorable calling." Such a sense of the term implies that compatriots engaged in trade would have been relegated to the "low-class" section. However, I am persuaded that the distinction being made is better defined by the virtuous/base (*liang jian*) entry in *Ci hai* (Taipei: Zhengye shuju, 1984), 1390, which defines virtuous

Over the years, numerous drives were organized to raise funds for the upkeep, repair, and expansion of the cemetery. Since the lists of contributors give only personal names, we cannot determine the social/occupational position of donors for most of the first several centuries of the cemetery's existence. There is therefore no direct evidence of merchant participation in the financing or management of the cemetery during this period, but not a few compatriot businessmen are probably recorded on the long lists of donors. Merchant involvement in the Shexian graveyard became much more open in the eighteenth century, however. One document from 1770–71 notes the absence of any effort to manage the cemetery, even though there had been sufficient funding for several decades previous to that date. The text states that only those annual rituals performed within the huiguan on behalf of those of metropolitan-official rank had been maintained.[10] This complaint regarding the apparent indifference of compatriot officials to the operation of the cemetery and the performance there of proper funerary rituals cannot by itself be taken as a sign of a general trend among scholar-officials toward increasing indifference to such activities, but I find it suggestive. In any event, as subsequent documents reveal, from that time on merchants of the Shexian community, chiefly those from the tea and banking trades, played a much greater role in the financing and the management of the cemetery.

Cemeteries were not only a space within which scholar-officials engaged with compatriots of other social backgrounds; they were also, in many cases, nexuses of interaction for compatriots of more broadly defined regions than that represented by their county huiguan. In some cases, several administrative districts jointly operated cemeteries; many were organized at the prefectural level and thus served all those from the multiple counties below it. Li Wen'an 李文安 (1801–55), the father of the famous statesman Li Hongzhang 李鴻章 (1823–1901), for example, led the effort to establish the Lu-Feng graveyard in Beijing, which served the two neighboring Anhui

---

people as those engaged in the four occupations of scholar, peasant, artisan, and merchant; and the base people as prostitutes, actors/male prostitutes, yamen runners, and slaves.

10. *Shexian huiguan lu*, 2.12.

prefectures of Luzhou and Fengyang.[11] A number of cemeteries served whole provinces. The Guangdong community in Beijing, for example, had two cemeteries: one established during the Ming period and the other in the early Qing (a third was added in the early 1940s).

Many charitable cemetery shrines were dedicated to the veneration of "former worthies" (*xianxian* 先賢), or departed notables who had been apotheosized into sacred figures, who had hailed from the native place represented by a particular lodge and its community. Bonds of kinship did not tie native-place communities together, but the veneration of former worthies served much the same function in native-place lodges that commemoration of departed lineage elders did within corporate lineages. An example of one such shrine is that to Yuan Chonghuan 袁崇煥 (1584–1630) located within the "new" Guangdong native-place graveyard. Yuan was a late Ming general who fell victim to rumors at court and was cut to pieces in the capital on orders by the emperor. According to tradition, his severed head was salvaged by a loyal servant and placed in a grave in the southeast periphery of the Outer City, where it was tended by the servant's descendents for generations.[12] One of the main Guangdong native-place graveyards in Beijing surrounded the grave/shrine, and it served as a central point of Guangdong community solidarity through the late imperial and Republican periods. Likewise, the tomb of Li Dongyang 李東陽 (1447–1516), a Ming dynasty grand secretary, served as the core of the (Hunan) Changsha prefectural cemetery and as a shrine and symbol of the collective interests of that community.[13]

Huiguan management of cemetery rituals continued until the forced disbandment of the organizations in the mid-twentieth century. In the 1940s, for example, the annual Qingming festival was an occasion to bring the children of the Guangdong compatriot

---

11. *Luzhou fu zhi* (1885), 34.12; see also *BJTSGC*, 82: 71. For Li's patronage in other contexts, see Chapter 9.

12. She Youzhi, "Guanyu Yuan Chonghuan cimu qingquang de jieshao," 298–300. This site is preserved in Beijing's Longtan Park.

13. See Beijing Municipal Archive, 19: 132: "Hunan Huiguan cimu yiyuan huiluo ji huixin lu"; see also stele inscription texts and diagram of cemetery in *Chang jun huiguan lu*, 13–16.

community to the "new" Guangdong cemetery for sacrifices and grave sweeping.[14] All compatriot communities performed similar cemetery rituals at Qingming. In addition, many huiguan carried out biannual cemetery sacrifices. Subsidiary funerary ritual dates varied according to regional custom. The 1935 regulations of the (Fujian) Zhangzhou huiguan, for instance, called for grave sweeping on Qingming and Zhongyuan (the Yuanxiao festival, celebrated on the fifteenth day of the first lunar month).[15] Other huiguan called for spring and autumn activities related to their cemeteries.

Ritual Activities Within
the Lodge Compounds

Within lodge compounds, ritual sacrifices were periodically offered to some deities that all scholar-gentry huiguan worshiped, some that a great many worshiped, and some that had purely regional significance. Nor was veneration of former worthies confined to native-place cemeteries. For example, a shrine located on the premises of one lodge held votive tablets for five former grand secretaries, eight governors-general, four governors, ten board presidents, and those who had passed the civil service examination with the highest honors.[16] This lodge was one of a number that even took its name from the shrine rather than calling itself a huiguan—although in terms of functionality little distinguished it from other lodges. At least eight different scholar-official huiguan (not including the Zhengyi ci, the Zhejiang native-banker's guild and thus a merchant rather than scholar-official huiguan) took their names from such shrines.[17] A few of these lodges were first established as

---

14. Personal interview with He Zhenqiang, who was raised in the (Guangdong) Zhaoqing huiguan.

15. *Minzhong Huiguan zhi*, "Zhangzhou huiguan."

16. *Yue Ci jilüe*, 32–33.

17. These included the (Jiangxi) Xiao gong ci 蕭公祠 (also known as the Jiangxi gongsuo); (Jiangxi) Xie gong ci 謝公祠; (Jiangxi) Ji'an erzhong ci 吉安二忠祠 (which worshipped Wen Tianxiang and Li Maoming; see *Jiangxi huiguan lüezhi*, 1, 4); (Shanxi) Sangong ci 三忠祠; (Yunnan) Zhao gong ci 趙公祠; (Zhejiang) Yuyao xiang ci 餘姚鄉祠; (Zhejiang) Zhe-Shao xiang ci 浙紹鄉祠 (also called the Shrine for the Veneration of Zhejiang Former Worthies [Yuezhong xian xian ci]); and the Zhili xiang ci 直隸鄉祠.

shrines and only later grew to provide the other range of services associated with native-place lodges.

In some cases, huiguan grew up around pre-existing shrines to eminent compatriot personages.[18] The Sichuan huiguan 四川會館 at Sichuan ying 四川營 was one such example, and a somewhat unusual one in that the local hero being memorialized was a woman. The site began as a shrine to the famous Ming-period Sichuan female commander, Qin Liangyu 秦良玉 (1574–1648). Qin encamped her men and her horses at this site while passing through Beijing after fighting against the Manchus in the northeast. During her time in the capital, Qin was granted the honor of an audience with the Chongzhen emperor, who presented her with four poems commemorating her bravery. The reception of Qin and her army was a notable event for Sichuan natives in the capital. Indeed, the name of the street on which the huiguan was located means the Sichuan military camp. The (Jiangxi) Huaizhong (embracing loyalty) huiguan 懷忠會館 is another example. The shrine around which it formed had been established by imperial edict. Located to one side of the Shuntian prefectural academy, not far to the west of the Imperial Academy, the compound consisted primarily of a shrine to the Song period patriot and prime minister Wen Tianxiang 文天祥 (1236–82), who died there while imprisoned by the Mongol rulers of the Yuan dynasty.

When the Wen Tianxiang shrine evolved into a huiguan is not absolutely clear. Several Ming-period texts note the existence of a huiguan at this site. The *Di jing jing wu lüe*, a late Ming book-length descriptive essay on Beijing, refers to the Huaizhong huiguan as located just outside the shrine proper.[19] This suggests that the shrine to the hero served as a nucleus for the subsequent development of the lodge, much as an eminent tomb might serve as the core of a native-place cemetery. But the early Qing text *Tian fu guang ji* describes a slightly different relationship between the original shrine and the huiguan. It states that in 1580 the shrine was moved from the west to the east side of the prefectural academy, and at that time

---

18. See Zhao Lingyu, "Zhongguo huiguan zhi shehuixue de fenxi," 14a–b.

19. Liu Tong and Yu Yizheng, *Di jing jing wu lüe*, 1.14.

the scholars and officials of Jiangxi established the lodge on the old site.[20]

What happened to this lodge during the Qing period is not clear. The various editions of the late Qing *Jing shi fang xiang zhi* by Zhu Yixin and Miao Quansun note the former existence of a huiguan there.[21] This source also relates the story of the Ming imperial censor Li Banghua 李邦華 (1574–1644), who hanged himself at the shrine shortly after moving into the huiguan. However, other late Qing sources deny the possibility of a huiguan at this location. The "amended" (*kaozheng*) edition of Zhu Yixin and Miao Quansun's work, edited by Liu Chenghan, states that there was not enough room for a huiguan there.[22]

I have visited the site, which is now maintained by the Beijing municipal government as a memorial to Wen Tianxiang. The compound, at least as it stands today, consists of only a courtyard and a one-room museum dedicated to Wen.[23] The small size of the site indicates that it could not have supported a full complement of huiguan functions. Nevertheless, that it functioned as a center for native-place gatherings at one point remains beyond doubt, and from the account of Li Banghua it is clear that there was once enough room to lodge there temporarily.

The Zhe-Shao xiang ci 浙紹鄉祠 (Zhejiang-Shaoxing native-place shrine) is another example of a huiguan that developed from a shrine to former worthies. It was originally proposed by two compatriots in 1681; money was raised, and construction was completed in 1686.[24] In the years that followed, the shrine underwent restoration, and a stele commemorating its establishment was erected. In 1766 and again in 1788 additional property was purchased on the south and

---

20. Sun Chengze, *Tian fu guang ji*, 93.

21. Zhu Yixin and Miao Quansun, *Jing shi fang xiang zhi* (1918), 4.34. Note that Ji'an is a prefectural city in Jiangxi and was the home town of Wen. Based on this account, it is not clear whether this huiguan served just Ji'an prefecture or the entire province.

22. Zhu Yixin and Miao Quansun, *Jing shi fang xiang zhi* (1918), "Kaozheng," 31a–b.

23. It means little, but the caretakers of the site knew nothing of its former existence as a huiguan, although they seemed surprised and interested when I brought the matter up.

24. *Yue ci jilüe*, 1.

west sides of the shrine, and native-place compatriots began to live there. In 1801 the Zhe-Shao huiguan opened in this area, under the management of the shrine. Finally in 1885 the name of the shrine/lodge was changed to the Shrine to the Former Worthies of Yuezhong (Yuezhong xianxian ci 越中先賢祠).

Huiguan altars were also dedicated to deities other than "former worthies" of particular local significance. For example, the Spirit of Poyang Lake was worshiped at the (Jiangxi) Xiao gong ci 蕭公祠 (also known as the Jiangxi gongsuo 江西公所).[25] Numerous lodges maintained altars to earth and city gods and other spirits connected with their home regions. Most huiguan had numerous altars within their premises and venerated not one god but a number of different gods. For example, the Anhui huiguan 安徽會館 (established by Li Hongzhang in 1870) maintained altars for the worship of Min Zi 閔子, a disciple of Confucius whose native place was in Anhui, and Zhu Xi 朱熹 (1130–1200), the Song-period neo-Confucian philosopher, who also hailed from Anhui.[26] An altar to the Dragon Spirit (Long shen 龍神) was erected beside a well within the compound as was a niche for an earth god (*tudi kan* 土地龕). The former was presumably intended to secure divine protection for that source of water. Whether the latter deity was considered to preside over the area where the lodge was located, or was instead an Anhui earth god is not made clear in any extant texts. If it was an Anhui earth god, then that is intriguing, because although it was not unusual for lodges representing counties to maintain altars for the city god of the county seat, I am unaware of any other earth gods that presided over province-sized territories. The lodge additionally venerated three deities that held not local but scholar-official significance: Wenchang di jun 文昌帝君, also known simply as Wenchang; Guandi 關帝; and Kuixing 魁星. More deserves to be said about these deities because they served as an important focus of huiguan ritual.

Undoubtedly, the spirits most commonly worshiped within Beijing scholar-official huiguan were Wenchang and Guandi. Huiguan records sometimes referred to the pair as the "Wen-wu sheng

25. Zhu Yixin and Miao Quansun, *Jing shi fang xiang zhi* (1918), 8.2a.

26. *Jingcheng Anhui guan cunce*, n.p.

文武聖" (Sages of civility and martiality).[27] Wenchang was popularly considered to be the patron spirit of examination candidates. The foundational text of the Wenchang cult, the *Wen Chang hua shu* 文昌化書, recounts the transformation of the god from a local protector spirit from Zitong county in Sichuan to a deity who served as the focus of an empirewide cult.[28] The special regard for the god held by scholars is explained in the seventy-third chapter of the text. It records the appointment of Wenchang as supervisor of the Cinnamon Record. From that position, the spirit reigned as master of the fates of the literati and overseer of the civil-service examinations. The text even held out that promise of possible visits by Wenchang to the dreams of worthy examination candidates and the revelation of answers to impending examination questions.[29]

The worship of Wenchang by the scholar-official huiguan received direct state encouragement, according to an 1858 text included in the annals of the (Hunan) Shanhua huiguan.[30] Entitled "An Investigation of Ritual Sacrifices to Wenchang," the passage describes how the lodge set up votive tablets to Wenchang in accordance with a communication received from the Board of Rites. Per the board's instructions, the tablets were done in red and inscribed in gold with the text "The Qing and the Han: two parts that form a whole" (*Qing Han he bi* 清漢合璧). On one level, the inscription might have been read as a boast that the Qing dynasty and the model Han dynasty were equals in glory and legitimacy. But another evident implication is that the Manchu rulers of the Qing and the Han people—or, given the context, the Han scholars and officials gathered in the huiguan of the capital—formed a perfect match. Since at the time the empire was threatened by the massive Taiping insurrection against Manchu rule, the measure could not have been more timely.

This example of state/huiguan interaction in regard to the object and content of huiguan ritual worship is an instructive reminder not to seek historical significance solely in corporate autonomy and

---

27. See. e.g., *Beiping Jingxian huiguan lu*, 1.8.

28. For an excellent English translation, with historical introduction, of this work, see Kleeman, *A God's Own Tale*.

29. Ibid., 290–91.

30. *Shanhua guan zhi*, 1.1; Beijing Municipal Archives 19: 116.

opposition to the state, for the dynamics of corporate/state coexistence are just as telling and just as historically significant. On one hand, the instructions issued by the Board of Rites illustrate the mutually advantageous and relatively tension-free relationship between state and lodge in such matters. This was, after all, a god worshiped for his ability to help scholars pass the examinations and enter government service. By exhibiting concern over the ritual sacrifice to the god, the state further legitimated the deity and thereby boosted his perceived efficacy. At the same time, the state was able to co-opt the significance of the ritual by slipping its own message of Manchu-Han cooperation into the sacrificial services. The relationship between state and lodge is discussed in further detail and from different perspectives in Chapter 5, and, as will be seen, this view of corporate ritual existing within a state-shaped context complements the findings of that chapter.

Guandi, the god of war and of loyalty, is a more familiar deity. As Prasenjit Duara has masterfully demonstrated, Guandi has meant many things to many people.[31] He served as the patron spirit for a host of different trades, including gold gilt, leather cases, tanned leather, tobacco, incense and candles, silk and satin, finished clothing, cooking, salt, condiments, meat, cakes, dried fruits, barbering, banking, pawning, fortunetelling, and tofu (Lord Guan was a tofu peddler before swearing allegiance to Liu Bei, the third-century claimant of the Han dynastic throne, an act that led to many heroic feats and his subsequent canonization).[32] That such a versatile god should serve as an object of veneration in scholar-official huiguan is not surprising. His popularity within scholar-official lodges, however, was certainly promoted by the fact that among his many attributes Guandi was considered the patron spirit of essay writing.

The other god most closely associated with huiguan worship was Kuixing. His popularity stemmed from his association with examination candidates. According to one story, a scholar named Kui possessed great literary talent but was very ugly. Kui attained the first rank in the examinations, but the emperor was so repelled by

---

31. See Duara, "Superscribing Symbols," 778–95.
32. See Li Qiao, *Zhongguo hangye shen chongbai*, 479 (and passages indicated).

Kui's ugliness that he refused to award the degree. The heartbroken Kui threw himself into a river, but a mysterious fish picked him up and returned him to the surface. Later Kui ascended to heaven and became one of the stars in the Big Dipper.[33] It is notable that both gods of literature, Wenchang and Kuixing, were associated with the Big Dipper, which revolves closely around the northern pole star.[34] There were some differences between the two gods, however. Kuixing was a more exclusive god, worshiped only by examination candidates and scholar-officials.[35] Wenchang attracted a more diverse body of faithful, most of whom were involved in cultural trades. He was, for instance, a patron deity of paper makers, bookshop workers, seal engravers, stele inscribers, professional storytellers, embroidered-box makers, and the makers of paper clothes burnt for the dead.[36]

Chapter 42 of the classic eighteenth-century novel *The Scholars* (*Rulin waishi*) contains a literary description of scholar-officials paying ritual respect to Wenchang, Kuixing, and Guandi at the convening of the metropolitan examination. In keeping with the satirical nature of the novel, the description is presented in the voice of a scholar entertaining his friends at a gathering in a brothel. Before the opening of the examination, the metropolitan prefect first invites Guandi to impose order on the examination grounds, Wenchang to preside over the examination, and Kuixing to cast light over the proceedings. A fourth god, General Zhou, is also invited to inspect the premises, but I have not been able to determine the identity of this last god.[37]

---

33. This story is from Liu Wu-chi et al., eds., *K'uei Hsing*, vii.
34. According to Wolfram Eberhard (*Dictionary of Chinese Symbols*, 34), this constellation was of special significance to the Chinese, in part because "the word *dou* = dipper refers also to an altar vessel used in religious ceremonies" and in part because the shaft "symbolizes the penis in the marriage ceremony." My (not necessarily exclusive) interpretation of the symbolic appeal of these stars would focus instead on the association of the north with power. Study for the examinations was a political act, and the sought-for success did bring power. It might be expected that divine help would be located there.
35. For an anecdotal account of Kuixing's special efficacy in influencing examination results, see *Minzhong huiguan zhi*, "Jianning huiguan."
36. Li Qiao, *Zhongguo hangye shen*, 140, 144–48, 166, 379–81, 420–28.
37. Wu Jingzi, *Rulin waishi*, vol. 3, 42nd *hui*, 6b–7.

Some scholar-official lodges worshiped a group of deities called "Wu Wenchang fuzi" 五文昌夫子. This group consisted of Wenchang, Kuixing, the Vermilion-Clothed Spirit (Zhuyi shen 朱衣神), Guandi, and Lü Dongbin 呂洞賓.[38] Not surprisingly, some scholar-official lodges, especially those representing regions of Fujian, worshipped Mazu, the Heavenly Consort. The main altar of the (Fujian) Jianning huiguan 建寧會館, for example, was dedicated to this deity, while a separate building was dedicated to Kuixing.[39] But the more telling fact is not that some Fujian scholar-official lodges worshipped Mazu but that, given the unsurpassed popularity of this god among the rest of the Fujian sojourning community, not more of them did. Instead, most Fujian scholar-official lodges worshipped Guandi and the gods of literature.[40] There is a clear contrast between the scholar-official lodges and the merchant lodges in this respect. The (Fujian) Shaowu huiguan 邵武會館, for example, maintained altars for Guandi, and for each of the four city gods of the counties in that prefecture, as well as for the former worthies of the region.[41] By comparison, the Yan-Shao huiguan, which served the paper merchants of Shaowu prefecture and neighboring Yanping prefecture, boasted an altar pavilion and a separate opera stage dedicated to Mazu.[42]

Both Guandi and Mazu were extremely popular religious figures, and the worship of both had received explicit court sanction; there

---

38. For a fuller discussion of the "Wu Wenchang," see Li Qiao, *Zhongguo hangye shen*, 381.

39. *Minzhong huiguan zhi*, "Jianning huiguan."

40. Evidence from the *Minzhong huiguan zhi*, which records the spirits worshiped at a number of Fujian huiguan reveals that the Quanjun huiguan, for example, worshiped the "Wu Wenchang fuzi" as well as Da xianye 大仙爺, Fude zhengshen 福德正神 (earth god), the former grand secretary and Quanzhou native Li Guangdi 李光地 (1642–1718; posthumously canonized as Li Wenzhen 李文貞), and the city god of Quanzhou; the Puyang huiguan 莆陽會館 worshiped the Wu Wenchang fuzi and a group of local worthies from that district; the Fuqing huiguan 福清會館 worshiped Wenchang and Guandi (Wen-Wu sheng) as well as the city god of Fuqing, the Fude star; and the Ming-period official who founded the lodge; the Jinjiang yiguan 晉江會館 worshiped "former worthies," the "Wu Wenchang fuzi," and the city god of Jinjiang; and the Longyan huiguan 龍巖會館 worshiped Wenchang. None of these lodges worshiped Mazu.

41. *Minzhong huiguan zhi*, "Shaowu huiguan."

42. Ibid., "Yan-Shao huiguan."

was certainly nothing heterodox about the worship of either. It is therefore especially interesting that whereas Guandi was widely venerated at scholar-official huiguan altars, Mazu did not receive the same level of attention. Given the well-known identification of Fujian people with Mazu in other situations, the relative lack of emphasis on this deity within the Fujian scholar-official huiguan is notable. Perhaps the explanation lies in some aspect of the underlying structuralist significance of Mazu. I believe it also suggests the degree to which the empirewide elite class of scholars and officials shared a ritual culture based on a broad foundation of common beliefs and practices that in some ways differed from more popular patterns of ritual activity. In at least this important respect, the ritual behavior of Fujian scholar-officials appears to have been closer to that of scholar-officials from other areas than it was to that of sojourning compatriots who were not scholars and officials. I return to this theme from another angle in the discussion of the significance of worship in these scholar-official lodges below.

One final observation on popular religious worship and the lodges—among the texts held by huiguan and handed over to the state in the 1950s and stored in the Beijing Municipal Archives today is a late nineteenth-century flier that shows the extent to which popular cults were transmitted through the lodges. The flier is entitled "The True Canon of the Holy Guandi Revealed to the World."[43] The wide circulation hoped for the text is reflected in an admonition on the first page: "After reading this, don't throw it away. Hand it to others, and receive unlimited merits." The text stresses the importance of faith in Guandi and lists twelve, easily memorized three-character rules of conduct, such as "Respect heaven and earth," "Be filial to both parents," "Sacrifice to ancestors," "Protect the princely way," and so on. Only one of these instructions, "Harmonize with native-place neighbors" (*he xiang lin* 和鄉鄰), has any particular relevance to huiguan. A further link with scholar-officials is found in a section recounting the types of situations in which the god had shown himself to be efficacious;

---

43. "Zhejiang huiguan guan shengdi jun jueshi zhenjing" 浙江會館關聖帝君覺世眞經, 19:1.2.1.

one of these is advancing to a higher-ranked civil service degree. To some extent, then, the scholar-official lodges did transmit popular religion.

Ritual Performances

There are relatively few descriptions of ritual proceedings within huiguan. The small number of extant prescriptive descriptions tend to envision fairly elaborate services. For example: "The playing of music; initial standing; four salutes [bows]; three offerings of incense; libation of wine; three offerings of wine cups; stop the music; reading of the invocation; playing of music; offering of food; urging [the spirits] to partake; offering of silk/wealth; offering of tea; four salutes/bows; burning of paper [money]; end of ceremony."[44] Another source describes the offerings to be presented to honored spirits in the twice-annual principal services of that lodge. In addition to reading an invocation, the officiants offered "five catties of pork, five catties of mutton, one rooster, five varieties of fruit, four kinds of pastries, two kinds of rice, rice wine, incense, candles, paper and silk, and fresh flowers."[45] Naturally a full complement of ritual vessels and equipment was needed to perform such ceremonies. In the case just cited, these were "a bronze incense burner, five candle holders and flower vases, 23 offering bowls and bronze ritual wine cups, eleven pewter bowls, five 7-inch pewter platters, three porcelain wine cups, and one porcelain wine carafe."[46]

No doubt the actual services within the lodges were not always performed in a manner as rich and elaborate as dictated by these prescriptive texts. Weng Tonghe referred in his diary to at least one instance of a service that apparently did not live up to the ideal. Weng described with obvious disappointment the main yearly ritual at the (Jiangsu) Chang-Zhao yiguan 常昭會館 as being marked by "mean instruments and simplified rituals."[47]

It was common practice among the huiguan of Beijing to follow such sacrificial ceremonies with a banquet (*tuanbai* 團拜) for the

---

44. *Yue ci jilüe*, 4.
45. *Shaoxing xian guan jilüe*, 3.
46. Ibid.
47. Weng Tonghe, *Wong Tonghe riji paiyin ben* (GX 18.2.18; 1892.3), 4: 1754.

members of the native-place community. The ceremony that disappointed Weng Tonghe, for example, was followed by a banquet of two tables (approximately sixteen to twenty people). Such postritual affairs served to consolidate the bonds of community further. Lodge administrators also took advantage of these semiannual gatherings to take care of more practical business. The formal initiation of important projects was often delayed so that they might be inaugurated during such occasions.

The diary of the celebrated early twentieth-century author Lu Xun offers an amusing reminder that the actual experience of rituals cannot be recreated entirely from their formal descriptions. Although Lu often noted the days on which huiguan services were held, he provided little further description of them. It may be unfair to read too much into Lu's mistaken record of the lodge carrying out the "autumn sacrifices" in April one year, but we do have other evidence that Lu Xun was not fully engaged with the ritual activities of his lodge.[48] According to his brother Zhou Zuoren, Lu arose especially early on the days the huiguan sacrifices were held. He then "escaped" to Liuli chang, where he spent the morning chatting in the bookstores. Only after a late and leisurely lunch in a teahouse would Lu return to the lodge, knowing that by then the ceremonies would be over and all the participants dispersed.[49]

Lu Xun's example aside, people did participate in the rituals associated with the lodges. These served a number of functions. They reminded participants of the accomplishments of past compatriots and fostered pride in the native place. They bolstered the connections felt with past worthies and with present compatriots. Native-place bonding was furthered in the rituals dedicated to purely local gods, such as the city gods of one's home city. At the same time, the services helped to consolidate the feeling among participants of belonging to a larger, empirewide group of scholars and officials. Thus the services also contributed to identification not only with the native place but also with the cosmopolitan elite that helped to rule China and with the ruling system itself.

---

48. Lu Xun, *Lu Xun quanji*, 14: 217.
49. Zhou Xiashou, *Lu Xun de gu jia*, 402–3.

Ritual Activities and Identification
with the Locality and the Imperium

In a manner somewhat reminiscent of Weber's argument (see Introduction), the Chinese scholar Wang Rigen has recently suggested that the deities installed in huiguan in Beijing were meant to showcase local persons of virtue and that this intention made the lodges "important bases for the development of regional identities."[50] In their considerations of ritual worship within native-place lodges, both Weber and Wang stress that these activities promoted identification with the native place. Both suggest that geographically delineated identification came at the expense of identification with non-native-place groupings. Insofar as the late imperial scholar-official lodges of Beijing are concerned, however, this characterization is flawed. In fact, the religious activities of these lodges simultaneously promoted identification with one's native region, identification with an empirewide elite, and even with the imperial project itself. Certainly the local spirits and former worthies worshiped in scholar-official huiguan reinforced a connection to local regions. But it is significant that the former worthies were figures whose accomplishments were primarily of an imperial rather than a local nature. Without exception, these apotheosized souls were noted for their scholarship, their achievement of high government positions, or, as is the case with Yuan Chonghuan and Wen Tianxiang (venerated by Jiangxi scholar-officials), their martyrdom for imperial causes.

The gods most commonly worshiped in scholar-official huiguan served in similar ways to promote identification with the empirewide elite from whom the ranks of civil officialdom were filled. For example, Terry Kleeman has described Wenchang as a "god that transcended regional limitations, and above all else, a god of the scholar-official elite."[51] The same is certainly true of Kuixing, who had an even more limited appeal to those not from the scholar-official class. Guandi, too, was a god who transcended geographic boundaries and who was commonly worshiped by non-kin-based

---

50. Wang Rigen, *Xiangtu zhi lian*, 332.
51. Kleeman, *A God's Own Tale*, 23.

communities. The symbol of loyalty and guardianship, Guandi inspired an ethic of trust and camaraderie that served repeatedly to hold together "societ[ies] of strangers."[52] It is therefore not surprising that so many Fujian scholar-official huiguan worshiped primarily Guandi or Kuixing instead of Mazu, even though Mazu was the spirit most commonly worshiped by Fujian merchant guilds and other non-scholar-official Fujian native-place organizations.

Religious worship in huiguan did not have a divisive impact on the ability of sojourning scholar-officials to identify with a collective larger than the native-place community. Indeed, religious worship promoted such an identity. Huiguan rituals served both to consolidate corporate coherence and identification with the native-place community and to foster identification with the civil imperium. Bryna Goodman's pathbreaking work on regional networks and identities in Shanghai has shown how native-place consciousness in that city played a role in the development of a national consciousness during the final years of the Qing and early years of the republic.[53] As she succinctly puts it, "The fact that people retained their native-place identity did not mean they could not also develop broader (particularly national) identities."[54] What the ritual activities of the scholar-official huiguan reveal is that a similar process had occurred in Beijing among the scholar-official elite well before the period with which Goodman is concerned. The consciousness reflected in the ritual activities should not be described as "nationalist." Yet the rituals do clearly represent identification on the part of the participants with an empirewide pool of elites who saw themselves as worthy to serve the throne and participate in the governance of the realm.

---

52. Huang Huajie, *Guangongde renge yu shenge* (The human and divine characteristics of Lord Gong) (Taibei: Taiwan shangwu yinshuguan, 1968); quoted in Duara, "Superscribing Symbols," 782.

53. Goodman, *Native Place*.

54. Ibid., 46.

SEVEN

The Corporate Character

of Lodge Property

Huiguan Property

Property was an essential feature of native-place lodges. The fact that the term "huiguan" refers both to the lodges as physical sites and to the associated social organizations reflects the degree to which the associations were conceptually linked to the property they owned, as well as the essential corporeality of huiguan.[1] Chinese native-place lodges were inextricably linked to their real property holdings. The provisioning of members of the sojourning community with the space and the facilities necessary to their activities was the raison d'être of huiguan. Living quarters, burying grounds, meeting places, and ceremonial areas required physical space. As sojourners, most huiguan members would have little access to such property if they did not collectively provide it for

---

1. He Bingdi, *Zhongguo huiguan shilun,* 11: "The narrow meaning of *huiguan* is the buildings publicly erected by fellow provincials; the broad meaning of *huiguan* refers to the native-place associations."

themselves. This they did through the founding and maintaining of huiguan.

Equally important for the associational character of huiguan was the *form* of that ownership. All native-place lodge property was held in common. This was essentially true by definition; organizations that did not hold property collectively were not huiguan. Fellow provincials came together in a variety of different circumstances, but scores of stele inscriptions attest that huiguan were considered founded only after property had been acquired and registered under the name of the association. The significance of the form of ownership goes beyond semantics. The common possession of property profoundly shaped the character of this institution.

Types of Huiguan Property

As noted in Chapter 5, the main compound was the central property holding of any lodge. In Beijing it was not uncommon for one lodge to possess several compounds. If the demand for association services—particularly the demand for living quarters—was high, and if conditions permitted, huiguan frequently expanded beyond the confines of the original compound. There were two principal ways of achieving this. A separate primary compound might be acquired and a new huiguan established, or alternatively, less autonomous, satellite property units might be purchased. The new huiguan were generally managed in a relatively independent way and took names such as "north hall" (*beiguan* 北馆) or "new hall" (*xinguan* 新馆) that reflected this autonomy. Satellite properties, on the other hand, were administered directly from the primary huiguan compound and did not receive a distinctive names. Efforts were generally made to acquire property close to the main compound, and this was true especially of satellite property. Physically adjoining property was, of course, the most highly desired, since the walls might be torn down or gates opened in order to provide direct communication. If adjoining property was not available, however, suitable premises were often sought nearby.

Huiguan also acquired properties in order to generate rental income. It is not clear how early rental properties were added to the mix of huiguan holdings, but we do know that it was a well-established strategy by the Qianlong reign. A detailed account of the establishment and rebuilding of the (Hebei) Hejian huiguan during the mid-eighteenth century, for example, shows that rental income was an important source of huiguan revenues by that time.[2] There are few equally informative records on huiguan finances before the late Qing, but numerous documents reveal that rental properties constituted a major portion of the total holdings of many huiguan by the late Qing and through the Republic. The records of the Zhejiang Association of the Zhejiang huiguan, for instance, reveal that by 1949 it owned 176 rental units.[3]

Real property was not the only property owned by huiguan. By the late nineteenth century and increasingly throughout the early twentieth century, huiguan also held such financial instruments as bonds and shares in companies. Records of the Shaoxing huiguan from the early Republic, for example, show that in addition to income from rents the lodge also held Zhejiang Railway stocks, stocks in one other company (the Guangxing gongsi 廣興公司), and government bonds.[4]

Huiguan administrators were also meticulous in their accounting of almost all physical items of any value owned by the association. Trees or other vegetation of significant size or worth were duly recorded in deeds of sale, and the private exploitation of these resources was strictly forbidden. The effort involved in managing minor articles of property was considerable. Account books were kept and periodically updated in order to keep track of furnishings and other miscellaneous articles. The variety of minor items listed in the following statement from the (Zhejiang) Zhe-Shao xiangci (also known as the Yuezhong xianxian ci), suggests how vexing the task of accounting for these objects must have been for huiguan administrators:[5]

---

2. "Chongxiu Hejian huiguan ji," in *Hejian huiguan lu.*
3. Beijing Municipal Archives, 19: 47, "Zhejiang huiguan Zhejiang gonghui fangzu shouru baogao." Note that not all these rental units were separate compounds. They were simply units whose rent was accounted separately.
4. *Yue ci jilüe*, 10a–b.
5. Ibid., 33a–b.

Six "safety lamps" with glass stands (three of which were lent out to a
   lecture hall)
Six "safety lamps" with metal lampshade frames
Five bookcases
65 eight-person tables
Three chairs
Five wooden *kang*
Six tea tables
Four "bull horn" lamps
Two "inverted flame" lanterns
Nine lamps with handle
Four square glass lamps
Three large long tables
Two wardrobes
98 two-person benches
Twelve plank beds
25 bed boards

Even this represents only a fraction of the many items of which
huiguan kept track. One eighteenth-century source states that
during the rebuilding of the Hejian huiguan over 800 articles such as
"tables, chairs, water containers, large and small iron pots, brass
basins, as well as brass, tin, and porcelain articles" were bought.[6] An
account of objects held by the Hunan huiguan 湖南會館 during the
Republican period runs to almost a hundred different categories of
items and includes everything from wash basins and tea sets to cal-
ligraphic couplets written by eminent late-Qing statesmen and fellow provincials Zeng Guofan 曾國藩 (1811–72), Zuo Zongtang 左宗
棠 (1812– 85), and Hu Linyi 胡林翼 (1812–61).[7]

Keeping track of smaller items was a perennial challenge for
huiguan managers. Indeed, keeping such articles at all was difficult.
There was a chronically high level of wear and tear, and a similarly
high rate of disappearance and destruction of huiguan minor property. Collective ownership proved to be less persuasive in moti-
vating the proper care of this sort of property than individual
ownership might have been. Huiguan regulations of all periods are
virtually of one voice in enjoining against the neglect of commonly

------

6. *Hejian huiguan lu,* "Xu," 4b.
7. *Beijing Hunan huiguan zhilüe,* 47–50.

owned items. The (Anhui) Shexian huiguan rules of 1738, for example, contain the following notice: "All chairs, tables, and other furniture procured by the huiguan have been entered into an account book. If items disappear, the huiguan watchman will investigate."[8] Similar warnings in other Qing and Republican-period regulations stipulate that those responsible were liable for the costs of replacing missing or damaged articles.

Acquisition of Property

Ho Ping-ti enumerated three ways in which huiguan property was obtained.[9] The first and second methods are similar, in that they consisted of property donations by a single patron, either a compatriot official or a merchant. The donor might give a personal residence belonging to himself (before returning to the home region upon retiring, for example), or he might buy a piece of property specifically for the purpose of handing it over to the huiguan. The third method was the most common. A group of fellow provincials would organize donation drives to raise funds to purchase property on the market. This, for example, was how funds were raised to establish the Anhui huiguan, an event discussed in more detail in Chapter 9.

A fourth method of huiguan property acquisition bears noting. Surplus funds accumulated from rents and other sources of lodge income were used to buy real estate. This was, of course, by its nature an option open only to huiguan already in operation. Since the decision to purchase property in this way could be made in the general course of managing a native-place lodge, special donation drives and the importuning of members were not necessary. Although the properties involved were relatively minor sites and bought one by one, it would appear that significant portions of the total holdings of some huiguan were purchased in this way. For example the (Hunan) Baoqing huiguan was founded in 1760 with property purchased from funds raised by donations from the "gen-

---

8. *Shexian huiguan lu*, 1.15.
9. He Bingdi, *Zhongguo huiguan shilun*, 17.

tlemen" from that prefecture.[10] It expanded its main compound with the purchase of abutting property in 1794, and continued to expand its holdings in 1860–61 with the purchase of four separate adjacent or nearby properties.[11]

Land Deeds and the Concept of Ownership

Among the most valuable of records kept by native-place lodges were land deeds and mortgage contracts. Original copies, known as "red deeds" (*hong qi* 紅契) because of the red official seal signifying that the transaction had been registered with the government, were kept in especially secure locations. Large numbers of these deeds were typically accumulated since not only sales but also mortgages, remortgages, and so forth were documented in this way.[12] Red deeds carried significant legal weight and served to protect property from outside encroachment. "White deeds" (*bai qi* 白契), or verbatim copies of deed texts without the official seals, were often reprinted in huiguan annals and other records. Fortunately, a great number of these have been preserved; as a source of information on huiguan holdings, they are invaluable to the historian.

The collective nature of huiguan property ownership is clearly revealed in deeds of sale. A certain amount of variation in the language denoting collective ownership, especially in deeds drawn up before the nineteenth century, is evident. A deed dated 1753, for example, recording the purchase of property in order to establish the (Anhui) Xiuning huiguan refers to the sale being made to the "entire county" (*he xian* 闔縣).[13] Other records use different wording. The 1738 sale of land to establish the Changsha prefectural huiguan was officially transacted with the "gentry of the huiguan" (*huiguan shen shi* 會館紳士).[14] Another mortgage contract with the same huiguan in 1752 was done "under the name of the gentry of the

---

10. *Jingdu Baoqing guan zhi, juan* 1 (preface) "xu," 1.

11. Ibid., 1.6b–11.

12. The *Lüping Chaozhou tongxiang lu* lists a total of 95 deeds and mortgage agreements, dating from 1666 to 1920, and even specifies the safety box they were stored in.

13. *Jingshi Xiuning huiguan gongli guiyue*, n.p. in this section.

14. *Jingshi Changsha junguan zhi*, 11.

huiguan" (*huiguan shenjin mingxia* 會館紳衿名下). Reference to "gentry of the huiguan" as opposed to the "gentry of the county" or the "entire county" might indicate that a distinction was being made between the community of sojourning gentry and those at home, but, in fact, no other evidence of this is available. In practice, the implication of all these forms of wording was that the property was held in common by compatriot gentlemen in the name of the lodge. By the nineteenth century, although some variation in language was still employed, most huiguan property was bought and sold "under the name of the huiguan" (*huiguan ming xia* 會館名下).[15] This, too, in effect implied that ownership was being vested not in any individual but in an abstract, legally recognized body organized as a native-place lodge.

Huiguan Longevity

A passage in the (Anhui) Jingxian huiguan annals remarks: "Since ancient times, it has been difficult to establish enterprises. Preserving enterprises has been more difficult, but preserving and maintaining commonly owned enterprises (*gong ye* 公業) has been extraordinarily difficult."[16] There is no doubt that the long-term continuation of collective enterprises presented formidable challenges. A fully functioning huiguan required a minimal level of support from the sojourning community. If the community was unable or unwilling to participate and contribute, the huiguan could not remain an active ongoing concern.

Perhaps because of the sensitivity of collective organizations to community fortunes, it is widely believed that huiguan were unstable and short-lived. G. William Skinner has suggested that "the life expectancy of a Landsmannschaft-cum-guild was apparently not long in late imperial China, few last[ed] for more than two or three generations without reorganization."[17] In fact, however, the opposite was true of Beijing scholar-official huiguan, which were remarkably stable and long-lived. Skinner does not explicitly define

---

15. Ibid., 16a–b; see also *Jingshi Xiuning huiguan gongli guiyue.*
16. *Beiping Jingxian huiguan lu, juan* 1, "xu."
17. Skinner, "Introduction: Urban Social Structure," 545.

"Landsmannschaft-cum-guild," but it seems to refer to merchant-dominated native-place organizations. Since my work focuses primarily on scholar-official lodges, my findings do not necessarily contradict Skinner's. However, Skinner's proposed short "life expectancy" is clearly inapplicable to Beijing scholar-official huiguan. I believe the relative longevity bestowed on corporate associations by their collective ownership of real property applies as well to merchant-dominated native-place lodges, but that issue lies beyond the scope of this study.

Evidence for the impressive longevity of the Beijing scholar-official lodges is provided by the 70 huiguan for which we have good evidence of Ming-period foundings.[18] Of this group, fourteen were originally located in the Inner City. These were abandoned following the 1648 edict prohibiting ethnic Chinese from residing in that area. The forced removal from these sites by a unique administrative fiat says little about the institutional longevity of huiguan, and we will leave these sites out of consideration for the time being. Of the remaining 56 huiguan, we can identify Ming-period street locations for 49 sites. Of that group, 38 (over 75 percent) were still operating at the same location several hundred years later in the late nineteenth century. Indeed, almost all continued to operate until forced to disband in the 1950s.

Few of the eleven known Ming locations that did host a continuously operating huiguan represent cases of short institutional life spans. One site, the Lingnan huiguan, remained in operation until at least 1718—a minimum of 160 years—before its disappearance.[19] Another site, the (Zhejiang) Jinhua huiguan 金華會館 on Xiaguoqiang hutong 下鍋腔胡同, was owned and operated by the Jinhua sojourning community through the mid-twentieth century, although it had been transformed into a charitable graveyard for

---

18. Discussed in Chapter 3; see Appendix for a listing of these huiguan.

19. The last record of this site is dated 1718. See *Beijing Lingnan wenwu zhi*, "Chongxiu shengou Lingnan huiguan ji," 1–2. The Lingnan huiguan was a Guangzhou provincial huiguan, several of which had been established by the late Qing. It seems likely that the disappearance of the huiguan from this site reflects either a relocation or a selling of the property for the purposes of consolidation with one of the other huiguan established by the sojourners of that province, rather than an outright abandonment.

Jinhua sojourners by the late nineteenth century.[20] Finally, four of the remaining huiguan sites, the (Guangdong) Yuedong huiguan, the Shexian huiguan, the (Jiangxi) Shang-Xin huiguan 上新會館, and the (Anhui) Xuancheng huiguan 宣城會館, continued in operation but sold their older, Ming-era properties and moved to better locations.[21]

Far from being short-lived, Beijing scholar-official huiguan were extraordinarily long-lasting. Unfortunately, reliable evidence of establishment dates is not recoverable for the majority of Beijing huiguan, and it is not possible to determine the average length of existence. Nevertheless, once established, Beijing scholar-official huiguan were likely to last a very long time. The reason for their longevity lies largely in the common ownership of huiguan estates. Once acquired, collectively held huiguan property was not that easily disposed of. Ironically, a legally binding sale of the huiguan estate required almost as much community coherence as did the operation of the lodge. Land held in an association's name could be sold only by the proper administrative leaders acting as agents of the association. When the community dissolved, there was literally no one empowered to sell huiguan land. Therefore, even though huiguan fortunes were subject to vicissitudes, the rights to the huiguan estate remained essentially inalienable.

When a sojourning community was no longer able to maintain its huiguan, services were curtailed; if no other solution could be found, the huiguan was boarded up and left vacant. At such times, the site might be rented out at market rates to non–fellow provincials. Such was the case, for example, with the (Shanxi) Xiangling nanguan 襄陵南館, which was rented out shortly after being established in 1751 and was not reopened as a huiguan until 1790.[22]

It was not always feasible to rent out lodge property when demand fell or community fortunes sank to a low ebb, however. The

---

20. Zhu Yixin and Miao Quansun, *Jing shi fang xiang zhi*, 7.26.

21. For the Yuedong huiguan, see *BJTSGC*, 87.190, see also Han Dacheng, *Mingdai chengshi yanjiu*, 407; for the Shexian huiguan, see *Shexian huiguan lu*, "Xulu jicun yuanbian jixi," *juan* 1; for the Shang-Xin huiguan, see *Shanggao xian zhi*, 3.42–53; for the Xuancheng huiguan, see *Xuancheng xian zhi*, "Jingdu xin she huiguan muzhu yin," 31.376–78.

22. Hu Chunhuan and Bai Hequn, *Beijing de huiguan*, 187.

failure to find a tenant was sometimes a matter of market forces, but it was just as often the result of the sojourning community's inability to maintain sufficient organization to oversee transactions, collect rents, and perform other administrative tasks. If a property remained unrented for long, it might be abandoned temporarily. Disturbances in either Beijing or the home region might lead to neglect of the huiguan. Sometimes a community was unable to rebuild an earthquake- or fire-damaged structure immediately. Disasters in the home region—a notable example is the devastation in south China during the Taiping Rebellion—also undermined the fortunes of a number of sojourning communities in the capital. In such circumstances, huiguan were left in disrepair or boarded up. Occasionally, squatters occupied abandoned lodge land. But community disuse did not imply forfeiture. Commonly held huiguan property could be reclaimed in court if necessary as soon as the community was able to come together again.

Reconstructing an abandoned site was a challenge, but not one on the same order as raising the necessary funds to buy a site in the first place. An inscription written in 1713 commemorating the restoration of the Shang Hunan huiguan 上湖南會館 relates that this lodge had been occupied by outsiders for a period after the founding of the Qing. The squatters made rough use of the premises: doors were taken down and used for beds, holes dug in the compound grounds for toilets, and columns toppled and sold. Nevertheless, once the community regained possession of the lodge, the site was refurbished, and it remained in operation until the disbandment of all Beijing huiguan in the 1950s.[23]

---

23. *Shang Hunan huiguan zhuanshu*, 1.2–3. For another instance of a lodge being reclaimed after having been "privately" disposed of, see *Minzhong huiguan zhi*, "Dingzhou huiguan," 1–3. In this case a donation drive was organized to redeem the property. See also *Shexian huiguan lu*, "Yizhuang yijie xingsong shimo," 2: 9–11b, for an account of a case in which part of a charitable cemetery lost to encroachment was regained through court action. See also No. 1 Historical Archive, Qing Xunjing bu dang'an, no. 214, "Shangbu dailang Gu Qingxing qing linghui jingcheng Wudao miao Jiangsu tongxiang huiguan gongchan fangwu chengwen" (GX 32.8.23), for yet another example of lodge efforts to reclaim property disposed of by an individual without proper authority.

Many huiguan operated in conditions that fell short of abandonment but betrayed a degree of chronic neglect. References to the sad state into which Beijing huiguan had fallen are especially common in twentieth-century writings. These comments reflect a decline in the financial well-being of huiguan, particularly because of the abolition of the imperial examination system in 1904 and the transfer of the capital to Nanjing in 1928. On the other hand, shabby huiguan were not always huiguan in decline. Peter Golas points out that it was common throughout China in the early Qing for merchant huiguan to be left empty and neglected for stretches of time during the course of the year.[24] Functioning Beijing huiguan were rarely left empty, but they were often undeniably run down. The stability and institutional longevity bestowed on huiguan by the commonly owned estates is further demonstrated by their impressive stability during the tumultuous last century of their existence. Despite all the upheavals of that time, huiguan holdings remained relatively unscathed. There is no denying that the years of warfare, the social and political unrest, and the transfer of the capital took their toll on huiguan in Beijing. During the 1930s and 1940s especially, some huiguan ceased to function, and others continued on as best they could in reduced financial circumstances. Some even fell victim to predation by their own caretakers. Yet the institutional resistance to complete disintegration of these associations is impressive. The commonly owned huiguan estate was largely responsible for this stability. During this period, the character of huiguan membership shifted dramatically, and huiguan functions and finances evolved correspondingly.

The corporate ownership of Beijing native-place lodges posed problems for the new communist government after 1949. On one hand, collective ownership prompted the administrators of some lodges to argue that the huiguan were by nature progressive institutions dedicated to selfless good works. The municipal government quickly decided that the lodges were "feudal remnants" that should be disbanded and their property taken over by "the people" as represented by the Beijing municipal government. This process is discussed in more detail in the final chapter of this book.

---

24. Golas, "Early Qing Guilds," 580.

The notion of property held in common by an abstract collectivity of people from the same region also contributed to a bureaucratic dispute following the dissolution of the lodges in the 1950s. At issue was how the old notion of collective ownership would be translated into the new system of socialist ownership. In the early years of the People's Republic, the answer to this question was still in flux. For example, the minutes of a meeting of the joint Zhejiang huiguan property committee, which was one of the many provincial committees established under the direction of the municipal government to facilitate the orderly transference of huiguan property belonging to the natives of each province to municipal authorities, record one member suggesting as late as 1954 that although in the past huiguan property was managed only by Zhejiang sojourners resident in Beijing, under the new socialist system the Zhejiang huiguan should be understood as belonging to all the people of Zhejiang, and thus their management should not be limited only to those in Beijing.[25] Such a suggestion seems reasonable enough, in that it recognized the degree to which the lodges represented the people of the locality they served, but had that notion been accepted, it would have complicated the claims of the Beijing municipal government to full administrative authority over the properties. In the case of Zhejiang this understanding of ownership was successfully ignored, but in another case a similar claim led to a bureaucratic standoff lasting several years about who might properly claim rights to the property.

The dispute arose from a clash between the Beijing municipal government and the Shanxi provincial government, both of which claimed, as "people's" governments, to be the legal inheritors of native-place lodge property held by Shanxi people in Beijing.[26] The Beijing municipal government left itself open to challenge in September 1950 when it formally notified all regional governments in China of its decision to appropriate all native-place lodge property in the city. One clause in the notice stated: "If any provincial, city,

---

25. Beijing Municipal Archive, 19: 1.68, "Zhejiang huiguan caichan guanli weiyuanhui" (1958.4).
26. For a series of documents relating to this dispute, see Beijing Municipal Archive, 19: 1.427.

or county people's government wishes to administer a public lodge (*gong guan*) belonging to that province, city, or country, then this must be raised with the responsible authorities and the matter handled after coming to an agreement through consultation." All other regional governments appear to have acquiesced, but the Shanxi provincial government politely but firmly informed the municipal government that it would assume control of the main lodge properties of the 37 Shanxi huiguan in the city and administer them through the Shanxi Capital Liaison Office (Shanxi zhujing banshichu). The Beijing municipal government strenuously objected, and the standoff lasted for four years. In 1954, the Shanxi provincial government compromised and turned all but three properties over to the municipal government.

Huiguan Finances

The day-to-day finances of scholar-official native-place lodges—how these organizations supported themselves, and what they spent their money on—can reveal much about their roles within the sojourning communities. Unfortunately, for the Ming and Qing periods, it is nearly impossible to reconstruct the financing of Beijing native-place lodges in detail. Stele inscriptions give us an occasional glimpse of some sorts of income, but by their nature they tend to record only the donations associated with special projects, such as major construction or refurbishing projects. Some lodge regulations include sections on regular donations and expenditures, but the picture they paint is an ideal one that needs to be checked against other evidence. Fortunately, the financial records of one lodge, the (Anhui) Qingyang huiguan 青陽會館, remain extant, for these records track with impressive detail contributions made to that lodge from the year 1598, when the lodge was first established, to 1832 when the records stop abruptly, presumably because the lodge annals in which they are found were printed shortly thereafter.[27] Qingyang county is lo-

---

27. *Qingyang huiguan lu*, n.p. The only extant copy of this work known to me is in the library of Beijing University. The work comprises four *juan*, and the findings discussed in this section are spread throughout the entire work. Because there is no consistent page numbering, all references to Qingyang huiguan finances are based on this work but are not separately cited.

cated in the part of Anhui south of the Yangzi River. In addition to the lodge established in the Inner City in 1598, another lodge, located on Shijia hutong 施家胡同 in the Outer City, was established in 1630. Both sites were jointly maintained until the 1648 edict banishing Han from residence in the Inner City; thereafter only the Shijia hutong site remained. Although the preservation of such detailed donation records is unique, there is no evidence that this lodge was particularly unusual in other respects; we may take the donation patterns found in these records as broadly representative of other county-level scholar-official lodges in the capital.

Donations made to the Qingyang lodge were categorized into two main types: (1) those expected to be made by examination candidates from Qingyang during their stay in the capital or by officials upon their promotion in official rank or appointment to office and (2) voluntary contributions (*leshu* 樂輸).[28] Of the two, donations in the first category represented the lion's share of the lodge's recorded income; over the period covered by the records, they totaled 10,331 silver taels. In comparison, voluntary donations amounted to 1,540.6 taels of silver and 1,772,286 copper cash. If we accept the general ratio of 1 string (1,000 coins) of cash equaling one tael—a ratio that varied significantly in practice—then the total value of the voluntary donations was about 3,313 silver taels. Thus roughly 75 percent of the total of 13,644 taels came from the expected contributions and 25 percent from voluntary contributions.

Voluntary contributions were intended to fund specific projects and appear to have been raised in coordinated fund drives. In contrast to the contributions made by scholar-officials on the occasion of their advancement, voluntary contributions occurred irregularly and raised varying amounts of money. Records of the voluntary contributions to the Qingyang lodge begin at an unspecified point

---

28. A few texts produced by other lodges refer to both types of contributions as *leshu*; thus the distinction was clearly not universal; see, e.g., "Jixi huiguan tiaoyue" of 1826, in Beijing shi dang'anguan, ed., *Beijing huiguan dang'an shiliao*, 283–86, which refers to what we treat here as "expected" contributions as *leshu*. Nevertheless, the distinction made in the *Qingyang huiguan lu* is a valuable one for analytical purposes, and the sense of *leshu* as used in the Jixi lodge regulations is reflected in the insistence that such contributions "must" be made according to guidelines provided.

during the Kangxi reign and continue to 1828. They do not include whatever donations were involved in purchasing either the original Inner City site or the Shijia hutong site. Altogether 30 separate sets of contributions were made; in most cases each set represented a sum gathered from several dozen or more individuals. In many cases, the name of each donor and the amount each contributed were recorded. The number of contributors as well as the amounts collected varied considerably depending on the project for which the funds were earmarked. Expensive projects such as major renovations, construction projects, and the purchase of new property naturally tended to generate higher donations. For example, in 1750, 146 people contributed 41.2 taels of silver and 54 strings of cash for the repair of the front gate, various buildings, and the walls of the lodge compound; and in 1771, 152 different donors contributed a total of 29.2 taels of silver and 72.4 strings of cash, which was also intended for the repair of lodge buildings. Other projects financed through fund drives include the construction or repairs of the altar hall (*xianghuotang* 香火堂), a horse shed (*mapeng* 馬棚), the purchase of lanterns for the Lantern Festival, the purchase of tables and chairs, and publication of a new edition of the huiguan annals.

Of all the projects for which voluntary contributions were solicited, the ones that attracted the most donors and generated the most income were those associated with the two Qingyang charitable cemeteries. The broad popularity of this cause confirms the suggestion made in Chapter 6 that the charitable cemeteries operated by the Beijing lodges tended to serve a broader cross-section of the sojourning native-place community than the exclusive scholar-official clientele directly served by the lodges themselves. For example between 1789 and 1795, 257 donors contributed 245.5 taels of silver and 587.5 strings of cash toward expenses associated with the establishment of the "new cemetery." Apparently only 360 strings of that amount were required for the purchase of that property; a property contract also included in the lodge annals records the purchase of a property for that amount at Sichuan ying in the Outer City in 1784. The remainder of the amount must have been used to tear down existing buildings on the site and to construct facilities appropriate to a cemetery there in their stead. That both cemeteries remained operational is reflected by the 151 taels of silver and 408.5 strings of cash contributed by 202 donors for the repair of the old cemetery in 1828. Altogether the records show that over the years a total of 436 taels of silver and 1,158.4 strings of cash were earmarked for the cemeteries, or roughly half the total value of voluntary contributions recorded and 12–13 percent of total recorded lodge income for this period.

The expected contributions were another matter. In contrast to voluntary contributions, lodge custom dictated that examination candidates and newly promoted or appointed officials contribute specific amounts. All donations were recorded. The obligatory nature of these contributions is conveyed in the recording of the names of those who failed to contribute what custom demanded. Next to the names of several Qingyang scholar-officials are comments such as "came to the capital, purchased the rank of imperial college student (*jiansheng*), and then absconded without paying the lodge fee." The use of the word "fee" (*fei* 費) here underscores the sense that these contributions were considered mandatory. The Qingyang lodge was not alone in recording the names of defaulters; for example, the regulations of the (Zhejiang) Wuxing huiguan 吳興會館 call for the recording of the names of those who make the expected contributions but warn: "If there are those who do not contribute, this should also be clearly entered into the account book in order to record such slighting of native-place feeling."[29]

The Wuxing huiguan regulations are a good example of the valuable information on contributions that can be gleaned from lodge regulations. Before we look more closely at the Qingyang records, it should prove helpful to get a sense of what was expected in other lodges. One of the earliest extant records of the amounts expected to be contributed is found in the 1649 (SZ 6) regulations of

---

29. "Wuxing huiguan juanxiang tiaogui (1847.10)," in Beijing shi dang'anguan, ed., *Beijing huiguan dang'an shiliao*, 209. For other sets of regulations that set out expected contributions according to rank, see also in the same collection: "Ren-Qian huiguan gongyi li juan gui tiao zhai lu (1853.2)," 210; "Jixi huiguan guitiao" (1826), 283; "Longyan huiguan guiyue" (n.d., Qianlong period), 337–38; "Longxi huiguan tiaoyue" (1848), 342–43.

the (Jiangxi) Ji'an huiguan 吉安會館.[30] Interestingly, this matter is covered in the section of the regulations that deals with lodge expenses. This is because the act of donation was embedded in a more complex customary gift-exchange process. As the regulations state:

It has long been customary for the lodge to present a "journey present" of two taels of silver to all officials and other gentry from our prefecture when they arrive in the capital. A "congratulatory gift" of three taels of silver is given to all officials who receive a promotion, new posting, or imperial commission, as well as to examination candidates who have recently passed the provincial or the metropolitan civil examinations. *The recipients customarily respond with a gift to the lodge that is worth twice as much.* For those newly appointed to the posts of circuit intendant (*daotai*), prefect, and district magistrate, it has been customary for the lodge to host banquets to send them off on their journey, all of which are to be held in their appropriate order.[31]   (Italics added)

Later regulations reveal a far more direct approach that did not imbed the donations in rituals of gift exchange. By the eighteenth century, if not before, the amounts scholar-officials were expected to donate were meticulously laid out in great detail. Although the lodge still hosted group celebrations for the community of hometown scholar-officials in the capital, lodges no longer practiced the custom of giving small gifts to members with the expectation of receiving bigger donations in return. The regulations of the (Zhejiang) Ren-Qian (Hangzhou) huiguan typify this approach:

Those who have recently passed the provincial examinations and come to the capital to take the metropolitan examination shall donate a tael of silver whether or not they stay in the lodge; those who pass the metropolitan examination, 2 taels; those who pass the palace examination shall donate according to the standards of the metropolitan examination. Those who have been appointed to a provincial post, who have come for an imperial audience, or who are expecting to fill a vacancy [shall contribute according to the following schedule]: magistrates of large autonomous departments and counties, 8 taels; magistrates of medium-size autonomous departments and counties, 6 taels; magistrates of small autonomous departments and

---

30. "Ji'an huiguan tiaoli," in Beijing shi dang'anguan, ed., *Beijing huiguan dang'an shiliao*, 373–74.
31. Ibid.

Table 7.1
Summary of Qingyang Lodge Donations, 1598–1832

Category	Amount in silver taels
Titles obtained by protection privilege, or posthumously appointed (封蔭敕贈)	
Ming period	120
Qing period	68
Third-degree graduates (甲科)	
Ming period	126
Qing period	476
Military third-degree graduates (武甲科)	
Ming and Qing periods	10
Provincial examination graduates (鄉科)	
Ming period	137
Qing period	158
Ming: military provincial examination	23
Qing (武鄉科)	47
Ming: military *xun* (武勛)	19
Imperial students	
Ming (歲貢)	96.9
Qing (貢)	500
Imperial College students (監生)	
Ming and Qing periods	3,617.5
Expectant officials (選官)	
Ming period	1,514.3
Qing period	3,418.1
TOTAL RECORDED EXPECTED DONATIONS	10,330.8

SOURCE: *Qingyang guan lu.*

counties, 4 taels; second-class subprefects, 4 taels; first-class subprefects, 6 taels; magistrates of independent departments, 8 taels; circuit intendants and prefects, 12 taels; ministerial department controllers, 24 taels; provincial governors, 40 taels; educational intendants, 12 taels; examination intendants, 6 taels; examination candidates who have been assigned a lodge room for either the provincial [i.e., Shuntian] or the metropolitan examination, 3 taels.[32]

---

32. "Ren-Qian huiguan gongyi li juan gui tiao zhai lu," in Beijing shi danganguan, ed., *Beijing huiguan dang'an shiliao*, 210; see also in the same collection, "Wuxing huiguan juanxiang tiaogui" (1847), 209.

The records of the Qingyang lodge provide a detailed overview of how these expected contributions worked in practice for one lodge between 1598 and 1832. Table 7.1 provides a breakdown of the thousands of donations made to the lodge over the course of more than two centuries. Expectant officials (*xuanguan* 選官) made up the single largest group of donors, giving 4932.4 taels, or 47 percent of the expected donations. In this group 2,242 donations are recorded, for an average donation of 2.2 taels. *Jiansheng* made up the next largest group. They accounted for 1,878 donations, averaging 1.92 taels, for a total of 3,617.5 taels. Donations varied widely from the average, however. Some donated only one tael or less, others donated several dozen taels or even more. Many officials donated a number of times; in some cases it is possible to track an official's career path from his donations as he was promoted or otherwise changed positions. Wang Yixiu 王懿修 (1736–1816), who is discussed below as a long-term director of the lodge, donated money on 34 different occasions, giving a total of over 200 taels. Wang Yixiu's son, Wang Zongcheng 王宗誠 (1763–1837), also discussed below, donated over 150 taels, spread out over twenty different occasions.

Administration

Finances and other corporate matters had to be overseen by some kind of lodge administration. Although the nomenclature differed, the pattern of leadership tended to be very similar across all huiguan. Lodge directors tended to be selected from the pool of fellow landsmen serving in Beijing as metropolitan officials. Typically the position was variously called, among other titles, *zhinian* (值年), *guanzhang* (馆掌), or *dongshi* (董事).

Lodge directors were in principle selected on a rotating basis for terms of one or two years. When an individual was willing to shoulder the responsibility for a longer period of time, however, the tendency was to defer to that willingness. For example, the 1770 regulations of the Hejian huiguan state: "It was originally determined that the director (*zhinian*) would change once each year, but over time it was left entirely up to the individual, and the term was not limited."[33] The detailed records on all administrators of the Qingyang huiguan from 1598 to 1829 provide unique insight into how such matters worked in at least one lodge in practice.[34] Although the administrative system of the lodge changed somewhat over time and was complicated by an evolving relationship of the three lodges representing the same area, essentially both a *zhuhui* 主會 and a *guanzhang* 館掌 were selected. The *zhuhui* was apparently more an honorary position and demanded less hands-on attention. The appointment of a more ceremonial *zhuhui* in addition to a *guanzhang* was uncommon; if nothing else, it serves to remind us of the various strategies employed by different lodges. In the Qingyang case, there was much less turnover in the post of *zhuhui* post than in the post of *guanzhang*. For example, the high-ranking official Wang Yixiu served as the *zhuhui* for a total of 50 years, from 1766 to 1816. Wang Zongcheng, a minister of the Board of Rites, served as the *zhuhui* from 1817 to 1829. The position of *guanzhang* changed hands more frequently.

How were lodge directors selected? The regulations of (Fujian) Longxi huiguan 龍谿會館, dating from the eighteenth century, set forth clear eligibility requirements:

Each year a metropolitan official will be appointed in a rotating fashion to serve as director to manage lodge affairs and to take control of the financial ledgers, as well as receive and pay out money. If at some point no metropolitan officials are available, than expectant officials may substitute; if there still is no one available, then an examination candidate may substitute. If there are two people of equal rank, than the elder should be selected so that the proper hierarchy may be presented clearly at all times, and negligence thus be avoided.[35]

Several sources indicate that once a group of suitable candidates had been determined, the actual choice of who was to serve was determined by drawing of lots.[36]

---

33. "Hejian huiguan zhinian zhike guitiao," in Beijing shi dang'anguan, ed., *Beijing huiguan dang'an shiliao*, 68.

34. *Qingyang huiguan lu*, juan 1, "Guanzhang" section, n.p.

35. *Minzhong huiguan zhi*, "Longxi" section, n.p.

36. Zhang Jixin, *Dao Xian huan hai jian wen lu*, 18; *Beiping Jingxian huiguan lu*, 1.59; reprinted in Beijing shi dang'anguan, ed., *Beijing huiguan dang'an shiliao*, 280; see also in same collection, "Ji'an huiguan tiaogui" (1848), 375–77.

As the passage from the regulations of the Longxi huiguan indicate, directors were placed in charge of overseeing the lodge, managing finances, and supervising the main ritual events. Indeed the same set of regulations reflects how ritual matters and more mundane administrative matters were often mixed together.

Each year on New Year's Day, piously prepare much sweet wine to sacrifice to our former worthies. Each person should contribute his portion of the cost, but if that is not sufficient, then it may be supplemented with the public monies of the lodge. After the sacrifice, those in attendance may enjoy the remains of what has been offered as a banquet, and the lodge director shall on this day open the yearly accounts to all and paste them on the wall to show that there has been no private misuse of funds. If the director is to be rotated, then the position should be handed over on this day also.[37]

When possible, the position of director was offered to a serving metropolitan official. Having the social/political elite in this role served a number of ends. This enhanced the respectability of the lodge, and if matters affecting the welfare of the lodge arose (a property dispute, for example), the huiguan benefited from such influential representation. On a more mundane level, men of such eminence were more likely to be trusted with managing lodge funds. Because the native-place lodges were such a central part of social and informal political interaction in the capital, many of those who served in the capital were called at one time or another to serve as lodge directors. Diaries and personal accounts reveal a veritable "who's who" of Qing political personages who served in that capacity. One such figure was the pre-eminent late Qing statesman and architect of the Qing victory over the Taiping Rebellion, Zeng Guofan. Zeng traveled to the capital twice in his early years to take the metropolitan examination, passing it in 1838. Although he must have had some interaction with the lodges of his region earlier, it is in the period after he passed the examination and began his rise through the ranks of officialdom that we see him most engaged with the native-place lodges of Beijing. His active involvement ended only with his departure in 1852 to conduct the Jiangxi provincial examination. It is an indication of the importance of huiguan in the

---

37. *Minzhong huiguan zhi*, "Longxi" section, n.p.

world of metropolitan officials that Zeng's close engagement with the affairs of his fellow Hunanese in Beijing was maintained even though he resided in the huiguan only for a matter of days during that time.[38]

Both his diary and his letters home show that Zeng paid considerable attention to the fortunes of his fellow Hunanese in the capital. His letters frequently report news of *tongxiang* in the capital. He recounts which *tongxiang* have died of smallpox, describes the misfortunes that have befallen this or that person, keeps track of how many have been retained in the Hanlin Academy, notes the actions of *tongxiang* who have come to the capital to buy posts, mentions how *tongxiang* have performed in the metropolitan examination. When there is no other news, he makes sure to remark that all the metropolitan officials from his region are doing "as usual" (*tongxiang jingguan bing jie ruchang* 同鄉京官并皆如常).[39]

One might wonder if Zeng's interest in the fortunes of his fellow Hunanese was not largely a function of the intended audience of his letters—after all, it is natural to write about those from home in letters to home, but Zeng's diary entries, particularly his accounts of Hunan candidates' fortunes in the metropolitan civil and military examinations, and even in the provincial examinations, show that he paid close attention to events affecting fellow Hunan scholar-officials.[40] However, the real proof of his close connections to his fellow Hunanese and to the native-place lodges of the capital is reflected in his social life. Zeng was a frequent visitor to several Hunan lodges, including the Hunan xinguan and the prefectural Changsha junguan 長沙郡館, as well as the lodge that served both Hubei and Hunan people, the Huguang huiguan. He met fellow Hunan scholars in his local lodge to practice his literary skills.[41] He

---

38. All citations from Zeng's writings in this section refer either to his diary, *Zeng Guofan riji* (hereafter cited as *ZGFRJ*), or to his letters to his family, *Zeng Guofan jiashu* (hereafter cited as *ZGFJS*). For the convenience of those using other editions of the letters, they are cited by the numbers conventionally assigned to them.

39. See, e.g., *ZGFJS*, 0001–5, 0010, 0018–20, 0025–26, 0030, 0039, 0060, 0133, and 0136.

40. See, e.g., *ZGFRJ*, DG 21.1.28, 100; DG 24.4.19, 298; and DG 24.9.24, 326.

41. See, e.g., ibid., DG 23.2.27, 246; and DG23.3.4, 249.

attended dinners, celebrations, and drinking parties at various huiguan.[42] He read the poetry of Du Fu in the library at the Huguang huiguan because he enjoyed the quiet there.[43] He ate everyday meals in his lodge.[44] And he hosted dinners both at his local lodge and at the Huguang huiguan.[45] He saw opera at the Huguang huiguan.[46] He went to the huiguan to visit examination candidates from Hunan and helped them in their efforts by correcting their draft examinations at his home and then delivering them to the several different lodges where they were staying.[47] And on occasions too numerous to list, he visited native-place lodges to see friends and acquaintances.

Zeng Guofan assumed the directorship of the Changsha junguan in 1841 and held that position for two years.[48] He clearly took his responsibilities seriously. In keeping with his charge to oversee the main ritual activities of the lodge, for example, Zeng made his way to the lodge on the first and fifteenth of almost every lunar month to lead the sacrifice to the spirits honored there. As director, he comforted *tongxiang* in need and helped make arrangements for the families of those who died.[49] He also was in charge of overseeing the finances of the lodge; this aspect of the position particularly interested him. As discussed in the next chapter, the financial situation of many metropolitan officials was very strained. Zeng was no exception. In his letters home, Zeng constantly bemoaned his need to borrow money to make ends meet. Clearly he hoped that taking charge of the lodge accounts would provide at least a temporary

---

42. See, e.g., ibid., DG 20.11.30, 85; DG 21.11.3, 161; DG 21.11.14, 163; DG 22.12.8, 215; and DG 25.1.14, 342.

43. See, e.g., ibid., DG 23.2.16–19, 243; DG 23.2.23–24, 245; DG 23.2.26, 246; DG 23.3.1, 248; and DG 23.3.24, 255.

44. See, e.g., ibid., DG 20.11.1, 78; DG 21.5.7, 131; DG 24.3.18, 292; and DG 24.4.23, 298.

45. See, e.g., ibid., DG 20.11.28, 84; DG 21.2.4, 102; DG 21.2.26, 106–7; DG 21.3.1, 108; DG 23.4.4, 258; DG 24.1.27, 283; DG 24.2.10, 285; and DG 24.5.6, 301.

46. Ibid., DG 21.1.19, 97.

47. See, e.g., ibid., DG 24.3.26 and 28, 293–94; and DG 24.4.10, 296. On an earlier occasion, he accompanied several candidates from his home county to and from the examination grounds; see ibid., DG 21.4.16, 21, and 28, 126–27, 129.

48. Ibid., DG 21.6.24, 137–38.

49. *ZGFJS*, 0065–66.

respite. As he had noted in his diary, with the acceptance of the directorship, he was now "in control of all its monies." So it was with disappointment only days after taking over the position that he wrote to his grandfather:

Recently the circumstances of your grandson in the capital have gradually become more distressed. The majority of metropolitan officials live from hand to mouth, neither enjoying times of abundance nor times of cold and hunger. The family must not concern itself about this, though. Your grandson has now taken over the management of the affairs of the Changsha junguan, although there is also almost nothing left in the lodge's public funds.[50]

If the funds were dry when Zeng took over, however, income was still coming in. In a letter to his parents four months later, Zeng struck a more upbeat tone.

Your son took over management of the huiguan finances in the sixth month. Every month [the lodge] collects 15,000 copper cash in rent. According to the regulations this money is under the control of the manager, and no accounting is called for until the time I hand over the position to my successor, and interest on the money is not calculated. In addition to that money, your son has another eleven or twelve taels of silver to use. If I am very frugal, next year I will not have to borrow money.[51]

The next month in a letter to his younger brothers Zeng related another positive development.

This year at New Year's I still had to borrow 150 taels of silver so that I could use 50 to pay back the Du family and use 100 for myself. Li Shiwu came to the capital and made a large donation to the Changsha junguan. I have already been borrowing from the public funds of the lodge, but it would be better not to mention this to outsiders. Otherwise, I will have to collect still more funds.[52]

Li Shiwu 李石梧 was an alternative name or style of Li Xingyuan 李星沅 (1797–1851), who had just been promoted to governor of Shaanxi. Although we do not have regulations for this huiguan concerning the donations expected from newly appointed officials,

---

50. Ibid., 0005.
51. Ibid., 0010.
52. Ibid., 0027.

to judge from customs in other lodges, he probably donated around 40 taels.

Zeng Guofan is remembered as a model of honesty and incorruption. Nothing related here should affect that perception. Although Zeng cautioned his brothers not to mention his "informal" use of the lodge funds under his control, one suspects that it was common practice. After all, as Zeng pointed out, there was no provision for calculating interest earned by the funds under the director's control. Indeed, control of lodge funds must have been one of the perceived benefits of being a director. As rotating credit associations prove, being able to control even relatively small amounts of capital can prove of enormous benefit, even if the original sum must be returned at a certain time. As discussed in the next chapter, native-place networks played a crucial role in providing income for metropolitan officials in chronic fiscal straits. It is clear that the metropolitan elite not only was led by duty and honor to take on the post of lodge director but also was attracted by the capital (and not just social capital) attached to that position.

Appraising the Corporate
Nature of Beijing Huiguan

The corporate nature of Beijing huiguan was an essential characteristic of that institution. The impressive longevity of huiguan was to a great extent a factor of the collectively owned lodge estate. As I have demonstrated, there were several reasons why estates bestowed such stability on these organizations. Another factor was the lack of property taxes on property located within the city walls during the imperial period. Tax revenues at the county level were raised through taxes on agricultural land alone, and the metropolitan government charged excise taxes on commodities coming into the city. With no tax burden, huiguan estates were in no danger of falling into arrears and losing their property to forfeiture during periods of neglect.

Another factor, described above, was the difficulty of legally selling huiguan property at precisely those times when a lodge was most vulnerable. It is for this reason that many huiguan were able to hold their property for centuries. Legal recognition of ownership rights was the main protection against one of the most dangerous threats to huiguan possessions, encroachment by other would-be claimants. The records are full of property cases fought between huiguan and those who either claimed outright ownership of a site or tried to enlarge adjacent holdings through expansion into huiguan-held turf. Moreover, it is clear from the number of cases upholding huiguan rights to property that the courts recognized the principle of corporate ownership.[53]

Clearly, huiguan estates belonged to abstractly conceived, legally recognized collectivities of compatriots. In this light, we must reconsider John K. Fairbank's remark "in old China there was no idea of the corporation as a legal individual."[54] If the legally protected possession of corporate property did not imply recognition of traditional corporations as "legal individuals," it is only because the Chinese legal system did not insist on locating in individuals alone all ownership rights. But corporate bodies were established, operated, and officially recognized as legal, if collective, entities by at least the eighteenth century, and the evidence suggests that de facto legal recognition came much earlier. By the Republican period, the administrators of at least one huiguan translated age-old notions into modern and unambiguous terminology. The 1922 charter drawn up for the (Anhui) Xiuning huiguan states: "This lodge is constituted as a corporation" (*benguan wei caituan faren* 本館爲財團法人).[55] More-

---

53. It has been argued that corporate property need not have been tangible property, i.e., the common possession of intangible resources, such as a valued tradition of knowledge, would serve in the same way as did ownership of real estate and other material possessions. See Watson, "Chinese Kinship Reconsidered." My research, however, indicates a qualitative difference between these two types of property: a "corporation" based solely on the common possession of intangible property would not seem to qualify as a corporation in the same way as did groups holding tangible property. I also maintain that this was an obvious distinction readily made in late imperial China. It is worth pointing out that rights over tangible and intangible property were accorded fundamentally different treatment under traditional Chinese law; see Alford, *To Steal a Book*.

54. Fairbank, *China: A New History*, 185–86.

55. *Jingshi Xiuning huiguan gongli guiyue*, n.p. The term *caituan faren*, literally "wealth-group legal-person" may represent a borrowing from the Japanese term employing the same characters, *zaidan hōjin*, which means "corporation" in the contemporary legal sense.

over, some degree of official recognition of this condition is reflected in the fact that the charter was submitted to the Beijing municipal authorities and received official approval.[56] Given the common possession of property and the clear legal recognition of huiguan, I believe the term "corporation," even in a legalistic sense, might arguably be applied to huiguan. In fact, huiguan satisfied both conditions: they held property in common (and practiced appropriate associated rituals), and they were legally recognized bodies.

One important area in which huiguan did not meet the modern legal definition of the corporation was in the extension of limited liability to the members of the huiguan. The evidence argues that such protection was not granted. William Kirby has demonstrated the absence of any language pertaining to limited liability in the legal codes. I have found no claim to limited liability in huiguan documents and know of no case that illustrates the principle of member liability for huiguan debts one way or the other. My own general sense of this issue is that debts in Chinese society were considered essentially indissoluble. Upon the death or disappearance of a debtor, the debt burden was frequently inherited by family members who had nothing to do with the original deal. The notions of legal amelioration of debt upon bankruptcy and limited liability for the owner of a business would appear to run counter to traditional attitudes regarding money owed.

More work needs to be done on the question of debt liability, but there is little reason to suspect that limited liability was considered particularly relevant to scholar-official lodges. Although there are numerous records of lodges mortgaging some portion of their property in times of need, records of total huiguan debt exceeding total estate value are rare, if they exist at all. The question of pursuing those associated with the huiguan for bad debts was therefore largely moot. In other words, debt was limited not by legal mandate but by customary conservative financial practice. Huiguan for the most part tended to invest in property, not in business ventures that might go bad (or return huge profits if they succeeded). Surplus funds were generally directed toward the purchase of urban property; these holdings generated small streams of regular rental income

---

56. Ibid., "Jingting li'an chenggao bing chaop'i," n.p.

and were not subject to the tax burden imposed on extramural agricultural land. Both the risk and the return on rental properties were low. These practices helped huiguan avoid debts.

Scholars and officials in the capital were tied to one another in many ways. Those who had passed the metropolitan examinations in the same year recognized one another as *tongnian*; the official supervising an examination became the "teacher" of those "students" who were successful on the examination, a bond especially important in the context of elite Beijing. However, only as native-place compatriots did metropolitan scholars and officials institutionalize their ties in corporate form, and not as an incidental attribute. Native-place lodge corporateness was expressed both in rituals that bolstered a sense of common identity and in the holding of huiguan property in common. The corporate form bestowed on the compatriot bond an institutional stability otherwise unachievable. Property held in the name of huiguan consistently received official protection from unauthorized appropriation. Although, unlike crimes against lineage estates, crimes against huiguan estates were not explicitly mentioned in the law codes, the courts obviously treated such crimes in much the same way. Native-place lodges thus benefited from the traditional rules against the unapproved alienation of estate land through private transactions.

If we consider Weber's premise (discussed in Chapter 1) that the historical significance of urban "oath-bound communities" lies in their ability to carve out spheres of autonomy from the state, then the striking feature of the scholar-official lodges of Beijing is the degree to which their "corporateness" was bound up with the state. To begin with, the lodge estate, which served as the foundation of huiguan, could not have been preserved over time without state protection. But the state-corporation connection did not stop there. The physical space provided by that estate facilitated the networking and socializing among compatriots that transformed abstract native-place ties into practically efficacious interpersonal bonds. Since the landsmen in question were scholar-officials sojourning in the imperial capital, efficaciousness most often involved interaction with the state, as we will see in subsequent chapters.

EIGHT

State-Lodge Cooperation in

the Maintenance of Order

One of the many functions of huiguan was to help maintain social order in the capital city. This chapter examines that role and analyzes the evolution of huiguan-state relations during the late Qing period. I have suggested that one key to understanding the native-place lodge as an institution lies in the close, complex, and ultimately complimentary nature of lodge relations with the state. We have seen, for example, that the concentration of lodges in the Xuannan ward contributed to identification among scholar-official sojourners with the imperium (Chapter 4), that state-lodge relations were reflected in and reinforced by the ritual activities of lodges (Chapter 6), and that the courts recognized and upheld the collective ownership of lodge estates (Chapter 7). The mutually beneficial interaction between the lodges and the state is further illuminated by the role of huiguan in maintaining order in the capital. The lodges were neither forced by the state into acting as instruments of public order nor allowed to operate autonomously in a government-free vacuum. Instead, social order was a joint project conducted by and on behalf of both the scholar-official compatriot community and the government.

The nineteenth and twentieth centuries saw tremendous changes in the relationship between huiguan and the state, culminating in the disbanding of the lodges at mid-century. At the heart of this process was the increasing state penetration of huiguan, which began in the late Qing and accelerated during the Republic. This shift fundamentally altered state-lodge interaction (for the history of this shift, see Chapter 11). Before we can fully appreciate the dynamics of that change, however, we must first examine the earlier relationship. This chapter seeks to illuminate the symbiotic relationship, beneficial to both the state and scholar-official native-place networks, that obtained in the capital during the late Qing period.

Of all the traditional social ties based on shared interpersonal qualities, the "*tong*-ties" or "*tong*-isms," the *tongxiang*, or compatriot relationship, alone was vested with an officially recognized and consistently applied element of mutual responsibility. As I discuss in detail below, *tongxiang* ties took on legally mandated functions in the capital that were found nowhere else. The special, quasi-official status of the compatriot tie in Beijing further undermines the notion that scholar-official huiguan acted as purely informal social organizations with no direct ties to government. The complex relationship between the scholar-official huiguan of Beijing and the late imperial government was, instead, formally and semiformally institutionalized in ways that benefited both the state and the metropolitan bureaucracy. Given the state's traditional wariness of factionalism within the civil bureaucracy and the prohibitions against scholars forming associations, huiguan might be thought to have run counter to the political constitution of the traditional imperial order.[1] Yet the lodges were not only tolerated, they were institutionally incorporated in several fundamental ways into the imperial administration of the bureaucracy and metropolitan Beijing.

Compatriot ties were an essential means by which the imperial regime implemented a system of mutual responsibility among civil

---

1. For a discussion of this prohibition in relation to the difficulty of gathering scholars together in order to change their views, see Kang Youwei, "Chronological Autobiography of K'ang Yu-wei," 71.

officials. By ensuring that the misdeeds of one would have repercussions for many, the court sought to prevent unacceptable behavior by all. Government recognition and co-option of these ties did not explicitly confer official status on huiguan, but the special significance of compatriot ties among the literati in Beijing greatly shaped the context in which scholar-officials operated. In certain cases, discussed below, the institutional organization of huiguan developed in accordance with this special circumstance. Scholar-official native-place lodges were the institutionalized expression of compatriot relations within the scholar-official class; the court not only sanctioned these relations but also encouraged and regulated them.

Chopped Bonds

The imperial court used compatriot ties as a central cord in a net of mutual responsibility thrown over the civil bureaucracy and petitioners of the government. One principal method of enforcing mutual responsibility was a document of guaranty called a "chopped bond" (*yinjie* 印結).[2] State regulations required a person seeking to conduct any of a broad range of activities in the capital to obtain such a bond. Only a compatriot metropolitan official of rank six or above was authorized to issue a *yinjie*.[3] The bond attested that the petitioner had the proper family background and examination credentials and affirmed his native-place registration.[4] The official

---

2. The *Cihai* dictionary defines *yinjie* as a type of certificate issued as a guaranty by government officials to their superiors. The certificate itself was called a *jie*, and those with a chop, or an official stamp, were known as *yinjie*. See *Cihai*, s.v. See also Li Pengnian et al., eds., *Qingdai liubu chengyu cidian*, 41, for a more detailed description. E-tu Zen Sun translates the term as "sealed bond of guaranty"; see *Ch'ing Administrative Terms*, 25.

3. Exceptions were allowed under certain circumstances: if there was no fellow-provincial official of the requisite level serving in the capital, for example, officials of lower rank were allowed to issue them. See *Qing huidian shi li, juan* 115, 2: 483. The precedent cited here was dated 1800 and dealt specifically with the guaranties required by examination candidates, although one suspects that the "rule of analogy" would have allowed this principle to be applied in all cases requiring the use of *yinjie*.

4. For a sample *yinjie* form, see Huang Liuhong, *Fu hui quan shu*, 1.22. However, the forms were excluded from Djang Chu's English translation of this work, *A Complete Book Concerning Happiness and Benevolence (Fu-hui ch'üan-shu): A Manual*

who issued the bond was held accountable. If the petitioner had misrepresented himself or if he used the bond to engage in inappropriate activity, the official was deemed to share responsibility. The case laws relating to the punishment to be meted out to an official who inappropriately or incorrectly stood bond are numerous and detailed.[5]

The *Collected Precedents* supplement to the *Collected Statutes of the Qing Dynasty* contains numerous references to actions that required chopped bonds. Anyone trying to purchase a rank or title, for example, needed a chopped bond.[6] An appointment to public office was conditional on presentation of the appropriate chopped bond to the Board of Rites.[7] A senior licentiate who did not meet the regular requirements but had acquired a chopped bond issued by a fellow-provincial official was allowed to take the Shuntian examination.[8] A student of the Imperial Academy seeking to change his status also needed one.[9]

A chopped bond was obtainable only upon payment of a fee, referred to as the *yinjieyin* 印結銀. These fees were collected by bureaus established by the metropolitan officials of each province and distributed among those officials according to rank toward the end of each year. The fees made up a substantial portion of the in-

for Local Magistrates in Seventeenth-Century China. Djang translates the term as "a reference letter from an official in the capital" (ibid., 86), which somewhat misses the formality and the degree of responsibility conferred upon the issuer.

5. See *Qing huidian shi li, juan* 115, 2: 482–85, for precedents relating to the inappropriate issuance of guaranties.

6. Zhang Dechang, *Qing ji yige jingguan de shenghuo*, 47. See also *Qing huidian shi li, juan* 115, 2: 484. See also Hu bu (Board of Finance), *Zengxiu Chouxiang shili tiaokuan* (Beijing: n.p., 1866), 4 *juan*, for a complete set of regulations pertaining to sales of office; see esp. 2.80–83b, for regulations related to use of *yinjie* in buying offices. New regulations added in 1852 and 1865 reflect both the growing incidence of such sales and, by implication, the growing demand for these guaranties in the late nineteenth century.

7. *Qing huidian shi li*, vol. 1 (*juan* 72–77), covers civil appointments; for specific precedents requiring the chopped bond of a compatriot metropolitan official, see, e.g., 932, 939, 943, 949, 950, 972, 975, 977, and 980.

8. Ibid., *juan* 337, 4: 979. For other cases involving senior licentiates and provincial graduates, see ibid., 960, 984, and 985.

9. Ibid., *juan* 358, 5: 269. The first case involved a student by imperial favor; the second military students by purchase.

come of metropolitan officials (who were unable to supplement their salaries in the innumerable ways, such as tax skimming, open to officials serving in the provinces). The highest-ranked officials received the lion's share of the fees, and this made a great difference in their living standards. A "bamboo branch" poem—a popular and frequently humorous or ironic verse form—described this benefit:

> Beijing is not an easy place to live in.
> Pay all your bills, and you're left a poor mandarin.
> Better to have a post in a ministry,
> Then you'll end up with most of the *yinjie* fee.[10]

The Hong Kong scholar Zhang Dechang has drawn attention to the importance of this source of income to metropolitan officials, especially during the period from the 1860s to the early 1890s, in his book analyzing the extensive and meticulously kept diaries of the nineteenth-century metropolitan official Li Ciming 李慈銘 (1830–94).[11] Li's detailed financial records reveal that chopped-bond fees accounted for approximately 79 percent of his recorded income during the cumulative span of 21 years he served as a metropolitan official between 1862 and 1889.[12]

In 1888, another, more lowly ranked metropolitan official, Liu Guangdi 劉光第 (1859–98) (one of six famous reformist officials executed in the wake of the failure of the 1898 Hundred Days Reform), briefly calculated what he considered the minimum financial needs of a metropolitan official. Liu figured that an official with family in the capital required at least 600 taels of income each year. Only somewhat more than 50 taels of that might come from one's salary. Liu's official rank relegated him to only a small share of *yinjie* income; thus he counted on a much smaller amount from that

---

10. Yang Jingting, *Xinceng Dumen jilüe*, 6.4b–5.

11. Zhang Dechang, *Qing ji yige jingguan de shenghuo*, see esp. 46–49.

12. Figures calculated from ibid., table 1, "Li Ciming de guanshi shouru," 64. The years Li spent outside the capital are not included in this calculation. Another way to estimate the importance of these fees in the livelihood of metropolitan officials is to calculate this income as a percentage of total expenses (Li lived well, but remained in constant debt; we may assume he also had some amount of unrecorded unofficial income). His chopped bond fee income amounted to approximately 27 percent of his recorded expenses for the same period.

source than did Li Ciming. Liu figured that the annual income from the *yinjie* fee for someone of his rank might amount to no more than 100 taels. This was more than double an official's salary, but it was still far from enough to meet expenses.[13]

The chopped bond bureaus were responsible for collecting, managing, and distributing fees to the appropriate compatriot metropolitan officials. Li Ciming noted that the administrators of the Zhejiang bureau were selected on a rotating basis from among officials from Zhejiang holding the *jinshi* degree and serving in ministerial positions.[14] Although there is little existing documentation on the chopped-bond bureaus, it is clear that in some cases these bureaus had direct relations with the respective provincial huiguan in the capital. Li Ciming, for example, recorded a contentious meeting of the Zhejiang provincial huiguan in which forty to fifty people deliberated matters relating to their chopped bond bureau.[15] Records of the Anhui provincial huiguan indicate that an institutional relationship between the huiguan and the chopped-bond bureau of officials from that province had developed by the later part of the nineteenth century at least. According to the Tongzhi period rules for this huiguan:

All incoming and outgoing expenditures plus revenue [generated] by the [rented] properties outside the compound will be collected by the chopped-bond bureau for management and accounting. Monies in excess of 300 taels will then, after public deliberation, be distributed to fellow provincial [officials]. If [after that] the actual figures show a surplus in all accounts, then it shall be agreed that after the sacrifice [on behalf of the gods and spirits worshiped in the huiguan] on the third day of the second month, the new huiguan administrator, the old administrator, and the chopped-bond bureau administrator will get together to decide what to do [with the surplus]. These funds should not be left for subsequent administrators.[16]

---

13. See Liu Guangdi, *Liu Guangdi ji*, 194.

14. Li Ciming, *Yueman tang guoshi riji*, GX 4.1.29. Zhang Dechang, *Qing ji yige jingguan de shenghuo*, 59.

15. Li Ciming, *Yueman tang guoshi riji*, GX 2.10; Zhang Dechang, *Qing ji yige jingguan de shenghuo*, 59n5.

16. *Jingshi Anhui huiguan cunce*.

This arrangement was changed somewhat in a revision of administrative procedure in 1886, but a direct tie between the lodge and the management of the fee remained. The administrator of the chopped-bond bureau was also a mandated participant in decisions regarding the spending of money on social/ceremonial occasions, such as the get-together held shortly after the start of each New Year.[17]

By the second half of the nineteenth century, *yinjie* fees had become so important to metropolitan officials that the practice had apparently developed beyond what was strictly demanded by the statutes. The various provincial groups enforced a system that required exorbitant fees and the obtaining of numerous bonds—at least for those who sought to purchase official positions. In a revealing passage, the noted official Wen Tingshi remarked:

The selling of posts is a flourishing practice of this dynasty, but in order to purchase a post one must first have metropolitan officials from one's native place issue a *yinjie*. Secretaries of the six ministries, directors of the Banqueting Court, assistant secretaries of the Court of Judicature and Revision, and doctors of the Court of Sacrificial Worship are all permitted to issue these bonds (as are the magistrates of Daxing and Wanping districts). One person may be required to obtain up to ten bonds. The fee for each bond varies from province to province, with some such as Guangdong requiring up to 300 *liang* per bond and some requiring no less than 70 to 80 *liang*. Since the number of bonds needed is not set, this province may require ten bonds, whereas that province requires as few as six or seven, depending on the level of native-place solidarity. Expectant ministerial secretaries in the capital [who have achieved the necessary rank but are waiting for a post] specifically depend on these fees to make ends meet, for although it is not a glorious way to earn money, salaries are so low that they cannot avoid having to rely on this for income, for otherwise they would be thrown into irredeemable debt. Officials of each province who have not risen through an orthodox career path may not issue *yinjie*. In addition to metropolitan graduates, "selected candidates" who have been awarded assignments as petty metropolitan officials or ministerial second-class secretaries may also issue the bonds. Although provincial graduates and those who received their rank from the *yin* privilege rose to these positions through proper channels, they are not allowed to administer the bonds. This being the case, among those of a given province it often happens that there arise numerous disputes leading to blows and cursing. In addition, once assigned to the

---

17. Ibid.

capital, officials compete to issue more bonds and frequently disparage one another. Alas![18]

The *yinjie* requirement was not the only instance in which the court called on metropolitan officials to vouch for the compatriots. Another similar, though less common guaranty was called the "quintet mutual-guarantee bond" (*wuren hujie* 五人互結). This bond allowed groups of five officials linked to one another either by compatriot (*tongxiang*) or same-examination-year (*tongnian*) ties to vouch for the background of the others. If discrepancies were later found in the records of one of them, all were held in some degree responsible.[19]

Under exceptional circumstances, huiguan administrators were also called on to vouch for the veracity (and loyalty) of examination candidates. When, following the Taiping invasion of Hubei, the court feared rebels had disguised themselves as examination candidates in order to infiltrate the capital, it issued an imperial edict ordering metropolitan officials from Hubei and those residing in the various Hubei huiguan to verify the candidates' identity.[20]

Huiguan and Social Control in the Capital

In administering order, huiguan did not operate in a supervisory vacuum. Regular interaction with the metropolitan administration was required. Alison Dray-Novey has contributed greatly to our understanding of the Beijing police system during the late imperial era.[21] As she has made clear, there were, in fact, separate systems established for policing the Inner City and the Outer City, with the control maintained over the Inner City much the stricter of the two. Dray-Novey mentions the role of huiguan in the Outer City only briefly, yet her conclusion is somewhat contradictory. She notes that in contrast to the Inner City there is no evidence of strict official registration of the transient residents of inns and huiguan in

---

18. Wen Tingshi, *Wen Tingshi ji*, 783.
19. Djang, *Complete Book Governing Happiness and Benevolence*, 75.
20. *Qing shi lu*, 41: 49 (XF 3.1.23).
21. See Dray-Novey, "Policing Imperial Peking"; and idem, "Spatial Order and Police in Imperial Beijing."

the Outer City. Nevertheless, she surmises, "the responsibility of proprietors for those living under their roofs suggest that all these transients were known to the Five Districts and Five Battalion police."[22] In fact, none of the criminal cases I have seen indicate that before the turn of the twentieth century metropolitan authorities attempted to keep track of the transient lodgers in huiguan. On the contrary, it appears that no official notice was taken of who inhabited huiguan unless trouble developed. However, huiguan were supervised in other ways.

The administrative structure of Beijing was fairly complex. The capital city was administratively divided into two districts: Daxing in the west and Wanping in the east. Both districts were incorporated into the Metropolitan Prefecture (Shuntian fu 順天府), which consisted, in total, of four subprefectures (*ting* 廳), five departments (*zhou* 州), and nineteen districts. For police and judicial purposes, Beijing city proper was divided into five wards (*cheng* 城), directed by two censors of the five wards (*wucheng yushi* 五城御史). Among the offices under the supervision of these censors was the Roadway Office (Jiedao ting 街道廳), which was charged with keeping the streets of the Outer City in repair (a responsibility largely kept in the breech according to the numerous accounts of the miserable state of the roads in the city). This office was also charged with the preservation of public order, although the major responsibility for this lay with the Office of the Gendarmerie (Bujun tongling yamen 步軍統領衙門).[23]

The construction or refurbishment of any property in the Outer City required approval from this office. A series of communications between the Anhui huiguan administrator and the Roadway Office

---

22 . Dray-Novey, "Spatial Order and Police in Imperial Beijing," 902. Dray-Novey cites an article by Albert S. J. Chan in which he suggests that the huiguan were invented during the Ming, partly to facilitate police control; see Chan, "Peking at the Time of the Wan-li Emperor (1572–69)," in *Proceedings of the Second Biennial Conference, International Association of Historians of Asia* (Taipei, 1964), 2: 119–47. I have been unable to track down Chan's article, but the late Ming authors Liu Tong and Yu Yizheng do portray huiguan as one element in the system of police control in the capital (see *Di jing jing wu lüe*, 180–81).

23. For a clear and concise description of the metropolitan administration of Beijing, see Brunnert and Hagelstrom, *Present Day Political Organization of China*.

provide a uniquely detailed picture of this process.[24] Since the degree
to which the metropolitan government exercised control over this
kind of activity is largely unknown, it is worth reviewing briefly
here. Beginning in 1869, the founders of this as yet not formally
established huiguan submitted a number of petitions requesting
permission to begin construction of buildings on newly acquired
land. The exacting detail of the petitions is extraordinary. Construction neither within nor without the compound could be undertaken without official sanction. In separate requests, the huiguan
sought permission to erect the altar hall and opera stage; to level
high ground within the compound and use the soil to shore up the
building foundations; to convert a nearby subsidiary property into a
carriage house; and even to replace old and crumbling horse-
mounting platforms in front of the compound.[25]

Permission was granted in each instance, but each permission
came with a stern warning that the organizers were not to take
advantage of the permit to engage in construction beyond the parameters of what had been granted. Petitions were apparently
submitted in person, for in each case for which the dates may be
determined, permission was granted on the same or the subsequent
day. One may speculate that the petition for approval was accompanied by the customary recompense (*lougui* 陋規) that usually
accompanied bureaucratic requests, but the superintendent of
the Roadway Office was not the only party to benefit, if
such was the case. Official sanction also protected the huiguan
from future harassment from the lower orders of those exercis-
ing administrative power. The documents granted by the Roadway Office explicitly state that the "policemen and yamen runners
of the respective five wards" were not to obstruct the activities described, and these official documents must have prevented such

---

24. *Jingshi Anhui huiguan cunce*, 17–20.
25. One is accustomed to think of officials of this period riding about the city in
palanquins or by carriage. These stones remind us that high-level gentry also rode
horses through the city. The platforms consisted of single blocks of carved stone.
Horse mounting (no doubt complicated by official robes) was facilitated by first
stepping up on to these carved stone blocks. The stones mentioned in the petition
may still be found today outside this site.

irritants.[26] Beijing appears to have been unique in the degree to which construction activity was regulated. As far as I know, other cities had no bureau equivalent to the Roadway Office.

Neither the Qing imperial legal codes nor the official compilation of legal precedents made reference to organizations such as scholar-official huiguan, merchant-oriented huiguan, and *gongsuo* (guilds).[27] Nevertheless, governmental custom and practice allowed for—indeed, at times demanded—the exercise of juridical authority by traditional corporate organizations. To date, scholarly examination of such authority has been confined mainly to studies of organizations such as corporate lineages and guilds. This section examines the corresponding functions of the scholar-official huiguan of Beijing. Comparison with guilds and lineages highlights the unique nature of scholar-official huiguan. At the same time, the focus on these issues contributes to our understanding of the mechanisms of social control in the capital and the functions of huiguan within this system.

The desire to have huiguan serve as agents of social order was as much a product of sojourners' interests as those of the state. Sojourners were frequent victims of crimes. Lacking the security network of clan and acquaintances that protected them at home and frequently unfamiliar with the scams and ruses of a big city, provincials in the capital often found themselves the unwitting marks of swindlers, cheats, and thieves. Countless examination candidates discovered that years of study and immersion in the wisdom of the classics proved poor preparation for the conniving and unscrupulous ways of a bustling metropolis. Examination candidates were, moreover, not the only victims; other visitors to the capital, including officials, found that rank provided no immunity from criminal predation.

––––––––

26. The translation of the reference to policemen and runners is suggested by Dray-Novey, "Policing Imperial Peking," 279.

27. The term "guild" is employed here strictly as a convenient means by which to distinguish merchant organizations from scholar-official huiguan. Despite its long-standing and widespread use, the appropriateness of this term has recently come under well-reasoned criticism from Bryna Goodman (*Native Place*, esp. 41–44).

Late imperial guidebooks to Beijing, written for visiting scholars and officials, warned their readers of the most commonly encountered scams and hazards.[28] These cautionary descriptions are superb reflections of the particular dangers faced by literati sojourners in the capital. Some of the pettier nineteenth-century nuisances may sound familiar to recent visitors to the capital. Although the "taxis" of the time were mostly horse and donkey carriages (rickshaws also became popular in the waning years of the dynasty), then, as now, hiring a vehicle to get across town was a problem.[29] The guidebooks warned against being taken by unscrupulous drivers, who exaggerated the distance to be traveled or purposely took circuitous routes in order to charge exorbitant amounts. Vexatious street shysters hawking sham articles were another phenomenon with modern counterparts.

Some villains specialized in bilking examination candidates. Guidebooks instructed candidates to turn a deaf ear to those who offered to have crib notes smuggled into the examination grounds. If caught, the books warned, the original instigators would surely escape, leaving the candidate to face the law alone. Nor did the potential perils end with the examinations. After the results had been posted and thousands of successful and unsuccessful candidates embarked on the long journey home, other criminals teamed up to waylay them on the road.

The interpersonal anonymity of a strange city lay at the heart of many of the sojourners' problems. Victims had few means of tracking down the criminals. Finding a safe place to keep money was an ever-present problem. Provincials were warned to make thorough inquiries into any native bank (*qianpu* 錢舖) no matter how big its signboard or how prominent its location before depositing their money. The banks of Beijing were notorious for closing

---

28. The examples related in this section are taken from *Chao shi cong zai, juan* 4, "Fengsu" (Customs), 2–3; and *juan* 7, "Fengsu," 1; see also Yang Jingting, *Xinceng dumen jilüe*, 4.7–9, which provides essentially verbatim versions in somewhat different order.

29. Other common means of transportation included being carried in a palanquin, riding on horse or donkey back, and walking. For an excellent contemporary discussion of Beijing street transportation, see Favier, *Péking*, 465–69.

without notice, leaving their hapless clients with nothing but worthless deposit receipts.

Guidebooks also encouraged sojourners to forgo buying slave-servants while in the capital. Anyone so purchased, the guides foretold, would soon disappear:

You may believe that the family [of your purchase] is dignified and respectful, but what you don't know is that those engaged in petty business outside your gate are in fact the relatives of the girl using the selling of needles and thread as a pretext to meet with her. At night they will call to her, and once together, she will be escorted away. This is called "flying a falcon" (*fang ying* 放鷹).[30]

Unfortunately, the walls of huiguan compounds served as imperfect defenses against criminal encounters in the streets outside. Guidebooks specifically warned huiguan lodgers of the ever-present danger of thieves making their way into the compounds. Most thieves gained entrance by climbing over the wall Other thieves slipped in through unguarded gates or even carved holes in the walls to squeeze through. Examination candidates lodging in huiguan were reminded that their valuables could disappear as easily in broad daylight as in the still of night: "In a moment, you will find your door opened, your lock broken, and your possessions stolen. Moreover you will not be able to determine from where the thief came or to where he went."[31]

Occasionally, thieves were caught, however, and files relating to their crimes were kept by the relevant authorities. Although most criminal records of petty crimes within huiguan have been lost, a few stray cases from the waning years of the imperial period have been preserved in the files of the Board of Punishments (and its 1906–11 successor, the Ministry of Justice) and are held in the Number One Historical Archives in Beijing.

---

30. Yang Jingting, *Xinceng dumen jilüe*, 4.8b. As the term—taken from falconry—implies, the servant was not all that vanished in this ploy. *Mathews Chinese English Dictionary*, entry no. 7479, offers a succinct description of how much was at stake, in its definition of *fang ying*: "To palm off a wife as a sister or other relative and sell her into the home of another family, from which she runs away, taking with her as much as she can lay her hands on . . . and other similar swindles."

31. Yang Jingting, *Xinceng dumen jilüe*, 4.9.

Many of the objects at the center of these cases were of little value, but there were always those desperate enough to risk much for so little. In 1888, for instance, a commoner was arraigned for the theft of two wooden boards from the Hunan huiguan on Lanmian hutong.[32] Another case from 1892 involved a destitute Zhili man who slipped into the (Hubei) Wujun shiguan 武郡試館 on Yuhe qiao in the Inner City, to the east of the legation quarter, and stole a sheepskin sleeping pad from the watchman.[33] He was arrested by a Beijing gendarmerie bannerman after pawning the skin for four copper cash. Some criminals favored huiguan as targets for petty theft. One thief arrested for stealing personal articles from the (Hunan) Shanhua huiguan on Xuanwumen dajie in 1911, later confessed to having previously robbed other huiguan. In his deposition, he admitted to previously stealing from the (Jiangsu) Nantong huiguan 南通會館 and the Guizhou laoguan 貴州老館, with the help of an accomplice.[34]

Ne'er-do-wells who jumped the huiguan walls or slipped in unnoticed were not the only ones the lodge needed to guard against. Some perpetrators lived in the huiguan already. At times servants were implicated. Close quarters, relatively secluded interior courtyards, and the absence of stay-at-home family members to keep an eye on possessions afforded plenty of opportunities for those inclined toward thievery. In 1908, for example, the servant of a *juren* staying in the Guangxi sanguan 廣西三館 on Haibo lu stole trousers, several miscellaneous articles, and over 100 taels of silver from another *juren* staying in the same courtyard. The servant noted in his confession that the close proximity of the residents had allowed him to observe his neighbor's habits and plan the crime accordingly.[35]

Menial laborers employed by the huiguan were also potential sources of trouble. In one notable case, a lodge cook was accused of a serious crime committed against a high official temporarily in residence there. In that incident, an official was granted temporary

---

32. Xing bu #475, 13325.
33. Ibid., 13336.
34. Fa bu #24788.
35. Fa bu #24592.

leave from his post in the northeast to tend to the family graves in Xiangshan county, Guangdong. En route, he stopped in Beijing and put up at the Xiangshan huiguan on Guancai yuan shangjie. Four female servants accompanied the official, one of whom, a sixteen-year-old girl, disappeared while they were lodged there.[36] A young man working as a cook in the huiguan was accused of kidnapping the girl and selling her to traders. Although he denied involvement, and the girl was never found, he was deemed guilty all the same. Others testified to his having boasted, only days prior to the incident, that the girl had expressed a desire to run away with him. Whether in fact he was responsible for the young girl's disappearance (it is easy enough to imagine other scenarios), the judicial authorities found the evidence sufficiently convincing.

Huiguan Watchmen

Watchmen (*kanguan* 看馆) were central figures in the effort to prevent crime and maintain social order within huiguan compounds. Their role in this regard was in fact much greater than that of the immeasurably more esteemed huiguan directors, primarily because directors typically did not reside on the premises. Directors were chosen, when at all possible, from among the most eminent figures of the native-place community. Men of suitably high standing typically resided in their own private residences, where they could live in greater comfort with their families (and away from the importunings of compatriots). A survey of huiguan in the western half of the Outer City undertaken by the Central Police Bureau of the Outer City in the last few years of the Qing dynasty illustrates this point. Only 70 (32 percent) of the 217 directors whose residences were recorded in that survey lived on huiguan premises.[37]

---

36. Xing bu #01134.

37. Archives of the Ministry of Justice (Minzheng bu dang'an): #28, "Waicheng huiguan diaocha" (held by the Number One Historical Archive of China); reprinted as "Qingmo Beijing waicheng xunjing youting huiguan diaocha biao," in *Lishi dang'an*, 1995, no. 2: 59–65. It is not known if the 32 percent rate of directors living in huiguan may be taken as representative of earlier periods. No anecdotal evidence indicates directors living in huiguan, but this is by far the most comprehensive source of such information. The social status of directors who did live within huiguan compounds varied greatly at this time. Sun Jia'nai 孫家鼐

Even when a director did live within the huiguan compound, the watchman was still the principal keeper of order. Directors, after all, were not expected to dirty their hands with the business of overseeing day to day affairs. Watchmen, on the other hand, as their name clearly indicates, were paid to watch. When the compound walls did not keep disorder out, it was the watchmen's job to take over.

The responsibilities of watchmen failed to confer much social respect. They remained mere employees, and as is true of other lodge employees, little is known about how watchmen were selected. There would seem to be reason to suppose that watchmen were selected from among the poorer compatriot sojourners in the capital. The bond of shared native place would presumably have encouraged upright behavior in dealings between the watchmen and the lodgers and would have allowed greater recourse against misconduct, since the connection would have allowed family and acquaintances to be enlisted in disciplining an errant watchman. However, there is little evidence to indicate that only compatriot watchmen were hired. Few sources indicate the geographic origins of watchmen; the records of two court cases involving huiguan watchmen (discussed in more detail below) do provide such records. In one case, the watchman of one of the Sichuan provincial huiguan was, in fact, registered as a Sichuan native.[38] But in the other case, the watchman for a Shaanxi provincial huiguan, the Guanzhong huiguan 關中會館, was registered as a native of Beijing (Wanping district).[39]

(1827–1909), a grand secretary, lived in the Anhui huiguan. (Sun simultaneously served as the director of the Fengyang huiguan on Paizi hutong, where, of course, he was not resident.) Other resident directors included an expectant district magistrate, a number of ministerial secretaries and cabinet secretaries, a Hanlin compiler of the second class, and other officials of varying rank, but college staff and one college instructor also served as resident directors at that time.

The exact period during which this survey was undertaken is not recorded. The Ministry of Justice, which supervised the survey, was in existence from 1906 to 1911. Most likely this survey was associated with a comprehensive survey of the Beijing population undertaken by this ministry in 1909; see *Da Qing fagui daquan*, 2: 981–89.

38. Xing bu #475, 13235.

39. Ibid., 10823. Wanping district incorporated the western half of Beijing. The possibility that the watchman was originally a Shaanxi native but later changed his

Watchmen were allocated one or two rooms on the premises, and they received small but steady wages. Their duties, as described in huiguan rules, included sweeping the grounds and keeping track of the huiguan furniture and other sundry items, so that those who damaged or made off with such property could be held accountable. They were also responsible for noting who entered and left the compound. Watchmen were a source of concern, however. It was clear that the potential for abuse was always present. This concern was reflected in a set of huiguan rules from 1738, one of the earliest extant sets. These rules from the (Anhui) Shexian huiguan state:

If [servants and watchmen] are neglectful or dirty; or if they take in bad elements; or steal the tables and chairs of the huiguan in order to sell them, or borrow them for their private use, or engage in other such evil practices, they will be handed over to the metropolitan authorities for punishment. They will, moreover, be expelled, and others will be found.[40]

In some cases, the malpractices of watchmen went beyond a lack of cleanliness and selling furniture on the side. One mid-nineteenth-century notice indicates that some watchmen might have been involved in a scam to dupe visiting provincials. An 1852 posting by the Tongrentang, the famous Beijing pharmacy (and supplier of traditional medicines to the court) alerted the Beijing public to "shameless persons selling fake medicines under the Tongrentang name in collaboration with inns and huiguan."[41] The notice is somewhat vague, but it seems to suggest huiguan watchmen or others with huiguan connections were foisting fake goods off on the lodgers. It is easy to imagine examination candidates buying presents to take home persuaded they had stumbled on a bargain for a famous Beijing "special product" when all they were getting was an overpriced knockoff.

----

county of registration while maintaining his original native-place ties cannot be ruled out. However, there is no positive indication that this was the case.

40. *Shexian huiguan lu*, 1b.15. An 1805 version of these same rules conveys essentially the same ideas, with the exception that in the case of infractions by the watchmen, the huiguan administrator was to mete out the punishment. Such wording does not rule out handing over the culprit to the metropolitan authorities; rather, it introduces a measure of greater leeway at the administrator's discretion; see ibid., 1c.15.

41. Beijing Tongrentang shi bianwei hui et al., eds., *Beijing Tongrentang shi*, 8–9.

The Judicial Authority of
Huiguan in Comparative Perspective

Proper understanding of how scholar-official huiguan did and did not maintain social order is best approached through a comparison with other corporate organizations. Traditional Chinese legal practice granted lineages and guilds broad regulatory authority over their affairs and considerable jurisdictional power over their members. Such organizational authority was by no means absolute; governmental authorities could and did intervene when it was determined that the greater social good was at stake. Yet, if the reach of the state did not stop at the front gates of lineage ancestral halls or guild compounds, the overall tendency was for government to adhere to a largely hands-off approach.

Previous scholars have addressed many aspects of the power exercised by corporate lineages over their members. The most comprehensive analysis of the mechanisms of lineage control remains the monograph by Hui-Chen Wang Liu.[42] Liu convincingly demonstrated the degree to which lineages were allowed to exercise a range of jurisdictional powers over members. In cases involving only members of the lineage, this authority included broad powers of adjudication and enforcement of punishments (for obvious reasons, inter-lineage disputes were quite another matter and fell largely outside the scope of lineage authority).

The jurisdictional authority of guilds has also long been recognized. Several of the earliest articles on guilds, dating from the late nineteenth century, specifically focus on guild regulations and legal authority.[43] Max Weber was also impressed by the degree of legal authority enjoyed by Chinese guilds, noting that "the guilds had often in reality appropriated absolute jurisdiction over their members."[44] To illustrate his point, Weber related the colorful (if suspect)

---

42. Hui-chen Wang Liu, *The Traditional Chinese Clan Rules.*
43. See K., "The Chinese Guilds and Their Rules"; and MacGowan, "Chinese Guilds or Chambers of Commerce and Trade Unions."
44. Weber, *The Religion of China*, 17. Weber continued: "Formally this seemed to be true of the huiguan guilds of officials and merchants who derived from other provinces," a supposition to which I seek to add nuance in this chapter.

story of a guild member who was "bitten to death for infraction of the rule defining the maximum number of apprentices."[45]

Numerous scholars since Weber have addressed the jurisdictional authority of guilds. Among them, Sybille van der Sprenkel's analysis still stands as a particularly cogent study of this subject.[46] Van der Sprenkel notes the range of sanctions available to guilds against misbehaving members and points out that fines were the most common guild sanction. Van der Sprenkel also follows up on the observations of much earlier scholars in noting that guilds, like lineages, exercised a very real delegated legal authority, arguing that in their exercise of judicial power, "*zu* [lineage] and guild tribunals may perhaps be thought of as subsidiaries of the official courts . . . [and as] part of the hierarchy of courts."[47]

Guild authority, in Van der Sprenkel's view, while enhanced by rituals associated with the group cult, was ultimately based on normative and coercive powers derived from the social and economic dependency of members of the guild. Expulsion was a severe, potentially catastrophic penalty, and members would under normal circumstances avoid it at great cost. Van der Sprenkel's insights effectively account for the dramatic differences between guild and scholar-official huiguan in respect to the relative jurisdictional authority they exercised. No precisely defined community of economic interests bolstered huiguan authority. Regulation of pricing, apprenticeship, and such matters was completely alien to these associations. Thus, as we shall see below, scholar-official huiguan

---

45. Ibid., 18. The source of this alleged incident was MacGowan, "Chinese Guilds or Chambers of Commerce and Trade Unions." The incident was apparently reported in the press of the day, although the story frankly strikes me as apocryphal. I know of no similar example of guild sanctions. For more on guild sanctions, see also Bradstock, "Craft Guilds in Ch'ing Dynasty China."

46. Van der Sprenkel, *Legal Institutions in Manchu China*, esp. chap. 7, "Jurisdictional Aspects of the Tsu and the Guild," 80–96; and idem, "Urban Social Control."

47. Van der Sprenkel, *Legal Institutions in Manchu China*, 96 (transliteration changed to *pinyin*). The concept of *zu* legal authority as delegated governmental authority was made by E. Alabaster, *Notes and Commentaries on Chinese Criminal Law and Cognate Topics, with Special Relation to Ruling Cases, Together with a Brief Excursus on the Law of Property* (London, 1899), lvi.

possessed comparatively less coercive power to bring to bear upon those who used their premises.

Huiguan Rules

Every scholar-official huiguan established rules or regulations and posted them publicly within the lodge compound. Such rules were referred to variously as *tiaogui* 條規, *guan'gui* 館規, or *zhangcheng* 章程. Huiguan rules governed a wide range of behaviors, including monetary donations and the performance of rites. Although the rules largely concerned the behavior of residents of the compound, some rules governed, or claimed to govern, the behavior of compatriot officials who did not reside in the huiguan or even in Beijing. As discussed in the preceding chapter, the rules on the sums to be donated upon promotion to specific posts, for instance, were intended to govern the empirewide community of compatriot officials.

No other corporate organization enacted the extra-local donation requirements associated with the Beijing scholar-official huiguan. Such sweeping coverage was made feasible by a combination of factors. First, all officials would necessarily have taken the *huishi* examination in Beijing earlier in their career, and during that time they probably lodged in the huiguan, thus establishing a personal connection with the facility. Second, scholar-official huiguan were both manifestations of regional pride and instruments of furthering regional objectives in the capital and thus were relevant objects of gentry largess even among those who did not live in or near them. Third, since officials serving in the provinces were called to the capital for imperial audiences both upon leaving an official posting and upon being appointed to a posting, every official would commonly have found himself in the capital for one reason or another at least several times during his career. Failure to donate sufficient sums while serving in the provinces would have led to uneasy relations with one's huiguan while in the capital (although presumably all could be put to rights with a generous donation at that time).

Most huiguan rules were intended to maintain the proper functioning of the organization and were not concerned with social control per se. Huiguan rules mandated that rooms be cleared to make way for examination candidates during examination years, for example. Other rules detailed payments to the watchman or exhorted residents to respect community property and specified payments for damaged items. Dates of ritual services and yearly banquets also constituted one standard element of the rules.

Some rules pertained directly to the overall comportment and civil behavior of the lodgers. This meant the avoidance not only of criminal behavior but also of any activities that threatened the order and reputation of the huiguan. These concerns were clearly expressed in an early example of huiguan regulations. The 1770 regulations of the (Hebei) Hejian huiguan decreed:

> It has been decided after due deliberation that if residents of the huiguan are unscrupulous persons (*feiren* 匪人); or are students of our prefecture who secretly reside in the huiguan and pretend to a respected reputation in order to cheat people; or who conceal or set up opera accouterments (*xiju* 戲具) or family members; or who gamble or drink to excess, and so on, upon investigation the director will be notified, and such residents will be expelled according to regulations. If those residing with the offender engaged in concealment or complicity, they, too, will be expelled.[48]

The prohibition against concealing or setting up opera accouterments is an intriguing element in this list of proscribed behavior. That sojourners were tempted to conceal opera props seems no more likely than professional opera players successfully passing themselves off as being scholars eligible to lodge within the huiguan. Most likely, the prohibition was intended to curtail "fraternizing" with boy opera players on huiguan grounds. Young opera performers often doubled as male prostitutes, and the regulation was directed at lodgers desiring to keep such young players in their rooms. The rules of other huiguan put the prohibition more clearly; one Jiaqing-era proscription stated: "The coming and going of prostitutes and actors is not allowed."[49]

Some rules proscribed behavior that was socially disruptive or impolite. One set of huiguan rules prohibited "becoming intoxi-

---

48. *Hejian huiguan lu*, 35b.
49. *Beiping Jingxian huiguan lu*, 1.1b. The regulation is dated 1817. For another prohibition against actors entering the huiguan compound, see *Shanhua guan zhi*, 1.3b.

cated and causing problems or singing songs in disregard of others; opposing one's betters, with impropriety and without regard to what is right; standing defiantly or squatting in the presence of the friends or relatives of the administrators."[50] Rules against excessive drinking, gambling, and other potentially disruptive behavior were common. However, the special emphasis given to respectful behavior in the presence of the administrators is unusual.

In comparison to the rules of lineages and guilds, what is most noteworthy about scholar-official huiguan rules is the relative lack of emphasis on regulating social behavior. The difference between guild rules and scholar-official lodge rules in this respect is quite striking and immediately apparent upon comparison.[51] Many sets of regulations make no reference to improper behavior beyond stipulating punishments for the destruction of property. The annals of the Shexian huiguan, for example, reprinted five complete sets of huiguan rules spanning nearly a century from 1741 to 1830.[52] Although these regulations were explicitly detailed in regard to operational matters, they said little regarding matters of social control beyond prohibitions against the misappropriation of lodge property. Moreover, the prescribed punishments were limited to reimbursement of the value of the lost property and expulsion.

Unlike the rules of lineages and merchant guilds, huiguan rules were extremely restricted in describing measures to deal with infractions. Clan rules stipulated punitive measures as various as "oral censure, ritual discipline, cash fines, corporal punishment, denial of clan privileges, expulsion from the clan group, and legal indictment."[53] Guild rules, too, frequently stated explicit measures, such as fines or extra ritual observances in cases of disobedience.[54] By

---

50. *Changjun huiguan zhi*, 20. This is another early example of huiguan rules. Textual evidence indicates that the regulations cited here date to approximately the mid-eighteenth century.

51. Zhao Lingyu, "Zhongguo huiguan zhi shehuixue de fenxi," 48, is the earliest work known to me to indicate this difference between guild and scholar-official huiguan rules.

52. *Shexian huiguan lu*, 1.16–20, 1b.17–21.

53. Hui-chen Wang Liu, "An Analysis of Chinese Clan Rules," 64.

54. See, e.g., "Chong jian Yaohang huiguan beiji" (Stele inscription commemorating the rebuilding of the Medicine Trade huiguan) and "Yuhang guiyue" (Jade

comparison, scholar-official huiguan rules, in general, call for no sanctions other than the restitution of the value of damaged property. If further punishment were deemed necessary, expulsion or notification of the authorities seems to have been the final measure.

Crime and Punishment

Scholar-official huiguan further differed from guilds and lineages in the handling of infractions of the rules and disputes between members. Unlike the other organizations, which convened formal tribunal sessions to adjudicate such matters, the response of scholar-official huiguan was much simpler and, again, more limited. I have found no evidence of a tribunal convened by any huiguan to decide issues of social control or mediate disputes between members during the imperial period. Rather, issues were settled in a much more direct and less autonomous fashion. Huiguan watchmen settled the most minor issues; more important issues were settled by the rotating huiguan administrators, and matters of any urgency or moment were handed over to the metropolitan government.

Unfortunately, among the records of cases extant today, there is no documentation of huiguan procedures in cases involving major disputes or infractions by legitimate huiguan lodgers. This lacuna surely reflects not only the lack of primary sources but also the relative rarity of instances in which examination candidates or officials became involved in disputes involving huiguan.

One court case from 1882, however, does shed light on huiguan handling of serious infractions, even though the accused in this case was not a legitimate tenant. The case involved the beating of the brother of the watchman of the Sichuan huiguan on Sichuan ying.[55] Among the anomalies of this case is that the accused was a bannerman, who, although a resident of Sichuan, was neither a scholar nor an official, and therefore did not qualify to reside in the huiguan.

Nevertheless, the bannerman showed up at the huiguan gate one day, luggage in hand, and requested a room for two or three days.

---

trade regulations), in Li Hua, ed. and comp., *Ming-Qing yilai Beijing gongshang huiguan beide xuan bian*, 93–94, 115–17.

55. Xing bu #475, 13235.

The watchman allowed him to move in. Upon informing the administrator of the unqualified tenant, the watchman was instructed to have him removed right away. However, in a telling admonition against too readily inferring social practice from formal regulations, the bannerman proceeded to continue lodging in the huiguan for, in the watchman's words, "two or three years."

Despite the illegitimacy of his tenancy and, if the subsequent testimony of the watchman can be believed, the bannerman's habit of whoring every night until the early morning hours and upon his return creating a racket to rouse the watchman to let him in, the situation might easily have gone on in that fashion indefinitely had not an altercation occurred. The incident developed when the sixty-year-old half-brother of the even-more-elderly watchman went to the bannerman's room to collect long overdue fees owed for meals prepared in the huiguan. When the bannerman refused to pay, or in any case disputed the sum demanded, an argument ensued, and the brother was badly beaten.

Of particular interest in this case is the almost total lack of huiguan administration involvement in the matter. No effort at sanction or punishment was brought to bear against the bannerman before the incident, and the only response after its occurrence was to contact the police. Also remarkable is the latitude extended to the watchman to handle affairs, so long as no trouble ensued. The bannerman's several-year stay in the huiguan may have been eased by private cash transactions between the bannerman and the watchman. Indeed, the Board of Punishments apparently suspected the watchman of complicity, because it criticized him for not living up to the responsibilities entrusted to him.

The principle by which authorities held huiguan watchmen responsible for the crimes occurring on their watch was displayed in another case as well. In 1903 a group of counterfeiters was discovered to be operating out of a large back courtyard in the (Shaanxi) Weinan huiguan 渭南會館 on Xihe yan.[56] This site had fallen on hard times and had largely ceased operating as a huiguan by the time. Management of the property had devolved to the Shaanxi provincial huiguan, the Guanzhong huiguan. The watchman of that site, Liu

---

56. Ibid., 10823.

Sheng, was instructed to take responsibility for the Weinan huiguan as well. Liu rented it out, as was appropriate under the circumstances, but claimed that the distance between the two sites prevented him from keeping close tabs on the activities of the occupants. He was, he said, unaware of the fact that the new tenants had set up a forge on the huiguan grounds and were fruitfully engaged in minting debased counterfeit copper coinage. Despite Liu's disclaimer, he was deemed negligent in his responsibilities and sentenced to 100 strokes of the bamboo (a sentence that was immediately reduced).

Neither of these cases represents a textbook example of transgression by a legitimate huiguan resident; however, both reveal characteristics of huiguan social control functions. In both cases, huiguan administration proved distant and disconnected from day-to-day activities within the huiguan compounds; practical management was left largely to watchmen. As long as no trouble arose, few questions were asked.

Most noteworthy is the absence of a clear autonomous judicial function located within the lodge. In both cases, serious matters were delivered directly to the civil authorities. Also striking is the relatively complete penetration of huiguan juridical functions by the metropolitan court system. This penetration is especially apparent in the punishment and castigation of the watchmen by the court for not living up to their responsibilities to the huiguan (no records indicate autonomous action by either huiguan in these or similar matters).

In the relationship between the Board of Punishments and huiguan, we find a clear indication that the scholar-official huiguan of Beijing differed qualitatively from such organizations as lineages and guilds in terms of the handling of social control problems. Rather than operate an autonomous if subservient intramural judicial system to deal with problems affecting those living within the huiguan compound, scholar-official huiguan were largely open to the judicial mechanisms of the metropolitan government. If scholar-official huiguan had ever possessed the kind of juridical authority characteristic of guilds (a supposition I find suspect), then that power had withered by the late nineteenth century. Nevertheless, the lodges did provide an important space for scholars and officials to come together, to socialize, network, and discuss issues important to them. Clearly, the state did recognize the legitimacy of such gatherings within the lodges and ordinarily did not interfere with them. Thus, although juridical authority was greatly limited, the lodges possessed a significant degree of spatial and social autonomy. This autonomy allowed scholar-official landsmen in the capital to come together to discuss and act on matters related to their interests and to the state in ways that would not otherwise be possible, as we shall see in the following chapters.

NINE

The Articulation of Regional

Interests in Beijing

Scholars of late imperial China have long been interested in the interaction between the imperial government and the regions that it administered. This interest has generated a large body of excellent literature on center-region relationships. We are, as a result, reasonably familiar with such issues as how revenue was extracted from the regions, how centrally appointed officials interacted with local societies, and how local societies, in turn, interacted with centrally appointed officials. To date, such studies have primarily directed our attention to how center and region interacted *in the regions*. Less studied is how center and region interacted *at the center*.

China's capital city was an important locus of dynamic interaction between center and region. The workings of the memorial system and other channels of official communication only begin to reflect on this side of the relationship. Provincial memorialists were, after all, centrally appointed officials themselves and thus represented regional interests only in a highly mediated fashion. However, more direct center-regional interaction in the capital was effected through other channels situated in the capital. Only recently has our attention been turned to this important site of interaction. One example is Madeleine Yue Dong's fascinating re-examination of the famous late Qing law case involving Yang Naiwu and "Xiao Baicai."[1] In that piece Dong argues that the key to understanding the dynamics of that case lies not in the formal legal processes that were the focus of an article written by William Alford ten years earlier.[2] Instead, Dong offers a revisionist analysis and stresses how much the final legal decision was shaped by "varied channels of communication," among which she particularly emphasizes newspapers and native-place networking.[3]

One of the outstanding features of Dong's article is her detailed reconstruction of a "private" network of influential elites in the capital who lobbied on Yang's behalf and who were mobilized largely through native-place ties. In this chapter, I explore in further detail some of the ways that native-place channels of communication were institutionalized in Beijing. Native-place ties not only shaped political action in exceptional cases such as the Yang Naiwu trial but were, in fact, a constant and significant factor in governmental action in the capital. Indeed, I believe they served as a *constitutional* mechanism of negotiation between state and society.[4] Whereas Dong describes such ties as "private" and explicitly contrasts them with the sorts of "public" actions that took place inside the offices of the various ministries in Beijing, I argue that in fact no such duality existed. In Beijing (and I believe the capital was something of a special place in this regard), native-place loyalties were not employed only "privately." Their use was encouraged, indeed demanded, by the state.

On one level, these circumstances further highlight the caution that must be exercised in applying terms such as "public" and "pri-

---

1. Dong, "Communities and Communication."
2. Alford, "Of Arsenic and Old Laws."
3. Dong, "Communities and Communication," 82, 113–15.
4. My sense of how "constitutional" applies to the Qing political situation is indebted to Philip Kuhn's use of the term in his essay "Ideas Behind China's Modern State" and his book *Origins of the Modern Chinese State*.

vate" to the Chinese political context. But, on another, more significant level, they demonstrate that a greater understanding of the political functions of native-place ties in late imperial Beijing is needed, given the sheer importance and volume of decision making in the capital. This chapter examines the functions of scholar-gentry native-place lodges in this process. That the capital city served as an important nexus between center and region should come as no surprise. As the seat of the imperial government, the capital city functioned as the heart of the national polity. It was in the capital that the emperor and his court resided, formed policies, and decided affairs of state. The capital's credentials as the locus of central power are obvious. That regional interests should seek to exert their influence within the capital city therefore seems natural, but little is understood about the channels and processes through which this was accomplished. Working in the opposite direction, the powerful officials and innumerable sojourners resident in the capital maintained strong ties with their home regions and also, naturally, at times sought to affect events there. In fact, Beijing native-place ties and native-place lodges facilitated both processes and thus constituted an important node of bidirectional interaction between center and region.

Given the many thousands of minor officials posted to bureaucratic positions in Beijing, it is not surprising that these metropolitan officials (*jingguan* 京官) played a key mediating role in these processes. Although vitally important to the functioning of the imperial administration, metropolitan officials are still a somewhat understudied component of the bureaucracy. The rules governing metropolitan officials differed from those applied to centrally appointed officials posted outside the capital (officials in the capital were not bound to the customary limit of three to five years in any particular office, for example). They participated in a unique cultural and social life, and, as discussed in the preceding chapter, they relied on a set of economic resources markedly different from that available to their provincial official colleagues.[5] Metropolitan offi-

---

5. The official wages of metropolitan officials were comparable to those of provincial officials. But an official's salary constituted only a small part of his overall income. As we have seen, many of the most lucrative methods used by

cials also retained strong ties to their native regions. They came from diverse localities throughout the empire, and upon retirement they were required by regulation (if not always in practice) to leave the capital and return home. The great majority of metropolitan officials were Han Chinese, and like native Chinese in all walks of life, their social interactions were greatly shaped by culturally constructed *tongxiang* bonds, which connected them to regional compatriots. Next to family and lineage ties, a common place of origin constituted the most important social bond in late imperial Chinese society. Those seeking favors, assistance, or influence were likely to turn to *tongxiang* fellows if family or kin could not help, and if a *tongxiang* fellow could help, he did. Shared native place was a recognized and honored social bond.

This chapter is divided into three sections, each composed primarily of a separate case study of a notable metropolitan official during the mid- to late nineteenth century. Each section focuses on the huiguan-related activities of the official in question. The first examines the political efficacy of *tongxiang* ties and the use of these ties by provincials visiting the capital in their dealings with metropolitan officialdom by looking at the activities of the powerful minister Weng Tonghe. The interactions between visiting *tongxiang* elite and Weng reveal how native-place ties served as conduits through which local interests were successfully communicated to Beijing officialdom. The second section analyzes the huiguan-related activities of Li Wen'an, the father of the powerful general and statesmen Li Hongzhang and a high-level metropolitan official in his own right. This study demonstrates the use of native-place lodges by a high-level official and other metropolitan elite *tongxiang* to affect events in their home region, in comparison to the previous section, in which we see the use of huiguan and *tongxiang* ties by provincial elites to influence the metropolitan bureaucracy. The last section examines the political functions of huiguan patronage by Li Hongzhang himself. In this case, Li's generous sponsorship of lodges in Beijing is considered in light of the extensive network of fellow Anhui natives, whom he actively promoted and helped to

---

provincial officials to generate income—tax skimming, customary gifts (*lougui*), for example—were unavailable to metropolitan officials.

place into positions of importance around the empire. In this case, the focus is on the role played by huiguan in facilitating such native-place patronage networks.

Tongxiang *Connections and Informal*
Access to Metropolitan Officials

Like government officials in any bustling capital city, metropolitan officials in Beijing faced many demands on their time. For visitors to the capital, gaining access to these officials presented a formidable challenge. Of course, high-ranking provincial officials may have had little trouble arranging meetings, but sure access was granted only to personal acquaintants, relatives, or those with proper letters of introduction. Without such entrées, non-officials or low-ranking provincial officials might find themselves in Beijing surrounded by bureaucrats and yet unable to meet any of them. One other, more-accessible channel to personal meetings with Beijing officialdom existed, however: shared native place. *Tongxiang* connections were an effective and frequently employed means by which prominent commoners and lower-level provincial bureaucrats obtained direct personal access to Beijing officials. Shared district, prefectural, or provincial origins did not provide instant access to everyone, of course, but any metropolitan official would have felt some obligation to accommodate those of acceptable social status from his native place. For visiting provincials, *tongxiang* ties opened doors.

Access to officials, moreover, readily converted into influence. Once the doors had been opened, face-to-face meetings with *tongxiang* metropolitan officials often produced politically significant consequences. Provincials appealed to officials to intervene on their behalf for widely varied reasons. On many occasions these undoubtedly involved personal favors, but issues of larger regional concern—matters that benefited not only the petitioner but also the shared native place more generally—were especially well received. The traditional dictates of propriety that governed particularistic relationships such as *tongxiang* ties ensured that these matters received a decent hearing and, within reasonable limits, an honest effort to assist on the part of the official. As long as no extraordinary excesses were involved, aiding one's native place was not considered a corrupt practice. Indeed, quite the opposite was true. Assisting one's native place was a virtuous act, in some ways similar to the filial behavior of sacrificing oneself for one's family so honored by Confucian values.

The diary of the prominent metropolitan official Weng Tonghe reveals numerous requests to Weng by visiting provincials for intervention on behalf of their shared region in the decades leading up to 1898 (when he was dismissed from office, apparently at the instigation of the Empress Dowager). During this period, Weng served as a grand councilor and a tutor of the emperor and held various high positions in the Six Boards. Weng served as president of the Board of Revenue from 1886 until his retirement twelve years later, a period during which he was unquestionably one of the most influential men in the empire.[6] Weng's diary records regular contacts with his native-place fellows, as well as instances in which he used the political clout of his office to intercede on their behalf. In neither respect is there reason to believe that his actions were unusual.

It is clear from Weng's diary that during his years in high office he often met with groups of *tongxiang* from his home city, prefecture, and province. Many of these meetings took place in the huiguan of his native city, Changshu.[7] A typical diary entry is that for April 1, 1889: "Went to the district huiguan to pay a call on all the gentlemen of my native place. Then went to the Caisheng guan [a banqueting facility frequented by the upper gentry of Beijing] for a get-together with Jiangsu *tongxiang*."[8] Numerous entries recording meetings with fellow-provincials for ostensibly social affairs are

---

6. Fang Chao-ying, "Weng T'ung-he," in Hummel, ed., *Eminent Chinese of the Ch'ing Period*, 2: 860–61.

7. Although Weng made numerous references to his local huiguan, he never referred to it by name or clearly identified it in his diary; rather, all references were to his "district-city lodge" (*yiguan* 邑馆). There is no doubt that the site in question must have been the Chang-Zhao yiguan on Lanmian hutong, which represented the adjoining districts of Changshu and Zhaowen. Weng also recorded visits to "Lanmian hutong" on numerous occasions; a good number of these may also have been visits to this huiguan.

8. Weng Tonghe, *Weng Tonghe riji paiyin ben*, GX 15.4.2, 1593. See also ibid., GX 15.6.9, 1603, for another meeting with Changshu *tongxiang* two months later.

found throughout the period of Weng's tenure in office.[9] A wide range of subjects, many of them relating to the affairs of Weng's native province, Jiangsu, and his home city, Changshu, were discussed at them. Such meetings served as an important if informal source of information concerning events in his home region. One native-place fellow, for example, reported to Weng on the problems caused by the influential secret society known as the Society of Elders and Brothers (Gelao hui) in their native district.[10] Another discussion concerned fellow provincials in need of financial assistance.[11]

Since Weng served as president of the Board of Revenue, it is not surprising that these discussions not infrequently revolved around the collection of taxes in his home province. Weng in turn provided special consideration to his *tongxiang* on tax matters. In the fall of 1892, for example, Weng recorded a visit by ten *tongxiang* from Zhenjiang, which was then suffering from a severe drought. The men asked Weng to do what he could to help gain approval for a memorial sent by the provincial governor requesting a suspension of tribute-rice collections in that area. Weng agreed and immediately forwarded instructions to those responsible in the Board of Revenue.[12]

Weng's response was by no means merely a polite but empty gesture. The efficacy of Weng's intervention was demonstrated when eight or nine of those provincial petitioners performed a ritual ceremony of thanks within the Forbidden City in appreciation for the court's mercy in remitting the taxes a month later.[13] The incident testifies to the power of *tongxiang* access to metropolitan officials. Weng's diary records at least four different instances in which officials from Jiangsu gathered to thank the court for other tax re-

---

9. See, e.g., ibid., GX 16.3.27, 1651; GX 17.1.6, 1695; GX 19.1.10, 1806; GX 19.4.27, 1821 (records native-place fellows paying respects to Weng on his birthday); and GX 20.1.9, 1862. Native-place-related visits were not limited to *tongxiang* natives. Weng also recorded the visit of the Changshu assistant district magistrate (*xiancheng*), who had served in Weng's hometown for fourteen years. See ibid., GX 17.6.19, 1718.

10. Ibid., GX 16.8.20, 1674.

11. Ibid., GX 16.3.27, 1651.

12. Ibid., GX 18.8.24, 1783.

13. Ibid., GX 18.11.27, 1796.

missions during the time Weng served as president of the Board of Revenue.[14] We may reasonably assume that Weng had a hand in each one of these remissions.

As a source documenting the use of *tongxiang* ties to influence central policies, Weng's diary is extraordinary in its degree of detail and in the pre-eminent influence of its author. But there is little reason to suspect that Weng's dealings with *tongxiang* seeking official favors were in any way out of the ordinary in other respects. Clearly *tongxiang* ties could be deployed to gain direct access to ranking officials and influence regional elites from throughout China.

The direction of political influence channeled through the scholar-gentry huiguan of the capital was not entirely unidirectional, however. Huiguan were also employed to channel information back to the region from the center and to influence events there. Metropolitan officials found huiguan to be useful tools in coordinating these efforts.

Huiguan in the Coordination of Regional Interests by Metropolitan Officials

When the Taiping armies broke out of south China and into the Yangzi River valley in the winter of 1852–53, all of central China was placed in imminent danger. Wuchang, the provincial capital of Hubei, fell to the rebels in mid-January 1853. Cities further downstream, including Anqing, the provincial capital of Anhui, fell in the weeks thereafter.[15] By the end of March, the Taipings had captured Nanjing. In the midst of these unfolding disasters, the court in Beijing struggled to find solutions to the successful defense of the Yangzi valley and other areas. Of interest to us is how the court and the *tongxiang* sojourners in Beijing interacted in order to affect events in the threatened regions. This process is effectively demonstrated by the actions of one metropolitan official who led his *tongxiang* sojourners in Beijing in an effort to strengthen the defense of Luzhou prefecture in Anhui province.

---

14. Ibid., GX 16.1.9, 1636; GX 16.12.14, 1691; GX 17.12.26, 1745; GX 18.11.27, 1796.
15. *Luzhou fu zhi* (1885), *juan* 22, "Bing shi zhi," 2.

On March 1, 1853, an imperial edict ordered Lü Xianji, the senior vice-president (*zuo shilang*) of the Board of Works, to proceed immediately to Anhui and implement appropriate defensive measures in cooperation with the leading officials there.[16] Upon receiving this edict, Lü petitioned the court to order a selected group of officials to accompany him.[17] The court quickly approved his request.[18] Among those whose services Lü requested was a young, second-class Hanlin Academy compiler (*bianxiu*), Li Hongzhang. As it turned out, Li's return to his native province constituted the critical turning point in his career. His subsequent rise to unparalleled wealth and power was inseparably linked to his Anhui-based military and political network of personal loyalties, whose foundations were laid during this period in his home province. There is, at first glance, however, something of mystery behind Lü's selection of Li.

When instructed by the court to return to Anhui, Li Hongzhang had just turned thirty, and he had no military experience. Li's *jinshi* degree and his posting in the respected Hanlin Academy marked him as a young man with a bright future, but he had served in no position of any extraordinary influence up to that time. Indeed, among the handful of officials Lü sought to have accompany him, Li Hongzhang was nominally the lowest ranked.[19] Lü's memorial to the court described Li's qualifications by noting that he was a native of Anhui and therefore familiar with the conditions there.[20] Li was,

---

16. *Jiaoping Yuefei fanglüe*, 25.16b; for an abbreviated version of the order, see *Qing shilu*, XF 3.1.22, 41: 47. The court did not yet know of the fall of Anqing and the loss of the governor at this point, since one of the officials with whom Lü was instructed to cooperate was the governor.

17. *Jiaoping Yuefei fanglüe*, 26.3b; for an abbreviated version, see *Qing shilu*, XF 3.1.25, 41: 53.

18. *Qing shilu*, XF 3.1.25, 41: 53.

19. Li's position as a Hanlin *bianxiu* carried a rank of 7a. The others mentioned in Lü's petition included an assistant deputy director of the Board of Punishments, an expectant second-class secretary of the Board of Punishments, and a brevet military licentiate of the fifth rank. Another of the men selected, Yuan Jiasan, was an imperial censor, a position with the rank of 5b. That the honorary rank of the military licentiate in fact conferred a greater political status than Li's is arguable; nevertheless, the licentiate's knowledge of military matters (mentioned in Lü's petition) more than justified his selection.

20. *Jiaoping Yuefei fanglüe*, 26.3b.

in fact, a native of Luzhou (present-day Hefei) in north-central Anhui, the location to which the provincial capital was moved following the fall of Anqing and an area Lü believed key to a successful regional defense strategy.[21]

Unless the term is very loosely interpreted, however, Li Hongzhang's "familiarity" with local conditions could not have been the primary consideration behind his assignment. Li had left the area ten years before as a young man of twenty and had had no noteworthy direct contact since then. Li's degree and imperial posting granted him some status and influence in his native community, but his principal value lay in the reflected authority conferred on him by his father, Li Wen'an, then serving in Beijing as a department director in the Board of Punishments. Although the elder Li held a more powerful position than his son, more important than rank was his leadership within the Luzhou native-place sojourning community in Beijing.[22] Of particular relevance to Lü's mission, and the reason behind the selection of Li Wen'an's son, was the elder Li's successful efforts to employ his influence in the cause of building local defenses in Luzhou.

Li Wen'an's prominence within the community of Luzhou *tongxiang* in Beijing was directly tied to his leading role in the establishment of the Luzhou huiguan 盧州會館. This project was begun in 1838 and completed in 1842, with the purchase and reconstruction of a 36-*jian* site in the west-central section of the Outer City.[23] Li had resided in Beijing since 1836. His efforts to lead the community in the construction of a native-place lodge began after he passed the metropolitan examination and earned the *jinshi* degree in 1838.[24] Li led the effort to establish the Luzhou huiguan and oversaw all aspects of its founding. In the words of the Luzhou

---

21. Ibid., 25.13. Lü himself was a native of the southern Anhui district of Jingde.

22. Stanley Spector (*Li Hung-chang*, 7), however, somewhat overestimates Li Wen'an's status in calling him "one of the hundred top officials in China." Li Wen'an's position as *langzhong* was ranked at 5a, and he was not a particularly influential political figure.

23. "Luzhou huiguan beiji," in *BJTSGC*, 84: 133.

24. *Luzhou fu zhi, juan* 24, "Huan xu zhuan 2," 12; "Luzhou huiguan beiji," in *BJTSGC*, 84: 133.

gazetteer, he "called for its establishment, collected the funds, and supervised the construction" of the facility.[25] Li's leadership entailed significant personal cost. As Philip Kuhn has noted, "leadership of voluntary associations in Chinese society involves a heavy personal commitment and particularly a financial commitment."[26] A sizable financial contribution was expected of association founders, who typically led community efforts by making large personal donations and thus setting a moral example for others to follow.[27] There is good evidence that, at least initially, Li assumed a heavy financial burden in establishing the Luzhou huiguan. A stele inscription written by Li Hongzhang in later years to commemorate his father's efforts to establish the huiguan claimed that records left behind by Li Wen'an revealed he had been reduced to pawning part of his wardrobe to raise money to found the huiguan.[28]

Whatever the debt incurred by Li, it is clear that his sacrifice elevated his social authority both within the sojourning community and back in Luzhou. The people of Luzhou were said to have been "moved" by his efforts.[29] Although such accounts might be dismissed as hagiographic, Li Wen'an's social authority was visible in his leadership of the Luzhou sojourning community. Li, for example, also led a drive to establish a charitable graveyard for sojourners

---

25. *Luzhou fu zhi, juan* 17, "Xuexiao zhi," 80b; see also Folsom, *Friends, Guests, and Colleagues*, 147n70. Folsom mistakenly describes Li Wen'an as "best remembered by his fellow *xian* members as having built the Luzhou examination halls, under imperial decree." In fact the Luzhou prefectural examination hall was built during the Shunzhi reign, destroyed in 1853 by the Taipings, and rebuilt under the order of Li Hongzhang in 1870. It was paid for by a special land tax surcharge labeled a voluntary donation.

26. Kuhn, *Rebellion and Its Enemies*, 87.

27. Note the similarity with the principle described by G. William Skinner in his discussion of the role of officers of voluntary associations in the Chinese community of Thailand: "They make the first contribution and generally the largest" (Kuhn, *Rebellion and Its Enemies*, 87, citing Skinner, *Leadership and Power in the Chinese Community of Thailand*, pp. 122–23). In some cases, huiguan were founded through an initial donation of property. This, of course, represented no less a contribution in value.

28. "Luzhou Huiguan beiji," in *BJTSGC*, 84: 133. Note that Li Wen'an is referred to in this text as "the late director of the Banqueting Court" (*xian Guanglu gong*). This position was bestowed on Li by the emperor in recognition of his services.

29. *Luzhou fu zhi*, 34.12.

from Luzhou and Fengyang, a neighboring prefecture, in Beijing.[30] Li's patronage thus had begun to extend beyond the natives of Luzhou prefecture.

Li Hongzhang's particular value to Lü Xianji's mission was tied to his father's leadership of an effort among the Beijing Luzhou native-place community to encourage the mobilization of local militia units (*tuanlian* 團練) in their native prefecture. Indeed, the elder Li's success in this effort led, later that year, to an imperial edict ordering him to return to Luzhou and lead *tuanlian*.[31] The memorial prompting this order specifically credited Li's efforts for the good state of defense forces in Luzhou despite the inroads made by the rebels in surrounding areas of Anhui: "The *tuanlian* of Luzhou prefecture are in good order. This is because Li sent a letter back to the prefecture exhorting the people of his native place to consider the calamity that might befall them and take measures to prevent it."[32]

More about Li's letter is found in a stele inscription written by Li Wen'an himself. This account demonstrates the concrete role huiguan could play in coordinating efforts by *tongxiang* in the capital on behalf of native-place interests. Li, in fact, directed the writing of the letter but was not its sole author. Rather, he called the entire community of Luzhou sojourners in Beijing to a meeting in the Luzhou huiguan. Li then rallied his native-place fellows to join in urging their compatriots in Luzhou to organize the defense of their native place. As Li recounted:

In the winter of the second year of the Xianfeng reign [1852], the Guangxi rebels invaded Hubei. Natives of our prefecture then resident in the capital assembled in this huiguan. Instructions were sent back to our prefecture urging compliance with the imperial directive calling for the raising of local militias (*tuanlian*). Now [the Anhui prefectures of] Chi[zhou], Chu[zhou], and Feng[yang][33] have been invaded by the bandits, yet Luzhou is secure due to the protection provided by the militia.[34]

---

30. Ibid.; see also "Luzhou huiguan ji," in *BJTSGC*, 82: 71.

31. *Qing shilu*, XF 3.11.10, 41: 732–33. The edict was issued on December 10, 1853.

32. *Luzhou fu zhi*, 34.12b. The memorial was submitted by Junior Vice-President of the Board of Finance Wang Maoyin.

33. The prefectures to the south, east, and north of Luzhou, respectively.

34. "Luzhou huiguan ji," in *BJTSGC*, 82: 71. Li Wen'gan, the author's name as written in this inscription, is the original *ming* of Li Wen'an.

Although the residents of Luzhou were the ones imperiled by the approach of the Taiping armies, the sojourners in the capital proved more capable of initiating an effective response. The court had only recently fully endorsed and encouraged *tuanlian* as a defensive measure. Proximity and access to the central government ensured that those in Beijing were more quickly and more thoroughly informed about possible forms of local defense and the emperor's views. The social prestige the sojourners enjoyed at home further facilitated their ability to lead their compatriots in Luzhou in a timely implementation of these measures.

The Luzhou huiguan played a vital and multifaceted role in these endeavors. The huiguan provided the Luzhou sojourners with a "public" place to gather and discuss issues. As a symbolic expression of commitment to the home region, moreover, the site explicitly promoted an obligation to action on the part of those assembled there. The huiguan was also an important element in the social prestige that enabled Li Wen'an to lead the community so effectively. Although Li's official position was not an insignificant element in his prominence within the community, his ability to call a general meeting and lead it toward a desired goal was surely based in large measure in his efforts on behalf of community-oriented charitable works. Li's sacrifices and efforts on behalf of the huiguan and similar projects were interpreted as righteous and selfless. In return for his efforts, the community bestowed moral authority on Li, which legitimized his leadership. In this case, the Luzhou huiguan served as both product and catalyst of community action and effectively channeled influence from center to region.

Huiguan and Regionalist Networks

The Taiping war, the imperial and regional response to it, and numerous other shocks and challenges to the imperial system led to dramatic shifts in relations between the center and the regions during the second half of the nineteenth century.[35] The implications

---

35. There is a voluminous body of work on or related to the reformulation of these ties: for a classic framing of this transformation under the rubric of the rise of "regionalism," see Michael, "Introduction." For an explicit counterargument to

of these shifts on the greater polity lies beyond the scope of this chapter; this section focuses instead on their impact on the native-place lodges of the capital. One aspect of the change in China's political system was the greater prominence of *tongxiang* provincial networks. The most notable of these was the extensive and well-nurtured network of officials and military men from Anhui united under the patronage of Li Hongzhang. Li Hongzhang was also an active patron of Beijing huiguan, and this section briefly examines the degree to which these huiguan were used to facilitate the interests of the Anhui network.

Li first came to the capital in 1843; he passed the Shuntian examination in 1844 and the metropolitan examination on his second attempt in 1847. Upon receiving his *jinshi* degree, Li was appointed to the Hanlin Academy. Despite his father's active involvement in the affairs of the sojourning community in the capital, there is little indication that the younger Li had particularly close interactions with his native-place community or its institutions during his initial ten-year stay in Beijing. On first arriving in Beijing Li may have stayed, albeit briefly, at the Luzhou huiguan, but he soon moved into the premises of a family friend.[36]

During the years of the Taiping Rebellion, Li Hongzhang occupied increasingly powerful military positions as he put together and expanded the Huai Army. Far from the capital and with more pressing concerns before him, the affairs of Anhui sojourners in Beijing did not greatly occupy his attention. Nevertheless, as his authority grew, he became more heavily involved in huiguan patronage there. In 1861, the *jinshi*, Hanlin academician, and fellow Luzhou native Liu Bingzhang 劉秉璋 (1826–1905) made a trip to Jiangxi,

---

Michael and an excellent discussion of the limits of regionalism, see Kwang-ching Liu, "The Limits of Regional Power in the Late Ch'ing Period."

36. Biographical information on Li given in this section is based on Dou Zongyi, *Li Hongzhang nian (ri) pu*; Lei Luqing, *Li Hongzhang xinzhuan*; Spector, *Li Hung-chang*; and Yuan Shuyi, *Li Hongzhang zhuan*. Yuan Shuyi (*Li Hongzhang*, 14) mistakenly depicts Li as residing briefly in the Anhui huiguan upon first arriving at the capital. This is not possible, since the Anhui huiguan had not yet been established. If Li did stay at a huiguan in Beijing, he no doubt would have stayed at the Luzhou huiguan.

where he met with Li and others.[37] Liu informed them that the Luzhou huiguan had for years lacked money for repairs and upkeep and now stood all but abandoned.[38] In response, Li and his associates contributed funds to have it repaired and expanded.[39] The purchase of adjoining properties resulted in an expansion of the site from 36 *jian* to a total building area of over 110 *jian*.[40] The near-abandonment of huiguan was a common phenomenon in the 1860s and 1870s. The devastation and destruction wrought by the rebellions and efforts to subdue them greatly undermined the vitality of sojourning communities in Beijing and their ability to finance native-place institutions. Throughout Beijing, huiguan were boarded up and temporarily neglected.[41] Li's activism and the ability of the community to rally to this cause reflect the rise in prominence and influence of both Li and the Anhui community in general.

Li first returned to Beijing from his extended duty in the south on a brief trip for an imperial audience late in 1868. However, he returned to the Beijing area more permanently in 1870, as the newly appointed governor-general of Zhili province, stationed in Tianjin, a mere seventy miles from the capital. Li remained in this post for the next 25 years. As Kwang-ching Liu has noted, "Li Hongzhang, in moving so close to Beijing, became in effect a metropolitan official."[42] The success of his leadership in the wars to suppress the Taiping and the Nian rebellions elevated him to a position of empirewide power. The Huai Army was widely recognized as the pre-eminent military force in China at that time, and its officers' ties

------

37. "Chongxiu Lujun huiguan beiji," in *BJTSGC*, 83: 22. The original stele is held at the Capital Stone Inscription Art Research Institute (Shoudu shike yishu yanjiusuo), located in the Five-Pagoda Temple (Wuta si) compound in Beijing. Liu Bingzhang became an important Huai Army commander, and later enjoyed an illustrious career in posts such as provincial governor (Jiangxi 1874–78; Zhejiang 1882–86), and governor-general (Sichuan 1886–94).

38. *BJTSGC*, 84: 133.

39. "Chongxiu Lujun huiguan beiji," in ibid., 22.

40. *BJTSGC*, 82: 7; *Luzhou fu zhi*, 17.81b.

41. The general impact and the relatively late recovery are reflected in a large number of sources; see, e.g., Zhu Yixin and Miao Quanshu, *Jing shi fang xiang zhi*, which was compiled in the late 1880s and lists over 60 huiguan as abandoned. Almost all these sites were restored to operation in later years, however.

42. Kwang-ching Liu, "Li Hung-chang in Chihli," 69.

to Li in networks of personal connections ensured their loyalty. Li's appointment as governor-general of Zhili invested him with the responsibility and authority of defending Beijing and the imperial domains. His position and his financial resources were further bolstered by his concurrent appointment to the office of the imperial commissioner of trade for the northern ports.

Soon after his return to the Beijing area, Li became actively involved in the establishment of the Luzhou shiguan 盧州試館 and the Anhui huiguan 安徽會館. The Luzhou shiguan was established in 1870, the first year of Li's return.[43] Li and his brother, Li Hanzhang 李瀚章 (1821–99), then serving as the Huguang governor-general, bought a compound over 100 *jian* in size located just to the east of the Imperial Examination Halls in the Inner City.[44] Its designation as a *shiguan* indicated that it functioned exclusively as a facility for examination candidates from Luzhou. The Anhui huiguan, on the other hand, stood on Hou Sun Gongyuan Lane just to the south of the Liuli chang, in the very heart of the scholar-official-dominated Xuannan district. Li Hongzhang, a group of top Huai Army commanders, and a large group of pre-eminent Anhui officeholders, including Li Hanzhang, played a leading role in establishing it. The emerging influence and power of Anhui natives was reflected in the impressive scope and grandeur of the lodge; although not the largest huiguan in Beijing, it stood out for its magnificence. Weng Tonghe, the prominent Jiangsu native discussed above, stopped by to see the premises on April 9, 1870. Noting that much remained to be done, he nevertheless described its rooms as "grand and beautiful."[45]

─────────

43. *BJTSGC*, 84: 133.

44. Ibid.; see also *Luzhou fu zhi*, 17.81b.

45. Weng Tonghe, *Weng Tonghe riji paiyin ben*, 2: 536. Weng describes it as "preliminarily completed." It would not be completely finished until September/October 1871. I visited the premises in 1994 and again in 2004. On my first visit the site was largely a run-down and overly crowded residential compound, but the original size and architectural presence of the site were still apparent. The stage, an impressive example of a traditional multistory Beijing style, was used as a warehouse for decades (and was thus, ironically, spared further damage). Although suffering superficially from neglect, it remained in fundamentally good repair. On my second visit I found the stage has been fully restored and the area immediately around it set aside and being prepared for opening to the public as a museum.

Such grandeur came at considerable cost. In order to raise the necessary funds, an empirewide fund-raising drive among Anhui officials posted throughout the provinces was held. Li Hongzhang himself recounted the origins of the huiguan soon after its completion. Li's central role in the establishment of the huiguan is obvious:

[Previously] when staying in the capital, I heard discussion among our community elders [regarding Anhui's lack of a provincial huiguan]. They had planned to build one, but nothing came of it. In [1868], with the western Nian rebels pacified and the imperial domain at peace, I came [to Beijing] to make a personal appearance before the throne. In my free time, I consulted on this matter with my native-place fellows, Mr. Hu, the vice-president of the Board of Civil Appointments, and Mr. Bao, the vice-president of the Board of Works, and others. All agreed that it was time to establish one, since we could not long continue lacking an association. The Huai Army was being disbanded in triumph, yet the majority of its commanders and leaders are Anhui natives. When they heard of this matter, they desired to contribute 10,000 taels of silver to set an example for others to follow. Since this was not enough, Governor-General Wu of Sichuan and then my brother and I each forwarded financial contributions. We also sent out an announcement to those Anhui natives serving as officials in all regions of the empire.[46]

The fund-raising drive, kicked off with the 10,000 taels contributed by the four top Huai army commanders, succeeded admirably.[47] Li Hongzhang himself contributed several thousand taels; in addition to the two governors-general mentioned by Li, four expectant provincial governors, two serving governors, the superintendent of Shaanxi military affairs, five provincial judges, nine department magistrates, eight prefectural magistrates, and 39 district magistrates made contributions. This list of contributors, all of

---

46. "Anhui huiguan bei," in *BJTSGC*, 84: 17; for a reproduction of a version apparently written in Li's own hand, see *Jingcheng Anhui huiguan cunce*; for a typeset version, see *Anhui huiguan zhi*. However, this version contains textual errors. It appears that Li's memory of the chronology of events was somewhat off. An announcement to Anhui natives calling for donations (and specifically mentioning Li) is reproduced in *Jingcheng Anhui huiguan cunce,* but it is dated 1866. The empirewide solicitation of funds must have begun before Li's return to Beijing for his imperial audience. It is, of course, possible that there were multiple solicitations.

47. They were Pan Dingxin 潘鼎新 (d. 1888), Liu Shengzao 劉盛藻 (d. 1883), Zhou Shengchuan 周盛傳 (1833–85), and Wu Changqing 吳長慶 (d. 1884).

them Anhui natives, testifies to the rising influence of the Anhui political network.

In a later depiction of the fund-raising effort, Li Hongzhang further injected an element of native-place chauvinism, extolling the professed qualities of Anhui people and linking their success in raising regional forces with the successful founding of the huiguan.

Although Anhui is small in size, the custom of its people has always been to esteem personal interconnectedness and to place value on one's word. Thus was it possible to raise local soldiers and go beyond our borders to suppress the bandits, all acting as with one heart. . . . Now, the army is being disbanded and sent back home. Yet, [the army leaders] were able to combine their efforts and accomplish the virtuous deed of rendering aid. If this is not true mindfulness of regional fraternity, what is it?[48]

In a brief article on this subject, the Beijing-based historian Li Qiao has argued that the huiguan was "a product [intended to] strengthen the internal coherence of the Huai Army clique."[49] Certainly, the Anhui huiguan both reflected and facilitated the interests of the Anhui network in the capital. Li Hongzhang portrayed the founding in an unusually political context, for example. He related the spirit of the founding to the substantial political reforms associated with the Tongzhi restoration, exhorting his native-place fellows to use the huiguan to contribute to that "great enterprise." He also explicitly stated that this huiguan was intended for more than just social functions:

The imperial realm is in the midst of reformation; thus must we take up the bequeathed tradition of Min Zi and Zhu Xi in order to perfect this great enterprise with discipline and determination. Those [Anhui natives] who have been appointed to office are innumerable. Certainly, [the establishment of this huiguan] is not undertaken merely to present the magnificent spectacle of lavish entertainments and banquets or for the affectionate talk that results from pleasure taken in seeing those close to us.[50]

----

48. Ibid.
49. See Li Qiao, "Anhui huiguan," 326.
50. "Anhui huiguan bei," in *BJTSGC*, 84: 17; see note 46 to this chapter for other versions of this text. For more on Zhu Xi, Min zi, and the other deities worshipped at this lodge, see Chapter 6, p. 129.

The Distinct Nature of Provincial Lodges

The Anhui huiguan founded by Li Hongzhang differed in some important ways from the majority of native-place lodges in the capital. For example, the Anhui huiguan did not serve examination candidates. In fact, candidates were forbidden from staying there. Huiguan rules stipulated that only those holding high office qualified to reside on the premises:

All fellow Anhui civil and military officials who come to the capital . . . and who are substantially serving civil officials [as opposed to being merely qualified to serve through the obtaining of a degree] at the department or district magistrate level and above, or are substantially serving military officials at the colonel or lieutenant-colonel level and above—although intendants and prefects need not necessarily be substantially serving—or are education and examination officials who have returned to the capital reporting on a commission, may live in the huiguan for the first three days of their return. Expectant officials, metropolitan examination candidates, and those who have purchased their posts may not obtain lodging.[51]

The Anhui huiguan was, in fact, not unique in its prohibition of all but high-ranking officials from its premises. Indeed, many of the provincial-level huiguan in the capital during this period increasingly directed their services to such an elite group. Li himself characterized this practice as consistent with that of other provincial-level huiguan in the capital:

Scholars come to take the metropolitan examination held by the Board of Rites, and each prefecture and district has temporary lodging places at which they may stay. Yet those gentry who have passed the examination

---

51. *Jingcheng Anhui huiguan cunce*, Li Qiao, "Anhui huiguan," 327. This exclusivity is reflected, as well, in the guidelines of the expected donations to be given to the huiguan upon promotion to a new post. Over twenty positions and ranks are given, ranging from 300 taels for an appointment to a governor-generalship to 160 taels for an appointment to any position on the Grand Council to 20 taels for appointment to the office of lieutenant-colonel. No lower amounts and ranks are listed, unlike similar guidelines for other Beijing huiguan, which typically included examination graduates and donation amounts as low as 1 or 2 taels. See "Zhuoding jingwai wenwu ge guan xizi yinshu" (Set silver amounts of celebratory donations to be given by various civil and military officials posted in and outside the capital), in *Jingcheng Anhui huiguan cunce*, 21–22b.

must also select suitable locations on which to build halls where they may be surrounded by friends during periods of rest and where they may mutually engage in banqueting, drinking, and entertainment. Zhili, Shaanxi, Huguang, Jiangxi, Zhejiang, and other such regions [so numerous] that it is difficult to list them out individually have such places, whereas Anhui, on the contrary, lacked one.[52]

Corroborating evidence indicates that some other provincial-level huiguan catered only to serving officials (although no pre-Republican period copy of rules regarding who might and might not reside at these other provincial huiguan survives). One account of the Fujian huiguan, for example, refers to a stage being torn down in order to make rooms for Fujian officials of the third rank and above.[53] A passage from an account of the Huguang huiguan, which served the (formerly linked) provinces of Hunan and Hubei, remarked: "Although officials from all the various provinces serving in the capital have established lodges as places of rest for examination candidates and expectant officials, *those who govern have, respectively, provincial* huiguan, as places [where they may] seasonally invite guests, perform sacrifices, and exchange toasts" (italics added).[54]

Clearly there was in Beijing a pattern whereby many provincial-level scholar-official huiguan were exclusively or at least primarily intended for the use of only the highest-level officials from the province. Many such luminaries were not in need of residential services, since those posted to the capital would, in general, have had their own residences. Even high-ranking officials posted outside the capital tended not to stay in native-place lodges, however, opting instead for such alternatives as temples, which were commonly available for rent. The emphasis within lodges catering to high-ranking officials therefore was given to the socializing and networking needs of such officials. This is why they were characterized by large opera stages and large banqueting facilities. Although a smaller amount of space within these lodges was given over to living

52. "Anhui Huiguan bei," in *BJTSGC*, 84: 17; see note 46 to this chapter for other versions of this text.

53. *Minzhong huiguan zhi*, "Fujian huiguan," 1.

54. "Xu" (Introduction), in *Beiping Huguang huiguan zhilüe* (reprinted in Beijing shi duiwai wenhua jiaoliu xiehui et al., eds., *Beijing Huguang huiguan zhigao*, 69).

quarters, some rooms were set aside for temporary visitors, although again there is a clear pattern among these huiguan of limiting lodging to high-ranking officials rather than mere examination candidates and so on.

It would be nice if I could say that provincial-level huiguan simply represented a particular type of lodge and that all provincial-level huiguan were characterized by the features described above. Unfortunately, the pattern was not quite so neat. Some provinces had multiple provincial-level huiguan and relatively few subprovincial huiguan. This tendency was most marked among the southwestern, western, and northwestern provinces.

Beyond the names and locations of the multiple provincial-level lodges established by those from the more peripheral provinces, very little else is known. What evidence I have on these lodges suggests that they operated much as subprovincial huiguan did and did not share the emphasis on serving high-ranking officials associated with the provincial huiguan of the central and southern Chinese provinces. I have found no evidence that any of these lodges catered to subprovincial territories, despite their provincial designations. My educated guess is that each of the lodges was open to all scholars and officials from the province. When one lodge filled up, a hopeful sojourner could try another site.

Why did the clientele of these lodges differ from that of the lodges representing the provinces of central and southern China? Economics might have had something to do with it. Compatriots from these areas, unable to raise the funds sufficient to establish huiguan at the subprovincial levels, established several provincial huiguan in their stead. For example, there were eight provincial huiguan and only three subprovincial huiguan serving Guangxi; seven of the eighteen Sichuan huiguan sites were provincial in scope, as were four of the seven Yunnan huiguan; Gansu sojourners built three provincial huiguan in Beijing and only one subprovincial one; and Guizhou could boast eight provincial huiguan yet no subprovincial one! Among all these provincial-level huiguan, only one, the Zhao gong ci of Yunnan, boasted an opera stage.

At least among Beijing sojourners from the more prosperous provinces of south China, a trend toward functional specialization was apparent by the late nineteenth century. All the provincial huiguan of these provinces exhibited certain common features expressive of their specialized functions. Such huiguan tended to be built on a more spacious scale than subprovincial association compounds. In general, less built space was devoted to residential facilities, and greater emphasis was given to ceremonial, social, and ritual functions. Provincial huiguan often boasted gardens, large meeting halls, and opera stages with enclosed viewing areas (see discussion of these features in Chapter 5). Architecturally, the Anhui huiguan was typical of this style of provincial huiguan, although somewhat grander in scale.

Conclusion

The scholar-official huiguan of Beijing served in a number of ways both to facilitate and to coordinate regional interests in the capital. Huiguan acted as nodes of bidirectional interaction. Communications through *tongxiang* channels flowed both from the regions to the center and from the center to the regions. Provincial elites used *tongxiang* ties to influence administrative decisions made in the capital, and elite Beijing residents used them to coordinate local administration in their native place. Furthermore, with the increasing prominence of regional political networks in the post-Taiping period, huiguan also facilitated the interests of those networks in the capital.

Informal *tongxiang* interactions were often intended to complement actions taken through official channels. Thus, for example, when the Jiangsu natives met with Weng Tonghe to seek a tax waiver, they requested that Weng expedite a petition that had already been submitted officially. This was in no way seen as subverting official administrative processes. It was, on the contrary, generally presumed that for the imperial system to function properly, the legitimate interests of regions deserved special attention. That *tongxiang* connections effectively communicated these interests and that *tongxiang* officials would be receptive to them seemed natural and ethical both to those in the region and to those in the center.

As demonstrated above, the articulation of regional interests in the capital was greatly facilitated and profoundly shaped by compatriot ties and the native-place lodges. The studies presented in this chapter offer us a look into some of the ways in which these processes occurred, but they only begin to tell the full story of how native-place relationships mediated informal regional-center interaction. Indeed, I believe huiguan must be seen as constitutional elements within the late imperial Chinese political system. Through them, local elites from the provinces were able to link up with their compatriots serving in the capital in order to influence decisions affecting them and their home territory. By the same token, as Li Wen'an's coordination of the raising of a militia in his home prefecture while still resident in the capital shows, huiguan also made it easier for compatriots in the highest echelons of power to influence events in their home territory. Although the "rule of avoidance" ensured that local administration was in the hands of outsiders, local elites and compatriot metropolitan officials could join to pressure (i.e., "suggest to") those administrators the adoption of measures of particular concern to them.

Huiguan and the *tongxiang* ties underlying them channeled information and influence back and forth between center and region. In either direction, this interchange effectively introduced a measure of native-place interest into the political operations of the empire. On one hand, this influence can be seen as representing the special interests of local elites. On the other hand, this influence can be seen as an effective means of introducing the legitimate interests of localities into the system, thus ensuring some measure of imperial responsiveness to the needs and demands of the localities. Both visions are correct, and both suggest that this informal channel of center-regional interaction must be taken into account in analyzing the late imperial political system.

This chapter has shown some of the ways *tongxiang* connections were incorporated both formally and informally into the day-to-day political process of late imperial Beijing. Although more work needs to be done on other cities, the available evidence indicates that Beijing was unique in the degree to which this was true. A variety of special circumstances in Beijing worked to ensure this. Among them were (1) the great numbers of sojourners in Beijing, many of whom were there expressly to access or influence state decisions; (2) the great numbers of metropolitan officials located in Beijing who manned the imperial bureaucracy; (3) the highly developed infrastructure of native-place lodges, which facilitated the making and the consolidation of native-place ties; (4) the use of native-place ties between metropolitan officials and those seeking to interact with the state as a means of promoting "proper" behavior through the imposition of mutual responsibility; and (5) the degree to which the metropolitan bureaucracy itself depended financially on *yinjie* fees for guaranteeing the behavior of fellow provincials. All these factors combined to envelop Beijing in *tongxiang* consciousness.

The historical implications of the political functions of native-place ties in Beijing during the nineteenth century are many. Given the obvious importance of Beijing as the center of critical political decision making, we must make a greater effort to understand how the processes of decision making were shaped by the particular characteristics of the capital. The incorporation of *tongxiang* connections into the constitutional political process of late imperial China should also be seen as encouraging a degree of responsiveness by the central state to provincial and local interests. To a considerable degree it did so successfully. These considerations also help to throw light on the period following the collapse of imperial rule, when new ways had to be developed to negotiate the interests of center and periphery, new ways that in some respects cannot be regarded as working effectively. In the next chapter, we shall see how these ties helped shape events in the capital when the old political order began to collapse.

TEN

Native Place and the Reform

Movement of the 1890s

The activist scholar-officials who led the reform movement of the 1890s that culminated in the Hundred Days Reform of 1898 failed in almost all of their overt objectives. Despite their protests against the terms of the 1895 peace with Japan, the Treaty of Shimonoseki was signed. Study societies and other reform groups formed in the wake of the war were suppressed. The Hundred Days itself ended in a countercoup, the revocation of the reform edicts, the execution of some prominent reformers, and the exile of others. Yet these obvious failures notwithstanding, the movement succeeded in introducing new political agendas and promoting visions of institutional reform that would ultimately transform China. The movement may justifiably be seen as the origin of much that came to characterize modern China.[1]

---

1. Karl and Zarrow, eds., *The 1898 Reforms and the Origins of Modernity in China.* A somewhat different version of this chapter is presented in that collection.

Although scholars have studied the reform movement for more than a century, the degree to which the sociopolitical urban ecology of Beijing shaped the movement has remained largely unappreciated. From 1895 to the suppression of the movement in 1898, many key events took place in the capital, and although important developments occurred in the provinces, Beijing truly served as the most important focal point. Yet even if we grant that the reform movement was centered in Beijing, we might still question whether the location per se was historically significant. After all, the events of 1895–98 were hardly unique in this regard; to some degree all late imperial matters of state took place mainly in the capital. Must such events be considered necessarily *of* the capital just because they were enacted *in* the capital?

The usual answer to this question is no. The city surrounding the palace and bureaucratic offices is considered largely irrelevant to Chinese political history. Yet there are two reasons to question this presumption. First, arguably, Beijing's significance in late imperial political decisions has been too readily disregarded in general. More work is needed in this area, but James M. Polachek's work on the debates surrounding Opium War policy is a notable step toward an approach that incorporates the local context of the capital in its consideration of political dynamics.[2] However, even if for the sake of argument we were to grant that Beijing had only limited relevance in the shaping of Qing political history generally, the 1895–98 reform movement must nevertheless be seen as an instance that demands fuller consideration of its urban context. This is primarily because a new mix of lower-level bureaucrats and non-ranked elite—chiefly, examination candidates and low-ranking metropolitan officials—emerged as an unprecedented influential political force at this time. As we shall see, the actions of this group were greatly shaped by the particular urban ecology of Beijing.

I focus especially on two factors: the patterning of urban space and the unique institutionalization of native-place ties in the capital. By "urban space," I mean not only the physical topography but also the structure of social space in the city. It is an important fact

---

2. Polachek, *The Inner Opium War*.

that the Han Chinese scholar-bureaucrats who dominated the movement did not reside evenly throughout the city but were instead concentrated in the Xuannan ward. The density of their residence there facilitated the exchanges of information and the gatherings of activists that were essential features of the movement. The actions of the reformers were further influenced and facilitated by the particular way native-place ties were institutionalized in the capital. By "institutionalization," I refer both to the co-opting of native-place ties by the imperial government through established regulations governing subject-initiated interactions with the government and to the extraordinary proliferation of corporately administered native- place lodges. Both the regulations and the scholar-official character of the lodges were unique to the capital, and both, as we shall see, profoundly shaped the course of events.

The most famous event associated with the upsurge in scholar-official protests against the court's war policy was the 1895 Petitioning of the Emperor by the Examination Candidates (*gongche shangshu*) in response to the humiliating Treaty of Shimonoseki, which brought the Sino-Japanese War to a conclusion. The action was significant for a number of reasons. As first stated by Liang Qichao and confirmed by later scholars, the petition drives and the public demonstrations accompanying them were the "first mass movement in Chinese history."[3] Word of the proposed settlement reached Beijing in late April 1895, just as thousands of candidates were gathered in the capital to take the examinations. News of the unprecedented concessions granted a foreign power (and former tributary) coupled with the thousands of idealistic and ambitious candidates waiting to sit the examinations then in the capital proved an incendiary mix.

The most celebrated petition was that signed on April 30, 1895, by 1,300 or so candidates from each of the eighteen provinces. The candidates gathered at Songyun an 松筠庵, a courtyard area in the heart of the Xuannan ward maintained as a shrine to the sixteenth-century official Yang Jisheng 楊繼盛 (1516–55). Since Yang had been

---

3. Ding Wenjiang, *Liang Rengong xiansheng nianpu changbian chugao*, 1: 24. Liang's assessment is cited and confirmed in Chang Hao, *Liang Ch'i-chao and Intellectual Transition in China*, 60.

martyred for his strong anti-appeasement stance in the contemporary conflict against the Mongols, the symbolism of the shrine was obvious. The candidates signed their names to a petition drafted by Kang Youwei calling for a resumption of the fighting, the transfer of the capital to the interior, and other measures of reform and resistance. The Songyun an "Petition by the Candidates" expressed the will of those normally excluded from voicing an opinion on state topics and served in turn as a model for popular protest for many years thereafter. It should, however, be appreciated for what it really was: one in a series of group petitions about the war submitted by scholar-officials.

For example, over 80 examination candidates from Guangdong and Hunan, organized by Liang Qichao among others, submitted petitions on April 22, eight days before the Songyun an meeting.[4] According to Kang Youwei, that action inspired other groups of provincial candidates to submit petitions as well.[5] However, protests, petitions, and calls for the reform of war policy began much earlier and emerged from a wider social-professional base than Kang indicated. The writings of the prominent reform official Wen Tingshi, for example, reveal that similar efforts to remonstrate with the government over war policy began among low-ranking metropolitan officials as early as September 1894. The officials drew up joint petitions advocating that Prince Gong 奕訢 (1833–98) be put in charge of the war effort and that China ally with England to strengthen its hand against Japan.[6] Groups of low-level metropolitan officials subsequently signed and submitted more petitions; among them were three petitions submitted by groups of Hanlin

---

4. According to the records of the Censorate, four petitions related to the war were submitted that day, one signed by 81 natives of Guangdong and three petitions signed by a total of 120 natives of Hunan. See Lin Keguang, *Kang Youwei*, 133.

5. Kang Youwei, "Chronological Autobiography of K'ang Yu-wei," trans. Jung-pang Lo, in *K'ang Yu-wei: A Biography and a Symposium*, 64.

6. Wen Tingshi, *Wen Tingshi ji*, 1495. Prince Gong had been cashiered in 1884. He was indeed called back in 1894 and placed in charge of the Office of Foreign Affairs (Zongli yamen) and the Board of Admiralty (Haijun yamen) to help direct the war against Japan.

scholars, one signed by 56 secretaries of the Zongli yamen, and one signed by 156 members of the Grand Secretariat.[7]

The actions of these bureaucratic remonstrators in late 1894 and early 1895 are particularly relevant to this chapter's focus on the connection between the unique characteristics of Beijing and the historical development of the reform movement. First, the thousands of metropolitan officials resident in Beijing from which the first protesters emerged constituted a social-professional group of a size found nowhere else. Second, the emergence of this early protest trend was clearly facilitated by the dense congregation of metropolitan officials in the Xuannan area. And third, those involved were able to take advantage of the uniquely plentiful space in Beijing's native-place lodges to meet and organize their efforts. Wen Tingshi, for example, recorded meeting in several different locations, including the Zhejiang huiguan and the (Jiangxi) Xie gong ci 謝公祠.[8]

In late April and early May 1895, with the city filled with examination candidates from around the empire, the terms of the treaty were made known, and the protest movement entered a new stage. The number of petitions submitted by low-ranked metropolitan officials and unranked examination candidates suddenly jumped in number. The Songyun an gathering was simply one of a number of such actions. In fact, a total of 32 separate petitions were presented to the Censorate by groups of examination candidates and metropolitan officials between April 22 and May 5, 1895.[9] The submission of the petitions was accompanied by a tumultuous popular protest that was, arguably, a harbinger of the student- and intellectual-led protests against government policy that so marked the twentieth century. Examination candidates and other scholar-officials gathered outside the Censorate to demonstrate their opposition to the treaty beginning on April 22 and continuing every other day after that for the rest of the month (since the censors reported to the court every second day, the protesters matched their schedule). During these demonstrations the street in front of the

---

7. Kwong, *A Mosaic of the Hundred Days*, 73.
8. Wen Tingshi, *Wen Tingshi ji*, 1495.
9. Lin Keguang, *Kang Youwei*, 132–35.

Censorate gates filled with carts and horses, and the throngs of scholars were so packed together that not even "sunlight could pass between them."[10]

The overwhelming organization of the movement along *tongxiang* lines is striking and was undoubtedly a reflection of the environment within which the protests arose. With the exception of the Songyun an petition, the petitions were submitted by groups of candidates from the same province. Approximately 3,000 candidates put their names to these thirty other petitions; the total number of signatures on all petitions was well over 4,000. What accounts for the compatriot character? The fact that the candidates were living, socializing, and meeting in their native-place lodges was certainly one factor. One can imagine how quickly the spirit of protest must have caught on among the candidates as news of the events circulated through lodges densely packed with fellow-provincial candidates.

The omnipresent influence of compatriot ties so characteristic of Beijing was not entirely absent from the Songyun an event. The symbolic significance of the site was largely bound up with the Ming patriot Yang Jisheng, but across the street from the Songyun an stood the Songyun caotang 嵩雲草堂, a hall with a capacity of 200–300 people. That site was the main building of the (Henan) Zhongzhou huiguan 中州會館. According to a later account by an eyewitness, the thousand-plus candidates who gathered for the mass signing were too numerous to fit into the Songyun an. The candidates actually assembled at both the Songyun an and the Songyun caotang to sign the petition and then met outside the Xuanwu gate and proceeded to the Censorate from there.[11] Even the Songyun an may have possessed a *tongxiang* connection to Zhili compatriots in the capital. It was certainly administered by Hebei sojourners in

---

10. Hushang yuanshi laoren, "Xu," *Gongche shangshu ji* (Shanghai: Shiyin shuju, 1895); cited in Kong Xiang ji, *Kang Youwei bianfa zouyi yanjiu*, 80–81.

11. Ye Zufou, *Beijing Fengqing zatan*, 116–17. For background on the Songyun caotang, see Lin Keguang, "Beijing Qiangxuehui yizhi." For background on the Zhongzhou huiguan (later renamed the Henan huiguan and also referred to as such in this work), see Hu Chunhuan and Bai Hequn, *Beijing de huiguan*, 216–18.

later years, although it is not clear whether a *tongxiang* connection existed in 1898.[12]

The unique system of mutual accountability imposed on the capital through the *yinjie* system was another major factor in determining the *tongxiang* structure of the protests. According to Qing statutes, examination candidates were not entitled to submit their views directly to the throne. The Censorate would accept a petition only if it had the proper chopped-bond guarantee from a compatriot metropolitan official. The rule mandating chopped bonds helps to explain why, of the 32 known petitions submitted at that time, the Censorate refused to accept only the one associated with the Songyun an gathering. In fact, the refusal of the Censorate to accept the Songyun an petition has long been something of a mystery. According to Kang Youwei, Censorate officials "refused to accept the petition, stating that the imperial seal had already been affixed [to documents accepting the peace treaty] and they could not be canceled."[13] However, the noted scholar Kong Xiangji, using Grand Council archives and other materials, has shown that Kang Youwei's explanation was wrong.[14] In fact, the Censorate accepted fifteen other petitions on May 2, the day that Kang claimed the Songyun an petition was presented. In explaining their reasons for accepting the petitions, officials at the Censorate wrote to the court: "Within each of these petitions are some imperfections. However, in consideration of the important and urgent nature of this matter, and as all these functionaries and examination candidates and so on have obtained chopped bonds from their *tongxiang* metropolitan officials . . . we do not dare to keep them from your attention."[15] However, Kong Xiangji has convincingly suggested that the Songyun an petition was not submitted to the Censorate on May 2 as Kang Youwei remembered but on May 4. Although we know that

---

12. For background information on the Songyun an, see Lin Keguang, "Songyun an yu gongche shangshu," 255.

13. Kang Youwei. "Chronological Autobiography of K'ang Yu-wei," in *K'ang Yu-wei: A Biography and a Symposium*, 65.

14. Kong Xiangji, *Wuxu weixin yundong xintan*, 10–11. The imperial seal was not affixed until May 3.

15. Zhongguo shixue hui, *Zhongri zhanzhong* (Shanghai: Xin jinshi chubanshe, 1956), 4: 58; cited in ibid., 11.

other petitions were submitted on that day and the next, there is good reason to suppose that the changing mood in the capital coupled with the challenge of securing *yinjie* from a compatriot official for each of the provinces represented in that document resulted in its submission without the proper paperwork.[16] Ironically, it seems that it was largely because of the multiprovincial origins of the signers of the Songyun an petition (rather than the timing or the content of the text) that it was not passed on to the emperor. It is worth noting, in this light, that when Kang submitted his Third Petition to the Emperor a few weeks later, a document that was essentially a rewritten version of the Songyun an petition, the Censorate accepted it. In doing so, the censors noted that among the most important reasons for its acceptance was that Kang had acquired the proper chopped bonds.[17]

Native-Place Lodges and the
Formation of Political Societies

The extraordinary presence of hundreds of native-place lodges in Beijing was an essential factor in the sudden outbreak of new forms of mass actions by the examination candidates and low-ranking metropolitan bureaucrats in the spring of 1895. Almost every one of the central figures in the reform movement lived in or was closely associated with a native-place lodge in the capital. Although Kang Youwei occasionally made brief use of Inner City quarters, his primary residence in Beijing was the (Guangdong) Nanhai huiguan on Mishi hutong. Liang Qichao stayed in the (Guangdong) Xinhui yiguan 新會邑館 on Fenfang liuli jie. Tan Sitong resided in the (Hunan) Liuyang huiguan on Kudui hutong. Lin Xu 林旭 (1875–98) and Yang Rui 楊銳 (1857–98) also maintained close ties to their native-place lodges. How closely these men identified with their lodges is revealed in the titles they bestowed on their now-famous personal writings. Kang's collection of poetry, *Han man fang shi ji* 汗漫舫詩集; Tan Sitong's *Mang cang cang zhai shi* 莽蒼蒼齋詩; and Yang Shenxiu's 楊深秀 (1849–98) *Xue Xu sheng tang shi chao* 雪虛聲堂

---

16. Kong, *Wuxu weixin yundong xintan*, 14.
17. Ibid., 43.

詩鈔 all took their names from courtyards in their respective Beijing native-place lodges.[18] Indeed, Tan's connection to the Liuyang lodge was especially close because the premises had once served as the private residence of his father, Tan Jixun 譚繼洵 (1823–1901), a prominent metropolitan official at the time. Tan Sitong had originally moved to that site with his family in 1865 when he was only two years old and lived there for the next several years.[19] His father donated the property to his fellow Liuyang sojourners to be used as a lodge in 1872, and Tan Sitong stayed there when he was in the capital. Any doubt about the importance of the lodges may be laid to rest by noting that when some government officials decided to put an end to the movement, they targeted the native-place lodges of the Xuannan ward. In the final days of the protests, a close associate of Grand Councilor Sun Yuwen 孫毓汶 (1833–99) was dispatched to make a round of the huiguan in the Xuannan ward to intimidate the candidates into withdrawing their support for the petitions.[20] Sun's representative was successful; many candidates withdrew their support, and in the end the signing of the treaty by the emperor deprived the movement of a focus.

The role of the native-place lodges in the reform movement was far from over, however. For example, Kang Youwei and others established the *Wan guo gongbao* 萬國公報 (later renamed *Zhong wai jiwen* 中外紀聞) in the Nanhai huiguan in August 1895.[21] This was the first private newspaper founded by Chinese (as opposed to foreign) residents of China. Additionally, one of the most significant developments in the period leading to the Hundred Day Reforms of

18. For Kang's description of moving into the courtyard and his bestowal of the poetic name on it, see Kang, "Chronological Autobiography of K'ang Yu-wei," 47; see also Wei Jingzhao, "Nanhai huiguan chunqiu"; on Tan Sitong, see Tong Xun, "Liuyang huiguan Mang cang cang zhai"; on Yang Shenxiu, see Hu Chunhuan and Bai Hequn, *Beijing de huiguan*, 196.

19. Gu Wei, "Tan Sitong zaonian jiqi jiazu ziliao *Tan shi jia shu* jianxi," esp. 308. For the establishment date of the lodge, see Wang Shiren et al., *Xuannan Hongxue tuzhi*, p. 136; for a site map of the premises today (with Tan's quarters indicated), see ibid., p. 118.

20. Kang Youwei, "Chronological Autobiography of K'ang Yu-wei," 65. For a thumbnail biography of Sun Yuwen, see Hummel, ed., *Eminent Chinese of the Ch'ing Period*, 685.

21. Cao Zixi et al., eds., *Beijing tongshi*, 8: 380, 470.

1898 was the founding of study societies that brought scholar-officials together in a new form of political association in order to discuss and advocate reforms. The first of these societies was the Society for the Study of Self-strengthening (Qiangxuehui 強學會). Founded in Beijing in October 1895, it was closed by the government, along with the *Zhong wai jiwen*, only five months later on the grounds that it contravened the Qing ban against the founding of private societies.[22] Though short-lived, the society proved tremendously influential. Later study societies were founded in other cities (including the Southern Qiangxuehui, the influential offshoot of the Beijing society founded in Shanghai), but it was no accident that the earliest reform society was founded in Beijing. As Kang later recorded, "If the societies were first organized in the provinces, they would be checked by the local officials. Therefore it [was] necessary to organize at first a society of scholars and officials in the capital."[23]

The Qiangxuehui was not organized along native-place lines, but it was nevertheless closely associated with two of the capital's native-place lodges. One was the Anhui huiguan, where the powerful official Sun Jia'nai 孫家鼐 (1827–1909) (who hailed from Anhui) made available space for the society members to meet.[24] The other site was the Songyun caotang in the Henan huiguan, which had earlier served as a meeting place for the candidates involved in the Sungyun an petition.[25]

The Qiangxuehui had been disbanded for only two years when the capital again witnessed the establishment of a new series of political organizations. These societies mobilized scholar-officials present in Beijing to advocate publicly for reform. They represented a vital step in the creation of a groundswell of elite opinion openly calling for a change in state policy. Founded on the eve of the Hundred Days Reform, their existence constituted a necessary step in the course of events that led to it. As one might expect, the particular urban characteristics of Beijing once again left an indelible

22. Hao Chang, "Intellectual Change and the Reform Movement," 293–95.
23. Kang Youwei, "Chronological Autobiography of K'ang Yu-wei," 71.
24. Lin Keguang, "Beijing Qiangxuehui yizhi," 263–64.
25. Kang Youwei, "Chronological Autobiography of K'ang Yu-wei," 72; see also Liang Qichao, *Wuxu zhengbian ji*, 126.

mark. The Beijing influence was especially apparent in the *tongxiang* organization of many of the societies, as well as the reliance of the societies on the native-place lodges of the Xuannan ward to provide relatively autonomous space for their gatherings. These elements are clearly reflected in Kang Youwei's description of the establishing of the earliest of these societies.

At this time I wanted to revive the former activities of the Society for the Study of National Strengthening (Qiangxuehui); and so as my first step, I organized a society of my fellow scholars from Guangdong, which, when it was formally established at a meeting of more than twenty of my friends at the Nanhai huiguan on the thirteen day of the twelfth month [Jan. 5, 1898], came to be known as the Guangdong Study Society (Yuexuehui粤學會).[26]

Two months after the founding of the Yuexuehui, other reform activists established new province-based groups. The Sichuan Study Society (Shuxuehui蜀學會), for example, was founded in the Sichuan huiguan on Pi ku ying by Sichuanese scholar-officials under the direction of Yang Rui and Liu Guangdi, both of whom were eventually martyred for their roles in the reforms.[27] Another martyred official, Lin Xu, founded the Fujian Study Society (Minxuehui 閩學會) in the Fujian huiguan 福建會館.[28] Other provincial study groups set up at this time included the Zhejiang Study Society (Zhexuehui 浙學會) and the Shaanxi-Shanxi Study Society (Shaanxuehui 陝學會); all were established on huiguan grounds.

Kang Youwei clearly recognized the potential role the native-place lodges could play in organizing the candidates and scholar-officials of the capital. Early in 1898 he sought to enlist the help of the court in recreating the lodges as centers not only for hosting scholar-official gatherings but also for propagating the latest knowledge gathered from abroad. As Kang later recorded in his chronological autobiography:

---

26. Kang Youwei, "Chronological Autobiography of K'ang Yu-wei," 79–80. Note I have substituted "huiguan" for the term "club" used in the original translation and converted the transliterations to *pinyin* spellings.

27. See Liang Qichao, "Yinbingshi wenji," in Zhongguo shixue hui, *Wuxu bianfa*, 4: 64–65. Yang Rui is given most of the credit for forming the society, but Liu was also involved; see Liu Guangdi, *Liu Guangdi ji*, 456.

28. Liang Qichao, "Yinbingshi wenji," in Zhongguo shixue hui, *Wuxu bianfa*, 4: 56.

Since the huiguan are places where officials in the capital often congregate and since I wished to take advantage of their presence there to guide them, I drafted a memorial, which I handed to the provincial censor Chen Qi-zhang to submit, requesting that the Zongli yamen and the Tongwen guan (College of foreign languages) distribute books to the various huiguan for perusal by officials of the capital. A decree was issued ordering that this proposal be carried out.[29]

Kang's proposal was not implemented; nevertheless, it not only underscores the importance of the lodges as meeting places for the scholar-gentry in the capital but also represents a fascinating vision of how the lodges might have been employed in the reform project. Intriguingly, the memorial suggests an imagined cooperation between the state and these independently established corporate bodies that would have in some sense co-opted the lodges into a larger national project.

A national project of another kind soon emerged in Beijing, and again it had close ties to the lodges. In April 1898 what would become the most influential study society, the Protect the Country Society (Baoguohui 保國會), was established.[30] Although organized along countrywide rather than provincial lines, it, too, utilized Xuannan area native-place lodges for its meetings. Over 400 scholar-officials attended the founding meeting, held on April 12, 1898, in the Yuedong huiguan, one of two provincial-level huiguan representing Guangdong. Like many provincial huiguan, the Yuedong huiguan boasted an impressive stage. Kang addressed the crowd from the stage in a rousing speech that touched on a range of reform pro-

---

29. Kang Youwei, "Chronological Autobiography of K'ang Yu-wei," 79–80. The memorial was, indeed, submitted by Chen on February 19, 1898 (GX 24.1.29). Entitled "Qing jiang yiyin geguo tushu ban'gei gexue geguan pian" 請將譯印各國圖書頒給各學各館片, it may be found in Kong Xiangji, ed., *Jiuwang tucun de lantu*, 21–22; see also *Qing shilu*, GX 24.1.29, 57.424. As the title of the memorial makes clear, the emphasis was on the distribution to the lodges of translated works from abroad.

30. Although often translated as "Protect the Nation Society," the sense of *guo* here surely does not entirely correspond to "nation" as *guo* would later come to be understood. By the same token, by 1898 its meaning just as assuredly had evolved beyond the earlier sense of "dynasty." Thus it is rendered "country" here.

posals.[31] The society met only three times before disbanding in the face of mounting criticism. After the first meeting, Kang was refused permission to use the Yuedong huiguan by the powerful fellow-provincial Xu Yingkui 許應騤 (d. 1903), the then-president of the Board of Rites, and the remaining meetings of the society met in other native-place lodges in the Xuannan ward.[32] The second meeting, on April 21, was held in the Songyun caotang, and the third on April 25 at the Guizhou huiguan. The last meeting attracted some 100 people.

The establishment of the Baoguohui, which had built on the previous founding of the various provincial study societies, led in turn to the establishment of more provincial societies in the capital. Among them were the Protect Yunnan Society (BaoDianhui 保滇會), the Protect Zhejiang Society (BaoZhehui 保浙會), and the Protect Sichuan Society (BaoChuanhui 保川會). Clearly, a newly charged atmosphere of political engagement had emerged from the concentrated gathering of the educated elite of the Xuannan district. In an address to the Baoguohui on April 21, Liang Qichao commented that whereas three years earlier only one in ten scholar-officials (*shi da fu*) in the capital had believed that the existence of the country was threatened, now the severity of the crisis was more generally acknowledged. Liang stressed the essential role of the scholar-officials gathered in the capital in meeting this crisis: "Whether the country will be able to continue as a country (*guo qi neng guo hu* 國其能國乎), I see as a matter that rests with the scholar-officials of the capital."[33]

It was no accident that the events of the early months of 1898, much like the petitions, protests, and meetings held in the capital three years before, coincided with the influx into the capital of

31. Hu Sijing 胡思敬, "Wuxu lü shuang lu" 戊戌履霜錄, in Zhongguo shixue hui, ed., *Wuxu bianfa*, 1: 374–75.

32. Xu was a native of Panyu county in Guangdong. Reference to his forbidding Kang to make further use of the provincial huiguan is found in the memorial submitted by Xu on June 22, 1898 (GX 24.5.4); see Dai Yi et al., eds., *Wuxu bairi zhi*, 71–73; see Kwong, *A Mosaic of the Hundred Days*, 184–87, for discussion of the context of this memorial.

33. Liang Qichao, "Baoguohui yanshuo ci," *Yinbingshi heji*, vol. 1, "Wenji," 3, 27–29.

thousands of examination candidates for the triennial examinations. Kang Youwei portrayed a direct link between this regular inpouring of candidates and his founding of the Baoguohui: "Many provincial graduates were at this time gathered in the capital, and among them were many talented men. I therefore wished to give expression to the sentiment of the entire nation."[34]

Soon after the Baoguohui was pressured to cease its meetings, Kang and others were able to direct this unique conversion of the talented and politically aware to pressure the court. Sparked by the defilement of a Confucian temple by German soldiers in Shandong some months before, in May 1898 hundreds of candidates submitted petitions and demonstrated outside the gates of the Censorate in a replay of the petition movement of 1895. Indeed, this group action by examination candidates in the capital in 1898 is sometimes referred to as the Second Petitioning of the Emperor by the Examination Candidates (*dierci gongche shangshu* 第二次公車上書).[35] As before, the petitions and demonstrations were largely organized along native-place lines. One of the initial petitions was signed by 369 candidates from Fujian under the direction of Lin Xu. Another was signed by 165 candidates from Hubei; 43 candidates from Hunan signed another; candidates from Jiangsu quickly followed with one of their own.[36] The movement culminated with a single petition signed by 830 candidates from all the provinces. There can be little doubt that this important mass action on the eve of the Hundred Days could not possibly have taken place without the unique set of circumstances afforded by the capital, the Xuannan ward, and the hundreds of native-place lodges found within that special district.

The importance of huiguan as residences and meeting places for reform activists persisted until the movement fell to counterforces. When the coup d'état led by the Empress Dowager put an end to the reforms, soldiers arrested several of the principal activists in their huiguan residences. Kang Youwei's younger brother, Kang Guangren 康光仁 (1867–98), was arrested in the Nanhai huiguan, Tan Sitong waited for his arrest in the Liuyang huiguan, where he had

---

34. Kang Youwei, "Chronological Autobiography of K'ang Yu-wei," 89.
35. Kong Xiangji, *Wuxu weixin yundong xintan*, 315–42.
36. Ibid., 319–20.

spent the early years of his youth, and Yang Shenxiu was taken into custody from his courtyard in the (Shanxi) Wenxi huiguan 聞喜 會館 on Ganlüshi hutong.

Politicization and Increased
State Penetration of Native-Place Space

As we have seen, the native-place lodges in the capital became centers of political networking and organization along provincial lines during the 1895–98 reform movement. At the same time, the meeting halls and spacious opera stages found in the more prominent lodges increasingly became areas for explicitly political meetings and public speechmaking for scholar-official gatherings that cut across native-place lines. Native-place lodges were not, of course, the only locus of politically charged events in the years following the reform. There were many such loci. But the lodges served as an important form of such space, both because they occupied extensive areas and because they benefited from what David Strand has called the "modicum of protection," which led the authorities to refrain from attacking corporate bodies directly.[37] Such relative insulation from state intrusion stemmed from both the location of the lodges in the Outer City (and the less intrusive police presence there) and, in Strand's words, "a tradition of corporate self-regulation," which accorded the huiguan an added measure of autonomy from the state.[38]

What began in 1894–95 with meetings of lower-level metropolitan bureaucrats and examination candidates to protest war policies expanded into further meetings and the establishment of political "study societies" in the years that followed. Native-place lodge space was increasingly used for political activities after 1898. This trend was especially pronounced from the eve of the Revolution of 1911 through the May Fourth period. Although this functional shift in the use of lodge space was too widespread to document comprehensively, a few representative examples of such meetings should illustrate the point. In the last year of the empire, for example, representatives from provinces across the realm attended a meeting

---

37. Strand, *"Civil Society" and "Public Sphere" in Modern China*, 11.
38. Ibid.

held in the Hunan huiguan advocating the convening of a parliament in conjunction with the establishment of a new constitution.[39] Indeed, as issues such as constitutional reform and protection of provincial railroad rights spurred local elites in China to active participation in political movements during the first decade of the twentieth century, they regularly maintained close contacts with compatriot officials in Beijing. In looking at activism in Zhejiang during these years, for example, Mary Rankin has shown how utilization of native-place networks, including ties to *tongxiang* provincials in Beijing, played an important role in political mobilization over the provincial railroad there.[40] Activists in other provinces, such as Sichuan, also found ties to their native-place brethren in Beijing equally valuable.[41]

The transformation in the political functions of native-place lodges became even more apparent once the Republic had been founded. Sun Yatsen proved a frequent visitor to the capital's native-place lodges at this time. In the summer of 1912, during his second trip to Beijing, Sun delivered public speeches at the (Anhui) Anqing huiguan 安慶會館, the Yuedong huiguan, and the (Guangdong) Xiangshan huiguan.[42] Over the years, Sun Yatsen also paid a number of visits to the (Hunan-Hubei) Huguang huiguan on Hufang qiao in the heart of the Xuannan ward and delivered political speeches to audiences assembled there.[43]

Additionally, a number of political parties and political societies were formed in the native-place lodges of Xuannan in this period. Among them were the Military Study Society (Wuxueshe 武學社) founded in the Hunan huiguan in 1912, the Administering Virtue

---

39. Number One Historical Archives of China, Minzheng bu, #30, Jingzheng ci, Xingzheng jingwu ke, "Minzheng bu deng guangyu jingshi baozhi, jicha ji tianceng zheng jing zhi xiangyin de wenjian."

40. Rankin, *Elite Activism and Political Transformation in China*, 263–76.

41. See, e.g., documents in Kui Yingtao et al., eds., *Sichuan Xinhai geming shiliao*, 1: 226–28.

42. Wu Zhezheng, "Huiguan." In *Beijing wangshi tan*, 90. Sun's speech in the Anqing huiguan was recorded in the Sept. 4, 1912, issue of the *Zhengzong aiguo* newspaper; for an excerpt, see Hu Chunhuan and Bai Hequn, *Beijing de huiguan*, 283.

43. Wang Canzhi, "Sun Zhongshan yu Beijing Huguang huiguan."

Society (Zhengdehui 政德會) established in the Sichuan huiguan in 1913,[44] the Great Center Party (Da-Zhongdang 大中黨) in the Sichuan huiguan, and the Society for the Establishment of a Constitution (Xianfaqichenghui 憲法期成會) in the Anqing huiguan.[45] No doubt the most notable of such party foundings was that of the Nationalist Party (Guomindang 國民黨) in August 1912. The new party was created from a merger of the reorganized Tongmenghui 同盟會 and several smaller parties in preparation for the first national elections in December of that year. The Nationalist Party was formed in a public meeting organized by Huang Xing 黃興 (1874–1916) and held in the (Hunan-Hubei) Huguang huiguan.[46] This site was chosen partly because it possessed one of the grandest and most spacious opera stages of all the lodges in the capital. During the Republican period, it was increasingly used for gatherings featuring public speakers. One such occasion occurred in 1916 when both Liang Qichao and Cai Yuanpei 蔡元培 (1868–1940) debated and addressed the crowd gathered there with political oratory.[47]

Native-place lodges also played a key role in events associated with the May Fourth Movement. Among the many political activities held around that time were the formation of the Youth China Study Association in the (Zhejiang, Ningbo) Yinxian huiguan 鄞縣會館 on Pen'er hutong.[48] Strand has noted that during the May Fourth protests of 1919 huiguan facilities played an important role both as places to organize and as havens when the army was brought out.[49] In the years that followed, the lodges continued to serve as favored places for political organization. The young Mao Zedong 毛澤東 (1893–1976), for example, delivered a speech rousing his compatriots to expel the warlord Zhang Jingyao 張敬堯

---

44. *Beijing dang'an shiliao* 1995, no. 3: 6–19; 1990, no. 1: 4–7.

45. Ibid., 1990, no. 2, 2–9; 1990, no. 3, 21–29.

46. Recognition of this meeting re-emerged over the past few years, largely in conjunction with municipal efforts to renovate the Huguang huiguan as a museum of and performance site for Chinese opera. Articles in the Sept. 26, 1992, issues of the *Beijing ribao* and the *Beijing wanbao* first directed renewed attention to this meeting. See also Hu Chunhuan and Bai Hequn, *Beijing de huiguan*, 161–63.

47. Beijing Municipal Archives, J181.

48. Wu Zhezheng, "Huiguan," in *Beijing wangshi tan*, 89.

49. Strand, *"Civil Society" and "Public Sphere" in Modern China*, 10–11.

(1880–1933) from their home province in the Hunan huiguan.[50] As late as 1925, in the (Sichuan) Tongchuan huiguan 潼川會館, Communist Party activists founded the Light of the Catalpa Society (Ziguangshe 梓光社) and the *Catalpa Light Journal* dedicated to the propagation of Marxist ideas.[51]

The growing use of huiguan facilities for politically charged events, however, led the state to interact with them in new ways. Previous tolerance of corporate autonomy increasingly lost out to new forms of state penetration and control of the lodges. Just as the initial rise in political activity within huiguan predated the establishment of the Republic, so, too, did the emergence of an increased state sensitivity toward these activities. In the years following the fall of the *ancien régime*, the new municipal government progressed from observation to increasing control and regulation. As early as 1915, the municipal government issued directives, with detailed organizational regulations, which all huiguan in the city were instructed to adopt. Subsequent government directives dictated precise administrative structures, elections by secret votes, and even membership criteria. Huiguan were instructed (and appear, by and large, to have complied) to adopt regulations establishing an elected board of directors and to designate one person, the director, to assume legal responsibility for the lodge—an incentive, naturally, for those who ran it to keep it free of punishable activities. Huiguan were required to open their doors to all fellow regional compatriots of good character, including women (who had been excluded under traditional rules), and were prohibited from serving the usual disreputable suspects, such as opium smokers, gamblers, those who engaged prostitutes, and those with contagious diseases. Socially disruptive activities were also prohibited. Subsequently, the government ordered all lodges to send a list of their administrative personnel to the police and the Social Bureau of the municipal government each year and to register all lodgers with the authorities on an ongoing basis. Lodges

---

50. Mao gave his speech on February 7, 1920. A plaque commemorating the event hangs on the outside wall of the original Hunan huiguan compound on Lanman hutong (formerly Lanmian hutong) in the Xuannan district.

51. Hu Chunhuan and Bai Hequn, *Beijing de huiguan*, 229. The catalpa is a symbol of one's native-place.

were also instructed to notify the authorities beforehand of any meetings or gatherings on their premises.[52]

Native-place lodge space was increasingly put to new uses during the early twentieth century, most notably, overtly political activities. Traditional notions of corporate autonomy facilitated this development, but in response the government began to encroach increasingly on that autonomy. This trend would greatly affect relations between the municipal government and traditional corporate bodies and alter state/society relations more broadly. Seen from this perspective, the new Communist government's dissolution of all native-place lodges and nationalization (or "municipalization") of their property in the early 1950s did not reflect communist dynamics alone, but grew out of a pattern of increasing state control over the lodges that began in the years following 1898.

Conclusion

The 1895–98 reform movement was inextricably linked to urban institutions uniquely characteristic of Beijing. If not for the triennial examinations, which periodically attracted thousands of examination candidates, or the imperial government, which employed many more thousands of low-ranking metropolitan officials, the movement would have been deprived of the social-professional base from which so many of its activists emerged. The scholar-official nucleus located in the Xuannan ward facilitated communication and organization because of the concentration of so many potential activists in a single area. Without the hundreds of native-place lodges dedicated exclusively for use by scholar-officials, the movement would have lacked the centrally located, relatively autonomous meeting places provided by lodge opera stages and meeting halls. The reform movement as we know it could not have taken place anywhere but Beijing because it was so profoundly influenced by the institutionalization of native-place ties unique to that city.

---

52. Documents reflecting the successive regulations issued by the municipal government during the Republican period are found scattered throughout the holdings on huiguan in the Beijing Municipal Archive; a selection of 30 such orders can be found in Beijing shi dang'anguan, ed., *Beijing huiguan dang'an shiliao*, 1–67.

ELEVEN

Beijing Huiguan in the

Twentieth Century

Native-place lodges were uniquely adapted to the needs of scholar-officials in China's late imperial capital, and the sweeping political changes of China's Republican years greatly affected the lodges of Beijing and the native-place networks they represented. Beijing huiguan continued to operate after 1911, and to some degree they evolved and adapted to the changing social and political environment. In addition to providing important space for the sorts of political activities discussed in the preceding chapter, they also began to provide vital new services in such areas as education. But on the whole, the first half of the twentieth century was a period of decline for the Beijing lodges. Thus even before the newly installed socialist state dissolved the lodges in the early 1950s, the institution had reached a low ebb. Among the most important reasons for this shift were changes in the demographic groups served by the lodges, an intellectual turn against traditional social forms, and a dramatic shift in the importance of Beijing as a national central place, capped by the moving of the capital to Nanjing after 1927.

The Shifting Demographics of Lodge Residents

In 1905 the examination system, which for a thousand years had served as the most important means of recruiting talent to serve in China's official bureaucracy, was abolished. This sweeping institutional reform changed the nature of the native-place lodges of the capital. As we have seen, the housing of examination candidates had been a primary function of huiguan, and abolition of the examinations led to a shift in both the functions of the lodges and the demographics of who stayed in them. With the examinations no longer periodically generating a huge demand for residential space in the lodges, many lodges began to allow women and families to take up residency.

The trend toward allowing women and families to reside in the lodges can be traced to the last years of Qing rule. The 1909 Ministry of Civil Administration survey found hundreds of women living on lodge grounds.[1] The survey recorded 540 females resident in the 233 huiguan that provided information. Some sites listed a surprisingly large number of women, including the (Anhui) He-Han huiguan 和含會館 (20 females) and the (Jiangsu) Rutai huiguan 如泰會館 (24). It is clear from textual evidence that the response to the survey was far from complete, and the figure for female residents must significantly underestimate the total number living in lodges even before the establishment of the Republic.

Very few, if any, of the female residents of the Beijing lodges were single women; rather, the growing number reflects the increasing lodging of families in huiguan compounds. A detailed survey of those resident in the (Hunan) Changsha huiguan in the mid-1930s by a Yenching University sociology student found that of the 84 inhabitants of that prefectural huiguan, only sixteen were single men living on their own. The remaining 68 persons (80 percent) were living with at least one other family member.[2] Although this ratio

---

1. Number One Historical Archives, Minzheng bu, Minzhi ci, Huji ke, "Minzheng bu guanyu diaocha jing waicheng huiguan, pu hu, miaoyu de biaoce," Minzheng bu an *juan* mu lu, 530/21–2, no. 28.

2. Zhang Xiaoxin, "Beiping huiguan diaocha," 44. There were twenty families resident there, not including the single men.

may not have prevailed across the general population of lodge residents at that time, much anecdotal evidence, including my interviews with past residents of the lodges, suggests that families represented a significant part of the lodge population during the Republican period.

The trend toward accepting women and families was, however, general but not universal. At least a few lodges continued to refuse women occupants well into the Republican period. The (Zhejiang) Shaoxing xianguan, for example, explicitly limited residency privileges to men, even after 1929, a time by which many, if not most, huiguan had opened themselves to resident families.[3] The well-known author Zhou Zuoren, who lived in the Shaoxing lodge (with his even more famous elder brother Zhou Shuren, better known by his pen name, Lu Xun), related that during the early Republican period, following the unsuccessful attempt at imperial restoration led by General Zhang Xun 張勳 (1854–1923) in 1917, a Shaoxing official caught on the wrong side sought to escape by temporarily hiding in the Shaoxing xianguan. No sooner had he moved into the lodge than the residents gathered in angry protest because the official was accompanied by his wife. In the end, a compromise allowed the fleeing couple to stay in the lodge one night, but they were obliged to move on the next day. The Shaoxing xianguan was atypically strict in its adherence to this point. Zhou suggested that the unbending adherence to the old restrictions was related to a suicide by a woman on the huiguan premises years earlier.[4]

The shifting demographics were reflected not only in the welcoming of women and family residents but also in the acceptance of male residents from different professional backgrounds. This trend began somewhat later, however. For several years following the Revolution of 1911, many lodges continued to restrict residency rights to a newly defined scholar-gentry elite. Officials in the Re-

---

3. Beijing Municipal Archives (hereafter BMA) 19: 32: "Shaoxing xianguan zhangcheng"; in contrast, the (Fujian) Zhangzhou huiguan regulations of 1935 extended residency privileges to compatriots "regardless of gender."

4. Zhou Xiashou (Zhou Zuoren), *Lu Xun de gu jia*, 401–3. The story of the hanged woman is mentioned by Lu Xun in his "Preface" to *Na han* (Call to arms). The tree from which the woman hung herself happened to stand immediately outside Lu Xun's rooms in the lodge.

publican government as well as all those associated with Western-style academic institutions were deemed the legitimate heirs of imperial officials and examination candidates. The 1915 regulations of the (Fujian) Fuzhou huiguan 福州會館 clearly strove to maintain continuity with the old lodge clientele, despite the ongoing changes in social categories. Natives of Fuzhou prefecture were allowed to stay in the huiguan for limited periods of times if they were in Beijing (1) to take the central government's civil service examination; (2) to sit the entrance examinations to any state-operated college or school; (3) to petition the government on a matter affecting the common good of Fujian province or Fuzhou prefecture; or (4) to take up an appointment to serve in the central government. Anyone in category 1, 2, or 4 was limited, in theory at least, to a stay of no more than 30 days; the maximum stay of petitioners (a less socially defined group) was 20 days.[5]

By the 1920s, many huiguan began to allow "respectable" businessmen to use their facilities as well. The (Jiangxi) Yihuang huiguan 宜黃會館, for example, restricted residents there to (1) students taking entrance examinations; (2) currently serving or expectant officials; (3) businessmen; and (4) those on official business.[6] The extension of lodge residency privileges to businessmen was by no means unique to this lodge. The number of businessmen, however, never amounted to a sizable portion of the overall mix; on the whole, the lodges of the Xuannan area remained overwhelmingly dedicated to serving students, officials, and those in the capital on official business of one kind or another.

There were three principal reasons the lodges continued to serve what may be considered to be the social successors to the scholar-official class. Self-selection on the part of those wishing to stay was certainly one reason. Although huiguan rooms were cheap,[7] they were far from luxurious. Moderately successful businessmen were only too happy to leave such accommodations to

---

5. *Minzhong huiguan zhi*, "Fuzhou huiguan."

6. BMA 19: 87: "Yihuang huiguan guiyue." This document is undated; textual evidence indicates it was written before 1929.

7. In the Yihuang huiguan, for example, room rent during the 1920s was only two yuan per month for the best rooms and one yuan for smaller standard rooms (ibid.).

poor officials and poorer students. Second, Beijing's sojourning population remained primarily scholar-official in character. The southern regions of China were disproportionately represented by huiguan, but there were not great numbers of merchants from these areas in Beijing.[8] The third and, I believe, most important factor involved traditional practices of social exclusion. When during the 1920s and 1930s compatriot communities organized native-place associations (*tongxianghui* 同 鄉 會), the members of this new form of organization were overwhelmingly scholars and officials, even though few of them resided on lodge property (and thus were not self-selected due to their need for cheap housing). In 1930, for example, the (Guangdong) Chaozhou native-place association 潮州同 鄉會 consisted of 155 persons, of whom 143 were either students, teachers, professors, or staff members of a school or college; five held government posts; two were businessmen; two were members of other professions (one lawyer, one editor), and the occupations of the remaining three members are not known. Of this group, 26 lived in the prefectural huiguan. Among those resident in the lodge, nineteen were students, teachers, or educational staff; four served in government posts; one was a businessman; and the occupations of the other two are not known.[9] The predominantly academic and governmental membership was preserved.

The survey conducted by the municipal Department of Civil Affairs in 1949 was greatly concerned with the professional and class background of huiguan administrators. Although the survey provides neither information on the residents of huiguan nor a breakdown of administrators by lodges, it is a valuable look at those associated with the lodges in their final years. One should keep in mind, however, the picture that emerges here reflects the great institutional stress resulting from the long years of Japanese control, civil war, and the flight of many elites in advance of Communist

---

8. Naturally the dozens of specifically trade-oriented huiguan discussed in Chapter 3 served businessmen and tradesmen from the beginning, although even the Beijing trade associations tended to serve less as lodges and more as meeting places and locations for social gatherings.

9. *Lüping Chaozhou tongxiang lu.*

Table 11.1
Professional Background of Those Serving as Beijing
Huiguan Administrators or Agents, 1949

Background	Total persons	Comments
Retired officials	42	Included an acting county magistrate and acting and retired civilian and military persons of equal or greater rank
Unemployed government employees and teachers	151	Included both those unemployed prior to "liberation" and those who lost their positions afterward
Lawyers	18	
Medical doctors	31	
Professors	49	
Government functionaries	174	Those serving at the time
Educational staff	85	Workers and staff at public and private schools
Students	73	
Workers	30	
Businessmen	354	
Discharged military personnel	9	Ex–Nationalist Army personnel
Housewives	11	Described as "a few petty-bourgeois heads of households."
The "retrained"	9	Those who previously served in the Nationalist government, who went on to serve in the post-"liberation" government/military after retraining
Office workers	10	Staff and office workers in private industry
Street peddlers	11	
Democratic personages	7	Those who had participated in affiliated party activity
Important government	3	
TOTAL	1,067	

NOTE: Huiguan administrators were huiguan directors, members of boards of directors and similar administrative bodies, and huiguan agents.
SOURCE: Beijing shi renmin zhengfu, Minzheng ju, "1949 nian Beijing huiguan qingquang diao-cha baogao."

takeover. Huiguan were administered in a variety of different ways. A handful maintained old-style administration by a single director, but some form of elected committee administered most lodges. Not all those who served on such committees necessarily lived on huiguan grounds, but their willingness reflects their close ties to the lodges. The findings of the survey are shown in Table 11.1.

The 1949 survey included all huiguan, not just those who had traditionally catered to a scholar-official clientele, and this partly explains why approximately one-third (354) of the administrators were merchants, but this level of merchant participation surely also indicates substantial participation by businessmen in the management of lodges that had not traditionally served trade interests. With the exception of a small number of workers and street peddlers (41, or less than 0.5 per cent), the lawyers, doctors, educators, and so on who made up the rest of those administering the lodges at that time constituted a broadly conceived class of intellectuals and professionals who may be understood as the social and political heirs of the late imperial scholar-official class.

Charitable Activities and Education

As the social and political environment of Beijing was transformed, many of the activities undertaken by the lodges shifted accordingly. Although some new functions represented breaks with the past, others developed more directly from traditional activities. The maintenance of native-place cemeteries, for example, was a traditional activity that by and large continued much as before. Possession of cemetery properties remained in the hands of the lodges. Grave-sweeping ceremonies and other activities associated with the operation of graveyards were retained. However, as the demographics of the lodges changed and more families became residents, children were systematically incorporated into rituals performed at the cemeteries on holidays such as the Festival of Light (Qingming jie 清明節), the traditional day for tending to graves and making ritual offerings to the dead.[10]

---

10. Personal interview with He Zhengqiang, a former resident of the (Guang-dong) Zhaoqing huiguan on Li Tiegui xiejie (1994); the informant grew up on the

Another activity that continued into the twentieth century was the granting of assistance to compatriots fallen on hard times. Indeed, such aid may even have increased in this period. A good example of how such support was managed is found in the charter of the (Jiangxi) Yongxin huiguan 永新會館, which lists charitable funds (*ci zhu fei* 慈助費) among the six categories of approved huiguan expenses.[11] These funds were set aside for impoverished compatriots who lacked other means of support. According to the charter, those who qualified were eligible for successive contributions if needed, although a cap of 50 yuan per person was placed on the total that could be dispensed in a single year without the approval of the representatives of the lodge.[12] Other lodge-related charitable activity was recorded in a report from the Central Police Station of the Southern City to the Ministry of Civil Administration submitted in 1911.[13] Among the fourteen charitable organizations it lists in that part of Beijing is the Charitable Association of the (Guangdong) Yuedong xinguan. Presumably this organization, too, was involved in dispensing funds to the needy, although the report did not specify its activities.

An increasingly prominent activity took the form of fellowships and grants to compatriot students. The (Jiangxi) Yongxin huiguan, for example, set aside funds for compatriot students studying in Beijing.[14] The Ningbo Native-Place Association, which operated from the premises of the Ningbo shiguan, financed a scholarship

---

premises and remembers that the children resident in all the Guangdong lodges in Beijing were brought to the Guangdong charitable cemetery to tend the graves of their fellow provincials each year on that holiday.

11. The other five categories of approved expenses were educational grants, repairs, social gatherings, emergency funds, and fellowships for students taking the examinations.

12. BMA 19: 87: "Yongxin huiguan zhang" (undated [pre-1929]).

13. Number One Historical Archives, Quanzong Minzheng bu 284, XT 3.10.11 (1911), "Waiting shenbao waicheng jiuji hui anlie qingbiao qing lian you," attached form: "Waicheng xunjing zongting."

14. BMA 19: 87: "Yongxin huiguan zhang." These funds were distributed twice yearly, in the winter and summer. For an example of Jiangxi scholarship funds from a somewhat later time (although prior to 1929), see BMA 19: 87: "Beijing Jiangxi tongxianghui zhangcheng." For an example from 1948, see Beijing shi dang'anguan, ed., *Beijing huiguan dang'an shiliao*, 415–17.

fund specifically earmarked for compatriot primary- and middle-school students. The Ningbo funds were limited to four students, who had earned superior grades, exhibited upright behavior, and wished to study or undergo professional training but could not do so due to economic hardship.[15]

Huiguan and their respective communities of *tongxiang* so-journers also became involved in the establishment of new schools. In the early years of the twentieth century, educational reform swept through China, spurred by the abolition of the examination system and the perceived need to provide effective means of education for China's youth. Richard Orb has demonstrated the leading role of Zhili province, which surrounded Beijing, in the implementation of educational reform in the waning years of the Qing dynasty,[16] and he provides figures from 1909 demonstrating the leading role of Zhili in terms of the numbers of new schools established; the numbers of staff, teachers, and students; and the income, expenses, and assets of the Zhili schools.[17] Orb did not specifically examine the response of Beijing to new school construction, but Beijing residents also responded impressively to the challenge. Huiguan played a leading role within the city in this respect.

According to another 1909 police report that focused on Beijing exclusively, 250 new-style schools had been established in Beijing. These were categorized at the time as private (*sili* 私立), official (*guanli* 管立), or public (*gongli* 公立). The institutions in the "official" category resembled American public schools in that they were established under the direct auspices of the state; the public category represented schools established through the collective efforts of social groups without state support (in today's parlance they might be called "nonprofit community schools"). Of the nineteen schools categorized as public schools, fifteen were operated by and on behalf of the respective provincial sojourning communities in the capital (see Table 11.2).

---

15. BMA 19: 32: "Ningbo lüping tongxianghui juban zhong-xiao xue buzhu fei guize" (1936).

16. Orb, "Chihli Academies."

17. Ibid., 231, 239.

Table 11.2
Huiguan-Operated Provincial Schools Established in Beijing as of 1909

1. Manchuria Middle School (Dongsansheng zhongxue tang)
   Location: Fengtian shiguan on Guanyin sijie (Inner City); established: 1906; 7 staff members; 7 teachers; 96 students; income: 8,000 *liang*; expenses: 8,000 *liang*; assets: 20,000 *liang*

2. Jiangsu Middle School (Jiangsu zhongxue)
   Location: Jiang-Zhen huiguan on Jiajia hutong; established: 1906; 2 staff members; 2 teachers; 53 students; income: 8,400 *liang*; expenses: 6,650 *liang*; assets: 11,000 *liang*

3. Anhui Middle School (Anhui zhongxue tang)
   Location: Housun gongyuan (site of the Anhui huiguan); established: 1906; 4 staff members; 12 teachers; 61 students; income: 10,607 *liang*; expenses: 15,406 *liang*; assets: 24,800 *liang*

4. Jiangxi Middle School (Jiangxi zhongxue [also called the Yuzhang xuetang])
   Location: Bajiao liujing; established: 1903; 1 staff member; 7 teachers; 19 students

5. Zhejiang Middle School (Zhejiang zhongxue tang)
   Location: Xiaxie jie; stablished: 1906; 6 staff members; 11 teachers; 44 students (+ 6 graduated); income: 7,175 *liang*; expenses: 4,640 *liang*

6. Fujian Middle School (Fujian zhongxue tang)
   Location: Xuanwumen dajie (site of the Quan-Min [Fujian] huiguan); established: 1907; 5 staff members; 13 teachers; 66 students; income: 14,175 *liang*; expenses: 10,574 *liang*; assets: 20,400 *liang*

7. Hubei Middle School (Hubei zhongxue tang)
   Location: Yongguang si (site of the Hubei huiguan); established: 1906; 5 staff members; 12 teachers; 83 students; income: 6,386 *liang*; expenses: 6,479 *liang*; assets: 21,300 *liang*

8. Hunan Middle School (Hunan zhongxue tang)
   Location: Xizhuanta hutong; established: 1909; 1 staff member; 12 teachers; 92 students; income: 12,801 *liang*; expenses: 8,319 *liang*; assets: 12,639 *liang*

9. Henan Middle School (Henan zhongxue tang [also called the Yuxue tang])
   Location: Dazhi qiao (also known as Zhazi qiao, site of Henan huiguan); established: 1905; 7 staff members; 7 teachers; 103 students; income: 31,633 *liang*; expenses: 15,761 *liang*; assets: 32,700 *liang*

10. Shandong Middle School (Shandong zhongxue tang)
    Location: Huashi qiao; established: 1906; 4 staff members; 10 teachers; 66 students; income: 7,800 *liang*; expenses: 7,680 *liang*; assets: 17,000 *liang*

11. Shanxi Middle School (Shanxi zhongxue tang)
    Location: Wulao hutong (site of the Sanjin huiguan); established: 1909; 5 staff members; 13 teachers; 45 students; income: 6,744 *liang*; expenses: 6,487 *liang*; assets: 76,600 *liang*

Table 11.2, cont.

---

12. Shaanxi-Gansu Middle School (Shaan-Gan zhongxue tang [also called the
Guan-Long xue tang])
Location: Baoan si (site of the [Shaanxi] Guannan huiguan); established: 1908; 1
staff member; 6 teachers; 34 students; income: 6,600 *liang*; expenses: 6,593 *liang*;
assets: 10,720 *liang*

13. Sichuan Middle School (Sichuan zhongxue tang)
Location: Piku ying (site of the Sichuan xinguan); established: 1898; 1 staff
member; 14 teachers; 70 students; income: 3,536 *liang*; expenses: 8,235 *liang*

14. Guangdong Middle School (Guangdong zhongxue tang)
Location: Guang'anmen nei dajie; established: 1906; 4 staff members; 10 teachers;
71 students; income: 11,000 *liang*; expenses: 10,000 *liang*; assets: 500 *liang*

15. Guangxi Middle School (Guangxi zhongxue tang)
Location: Beiliu xiang (site of the Guangxi xinguan); established: 1906; 4 staff
members; 10 teachers; 88 students; income: 2,280 *liang*; expenses: 4,340 *liang*

SOURCE: Number One Historical Archives, Quanzong: Minzhong bu: 28: "Jingshi duxue biao:
xuetang—jianbiao." The same report can be found in Quangzong: xuebu: 76. See also Yang
Jingting, *Xinzeng dumen jilüe*, 4.71–72 for a list of school names and locations, with some
minor variations.

In fact, the police report did not record all the schools known to
have been established by sojourning compatriot communities in
Beijing at the time. It missed the Yunnan School (known as the Dian
xuetang 滇學堂), set up on the premises of the Yunnan xinguan on
Zhu chao jie shortly after 1898.[18] It also failed to record the Zhili
School (known as the Yanji zhongxue 燕冀中學) established in 1898
and still operating into the 1930s.[19] Given the total number of new
schools established in Beijing in the last years of the dynasty, the
number of compatriot-operated schools may appear to have been a
negligible part of the new trend. In fact, however, they accounted
for a disproportional amount of the educational investment in the
capital, even if only the fifteen schools recorded in the 1909 police
report are considered. These schools were among the best endowed
of all the new schools in the capital. Out of the total 380,303 *liang* (of
silver) of reported income for all categories of schools, the provincial schools recorded 156,040 *liang*, or just over 40 percent of the
total. The value of the reported assets of the provincial schools is

---

18. Jian Enpei, "Yunnan ren zai Beijing."
19. Zhang Xiaoxin, "Beiping huiguan diaocha," 54b–59.

even more impressive. Provincial school assets amounted to 414,389 *liang* of the total of 667,501 *liang* for all the schools in Beijing.[20] Thus, according to the report, the compatriot schools possessed over 60 percent of all school-owned assets in Beijing.

Why were the huiguan-affiliated schools so much better off? First, the corporate holdings of the lodges provided them with an unusually solid foundation. As Table 11.2 reveals, many of the schools were established within huiguan compounds. But this alone does not explain the relative wealth of the schools, since the grounds and facilities were lent to the schools rent free, not signed over to them. In fact, the schools received a variety of different kinds of support from the lodges. Administrative support was one form of help. Because the administrative demands of schools required more time, effort, and even knowledge than could be reasonably expected from the volunteer lodge administrators, they did not typically directly administer the schools. However, some form of managerial link was generally maintained even with those schools that were not on huiguan premises. The charter of the Jiangxi native-place association, for example, which somewhat later in the Republican period managed all Jiangxi huiguan property, called for an independent administrative committee for the Yuzhang Middle School to be operated under the direction of the administrative committee of the native-place association. In this case, the members of the school's administrative board were unpaid, but they were reimbursed for all travel expenses.[21]

More substantial financial support from the huiguan was also typical. Rents collected from other huiguan-owned property were sometimes specifically designated as funds for the provincial school, as was the case with the Chunming Girls School (Chunming nüzi xuexiao) established in the Fujian laoguan.[22] Huiguan also coordinated countrywide fundraising for the schools. This is reflected in the unsurpassed libraries of the provincial schools, which surely ranked among the richest school libraries anywhere in China. Ap-

---

20. Number One Historical Archives, Quanzong Minzhong bu, 28. "Jingshi duxue biao: xuetang—jianbiao."

21. BMA 19: 81: "Jiangxi lüping tongxianghui zhangcheng."

22. *Minzhong huiguan zhi*, "Fujian huiguan."

proximately 900 sets of books were donated to the Guangdong xuetang in a two-month period in 1909, for example. The school received copies of the classics, gazetteers, and books of literature, history, and Western sciences. Among the donors were the Chao-Jia huiguan of Hankou, who contributed, among other things, a 720-volume set of biographical memorial texts (the *Guochao zhixian leihui*); a nationwide institutional network of compatriots apparently thought it important to support schools in the capital.[23] An accounting of the holdings of the Chunming Girls Schools from later in the Republican period (1943) seems somewhat paltry in comparison, but no doubt its library would have invoked the envy of innumerable schools forced to operate with much less. It owned sets of China's traditional dynastic histories, a 22-volume *Encyclopedia Britannica* (one volume was missing), and over forty other sets of classics, math books, art books, and so on. Additional possessions included anatomical models (an entire human body, a throat, an ear), some scientific equipment, a set of "foreign-style" (*yang*) drums, and an accordion.[24]

The New Culture Movement and
Shifting Perceptions of the Beijing Lodges

Bryna Goodman's fascinating work on native-place networks in modern Shanghai emphasizes the ways native-place institutions successfully presented themselves as legitimate and valuable contributors to a modernizing Shanghai at least through the first third of the twentieth century.[25] The story in Beijing was quite different, however. As we have seen, the native-place lodges and native-place networks of Beijing contributed in many ways to reform and modernization during the late Qing and the early Republic, but by the 1910s public opinion began to shift, and the lodges increasingly came to be seen as vestiges of a backward past with little or nothing to offer a modernizing China. No doubt some of this shift was due to the changing demographics of the lodges and the reduction in

---

23. Liu Dingfen, *Jingshi Guangdong xuetang shuzang juanshu mulu*.
24. *Minzhong huiguan zhi*, "Fujian huiguan."
25. Goodman, *Native Place*.

status that the introduction of families and women meant, but the reputation of the lodges also suffered from a growing feeling that lodges and the native-place ties they represented reflected a past that China had to leave behind in its march forward.

No single person better reflects the shift in regard for the Beijing lodges than Zhou Shuren, who came to Beijing as a petty official in the Ministry of Education and under his pen name, Lu Xun, went on to become the pre-eminent essayist and short-story writer of modern China. As noted above, Lu was a long-time resident of the (Zhejiang) Shaoshing xianguan. In one of his best-known pieces, the "Preface" to his first collection of short stories, *Na han* (traditionally translated as *Call to Arms*), Lu Xun referred to the lodge as "S guan" (S lodge). The reference was to the Shan-Gui yiguan, which took its name from the two counties of Shanyin and Guiji that together made up the city of Shaoxing. In 1913 these two counties were merged to form Shaoxing county, and the name of the lodge was duly adjusted to Shaoxing xianguan. Many people continued to call the lodge by its old name, and Lu himself frequently referred to it simply as *yiguan* ("city lodge," referring to Shaoxing city) in his diary. Lu Xun's brother Zhou Zuoren suggested Lu avoided public mention of the lodge's proper name in order to distance himself from Shaoxing's reputation as the hometown of innumerable clerks serving in the bureaucratic offices of the capital.[26]

In the preface, Lu described an incident that occurred on a summer night in the small courtyard outside his rooms in the Shaoxing xianguan. A friend, who had stopped by to visit, urged Lu to write a piece for the literary journal *New Youth* as a means of raising the political and social consciousness of its readership. Lu responded with one of the most famous allegories of modern Chinese literature:

Imagine an iron house without windows, absolutely indestructible, with many people fast asleep inside who will soon die of suffocation. Since they will die in their sleep, they will not feel any of the pain of death. Now if you cry aloud to wake a few of the lighter sleepers, making those unfor-

---

26. See Zhou Xiashou (Zhou Zuoren), *Lu Xun de gu jia*, 400–401. See also Cole, *Shaohsing*.

tunate few suffer the agony of irrevocable death, do you think you are doing them a good turn?[27]

Lu's friend replied that as long as some people inside were awake, there was hope. Lu Xun was persuaded, and there in a small court-yard tucked away at the back of the Shaoxing xianguan, he decided to begin writing.

Lu Xun moved into the Shaoxing xianguan when he first arrived in Beijing to serve in the new Ministry of Education at the request of the minister, Cai Yuanpei (a Shaoxing compatriot), in May 1912. He remained there until November 1919. During this period, Lu often mentioned the lodge in his diary, which he began on the day he arrived in Beijing. The first such reference is found in the initial entry.[28] Although not able to move into the lodge that first night, Lu stopped by to visit a close friend, Xu Mingbai 許銘佰 (1866–1921). Lu Xun was no stranger to native-place organizations: he and other overseas students from Zhejiang, including Xu Shoushang 許壽裳 (1883–1948; the younger brother of Xu Mingbai), had formed a Zhe-jiang Native-Place Association in Tokyo, when Lu had studied medicine there ten years before.[29] Reflecting his interest in the so-journing Shaoxing folk in the capital, during his first visit Lu obtained a copy of the *Yuezhong xianxian ci mu* (Catalogue of the Shrine to the Former Worthies of Yuezhong [Greater Shao-xing]), which described the Yuezhong xianxian ci, another lodge in Beijing.

Lu moved into the lodge the next morning and then rode off to the Ministry of Education offices on a mule cart. That night, however, he encountered a more pedestrian side of huiguan life. The entry for his first day in the lodge tersely notes: "In less than half an hour after lying down, I discovered thirty to forty bedbugs. I then

---

27. Lu Xun, "*Na han*: zixu," in *Lu Xun quanji* (hereafter *LXQJ*), 1: 418–19. English translation taken from Spence, *The Gate of Heavenly Peace*, 145.

28. Lu Xun, "Riji," in *LXQJ*, 14.1, entry for 1912.5.5.

29. "Lu Xun zhu ze nian biao," in *LXQJ*, 16: 5. This network of personal and *tongxiang* connections was an essential element in Cai Yuanpei's invitation to Lu to take up a ministerial post. When Cai was called on to form the new ministry, he turned to Xu Shoushang to assist him in gathering talent for the task. Xu recommended Lu.

slept on a table top to avoid them."[30] The next day Lu had the lodge caretaker replace the bed, and that night he finally got some sleep. Lu's diary shows other aspects of life rarely reflected in other sources. For instance, despite the rules against extended stays found in many lodge regulations, Lu's seven years in the Shaoxing xianguan indicates that residence could be semi-permanent. During the course of his stay, Lu moved several times within the lodge compound, first living on one side and then the other of an interior courtyard called Wisteria Flower Lodge (Tenghua guan) and then moving, in 1916, to another courtyard called the Replaced Tree Studio (Bushu shuwu).[31]

Lu's diary also clearly reveals that native-place lodges remained an important social center for the educated elite of Beijing in the early years of the Republic. A number of entries record visits from others as well as Lu's calls on others at their lodges.[32] These social calls often lasted for hours, involved many friends engaged in long discussions, and occasionally ended with one guest or another spending the night. Friendly visits were not the only social activity to occur in huiguan; Lu also recorded attending a wedding of a friend in the (Anhui) Anqing huiguan, for example.[33] Huiguan served as venues for other cultural events, too. At one point Lu paid a visit to the Quan-Zhe (Zhejiang) huiguan 全浙會館 to inspect its opera stage and the adjoining rooms to see if they might serve as an appropriate site for a national children's art exhibit sponsored by the Ministry of Education.[34]

Despite Lu Xun's lengthy seven-year stay in the Shan-Gui lodge, and the large role the lodges of Beijing played in Lu Xun's social life, in his published writings Lu tended to portray the lodges as backward and antimodern. Although Lu's diary is filled with references to Beijing lodges, his public writings are not, and what references

---

30. Lu Xun, "Riji," 14: 1.

31. Ibid., 14: 218, entry for 1916.5.6; see also ibid., 14: 221*n1*.

32. For more on Lu Xun's visitors in the Shaoxing xianguan, see Zhou Xiashou, *Lu Xun de gu jia*, 316–17.

33. Lu Xun, "Riji," 14: 80, entry for 1913.11.2.

34. Ibid., 14: 51–52, entry for 1913.3.31. The exhibit was delayed due to the instability created during the Second Revolution and was eventually held elsewhere in 1914.

there are tend to be at least obliquely negative. Not much is said about the "S guan" in his preface to *Na Han*, but the general image conveyed is that before his political awakening, Lu holed up in his huiguan and immersed himself in historical inscriptions in an attempt to escape from the imperative to become politically involved. As Lu described it:

There is a three-room apartment in the S lodge where, it is said, a woman once hanged herself from the locust tree in the courtyard. Although by the time I arrived the tree had already grown so tall you couldn't reach the lowest branch, there was still no one staying there. For a period of several years I lived in those rooms, devoting whatever spare time I had to making copies of ancient inscriptions. Very few guests came by to shake me from my lethargy, and of course I encountered nothing in the inscriptions—no social problems, plans for reform, and so on—to pull me out of it either. And yet the span of my years was in fact silently slipping away. But that was exactly the way I wanted it.[35]

Lu Xun's depiction of a native-place lodge as an antimodern force is most fully given voice in his short story "Shang shi" (Mourning).[36] This tragic tale depicts a young couple of the early Republican period who have come together in a self-arranged "free love" relationship. In the end, the couple's relationship is crushed, the young man's career is destroyed, and the young woman is reduced first to sickness and then to death, mainly as a result of conservative social pressure. The story is presented as written down by the young man in a "silent, empty, broken-down room in a forgotten corner of a native-place lodge." Without launching into a literary critique of each reference to the lodge, I think it is fair to say that the oppressive conservatism of the huiguan is so palpable that the lodge is essentially a symbol of the mean-spirited, heartless, and destructive reactionary impulses Lu Xun saw operative in China at that time.

Lu Xun's relationship with the native-place lodges of Beijing is both contradictory and representative of that period. On one hand, Lu made great use of his lodge during his early years in the capital. The Shaoxing lodge provided Lu with affordable housing for seven years, and, as his diary shows, much of his social life took place in

---

35. Adapted from Lyell, trans., *Lu Xun*, 25–26.
36. *LXQJ*, 2: 110–31.

lodges. As we have seen, the native-place networks that organized around the lodges used the facilities to establish new schools, and Lu himself considered using the grounds of his provincial lodge as a venue for an educational exhibition. But Lu also obviously had conflicted feelings about the lodges and the native-place ties that connected him to his home area. He shunned open association with Shaoxing, he avoided the periodic ritual ceremonies held on the lodge premises, and he depicted the lodges in his literary work as bastions of the values of a backward China.

Declining Fortunes During the Late Republic

Despite Lu Xun's use of huiguan as a literary metaphor for out-of-date social forms, his diary reflects significant vitality among huiguan during the second decade of the twentieth century. That native-place lodges continued to offer real-world benefits in the early Republic is further indicated by the fact that lodges continued to be established after 1911.[37] But by the late 1920s and 1930s, contemporary observers increasingly commented on the decline of the institution. This decline was greatly accelerated when the new government under Chiang Kai-shek transferred China's capital to Nanjing in 1927.[38] Although Beijing in many ways remained a national cultural center, the removal of the central government to Nanjing naturally resulted in fewer sojourners in Beijing. The demand for huiguan services thus fell accordingly. The reverse was true in Nanjing, where its new status as the national capital resulted in a sudden dramatic increase in the number of huiguan there. One contemporary source referred to the phenomenon with a standard

---

37. The (Guangdong) Dongguan xinguan (established in 1912) and the Fengtian huiguan (established by the Manchurian warlord and de facto military power of Beijing Zhang Zuolin in 1919) are prominent examples. The (Henan) Zhengyang huiguan was not established until 1921. A survey undertaken by the Beijing Municipal Civil Administration Bureau (discussed in greater detail below) records two Hubei lodges founded in the 1930s, the Tijiang huiguan (1930) and the Dazhi huiguan (1936).

38. The decision to move the capital was taken at the seventy-third meeting of the Guomindang Politburo (Zhongyang zhengzhi huiyi); see *Guomin zhengfu gongbao*, ningzi, no. 2 (my thanks to Chen Shiwei for directing me to this source).

Chinese idiom, describing the new native-place lodges in Nanjing as "sprouting up like bamboo shoots after a spring rain."[39]

In discussing the declining fortunes of Beijing's huiguan in the twentieth century, especially following the move of the national capital to Nanjing, Ho Ping-ti suggested that the impact was greatest on huiguan representing "culturally and commercially backward areas," which Ho appears to mean Gansu, the Northeast, Sichuan, Guangxi, Yunnan, and Guizhou. The huiguan of these areas, he argued, "could only tend toward deterioration. After the national capital was moved to the south, they became formless to the point of disappearing."[40] Citing as evidence a 1936 Beiping guidebook listing only 59 huiguan, Ho concluded, "After the moving of the national capital, it was not easy for ordinary huiguan to maintain themselves."[41]

There is a degree of truth in Ho's depiction of post-1927 huiguan, but Ho greatly underestimated the institutional resilience of native-place lodges. Had he consulted other sources from the same period, he would have found a very different picture. The *Beiping lüxing zhinan*, for instance, also published in 1936, listed 357 huiguan in Beiping at that time.[42] Huiguan did not disappear *en masse*, although they obviously encountered difficult times. Indeed, the *Beiping lüxing zhinan* included a photo of the dilapidated and seemingly abandoned main meeting hall of the Yangzhou xinguan, which speaks volumes about the complexity of the situation (see Fig. 11.1).

---

39. *Shoudu Yangxian yiguan luocheng jinian kan*, "Xu" (introduction), 3. Evidence of the positive impact the transfer of the capital had on native-place lodges in Nanjing can be found in *Guangdong lüjing tongxianghui gongzuo gaikuang*.

40. Ho Bingdi, *Zhongguo huiguan shilun*, 34–35.

41. Ibid., 35. The guidebook cited by Ho is Tian Yunjin, *Zuixin Beiping zhinan*.

42. Ma Zhixiang, *Beiping lüxing zhinan* (1936), "Huiguan" section. See also the map *Xince shiyong Beiping dushi quantu* (1930), which lists 475 native-place huiguan. Both sources include huiguan established in the Republican period, such as the Fengtian huiguan on Jiu Xingbu jie (founded 1918), an indication that these lists reflect the contemporary situation. The second source also includes the (Henan) Zhengyang huiguan 正陽會館, which was not founded until 1921. The *Beiping luxing zhinan* list includes many double listings of single sites under alternative names.

Fig. 11.1   Dilapidated main hall of the Yangzhou xinguan, ca. mid-1930s
(source: Ma Zhixiang, *Beiping lüxing zhinan*, 1936).

The photo at first glance seemingly supports Ho's description of lodges as "disappearing," but the very inclusion of the photo in the guide also reveals an ongoing effort of concerned sojourners to maintain and rebuild properties. Next to the photo is an appeal issued by the "Committee to Preserve the Yangzhou xinguan" (the editor of the guide was a Yangzhou compatriot and member of the committee) asking other Yangzhou natives to assist in restoring the property. The notice explained that the site had fallen victim to a dishonest caretaker who had sold everything of value, thus leaving it empty for ten years.

Although the fate of the Yangzhou xinguan may not have been unique, neither was it typical. By all accounts, the huiguan of the post-1927 era continued to provide housing for compatriots and their families; properties did not disappear; their ownership generally remained in the hands of compatriots; and the compounds were maintained, though not always well.

The Dissolution of the Beijing Native-Place Lodges

Less than ten years after the establishment of the PRC, the Beijing municipal government dissolved the native-place lodges of Beijing and took possession of all lodge property. There is no evidence that the new government planned the "municipalization" of lodge property from the beginning, but in retrospect it seems an inevitable development. As we have seen, huiguan had developed over the course of the late imperial period into autonomously run, corporately owned spaces constitutionally integrated into the imperial political system. During the Qing dynasty especially, the lodges worked to the mutual interests of both the state and the native-place communities that operated them. But the symbiotic relationship between state and lodge had already begun to change at the turn of the twentieth century and continued to change after that. New models of municipal administration resulted in greater penetration of lodge space by the city government, in terms of both information gathering and a greater police presence. By the second decade of the century, the city government had asserted its right to dictate acceptable forms of lodge administration and set the parameters of lodge rules. Thus in some ways the takeover of the lodges by the state might be seen as the logical end of a progression under way for many years. But it was more than that.

Although one might think that collectively owned operations dedicated to nonprofit welfare-orientated activities would have been welcomed by the Communist authorities, other characteristics of the lodge proved fatal. When the municipal government concluded the lodges were "feudal remnants" unfit for the new society, the characteristic they most stressed was the class background of those the lodges served. The scant numbers of working-class members and far larger number of those deemed "reactionary" cast suspicion on the whole institution. The flight of many of the prominent provincials associated with the lodges before the Communists arrived highlighted the questionable class nature of the lodges.

Other features surely contributed to the government's determination that the lodges were unfit for the new socialist society. The religious nature of huiguan altars was clearly associated with rituals the new state wanted to transcend. The vast property holdings of the lodges also no doubt proved attractive to a state with ambitious social engineering plans. But the greatest factor in the government's decision to dissolve the lodges and take over their property was that the relative autonomy of the lodges threatened the new government's intention to reach more thoroughly into the social structures of the nation, particularly of the capital. There was no room in the new capital for that.

The dissolution took a number of years. Native-place communities were first instructed to organize "property management committees" (*huiguan caichan guanli weiyuanhui* 會館財產管理委員會), which were charged with making accurate inventories of all lodge holdings and reporting the results to the government.[43] Given the extensive holdings and the incomplete documentation of many properties due to the several decades of social disruption and hard times, this was a time-consuming process involving the posting of public notices of claims to property that could not be verified by deeds.[44] Once the committees itemized and cataloged all properties, the process of state confiscation began. The lodge sites were used for various proposes: some became government offices; others schools and kindergartens; still others factories. Many sites were kept as residential properties, although with many more people than originally intended, and, of course, the state no longer assigned these residences on the basis of native-place background.

It is an irony of socialism that despite all the rhetoric of "destroying the past to build the new" characteristic of the Maoist pe-

---

43. Government directives and the reports of the individual property committees to the municipal government can be found in Beijing shi dang'anguan, ed., *Beijing huiguan dang'an shiliao*, passim.

44. Public notice of claims to property and announcements of meetings to be held by the various huiguan property committees may be found in the *Beijing ribao* of the period. For examples of specific notices, see the issues of 1952.11.1, 3, and 1952.12.12, 3 (Anhui); 1952.12.11, 3 (Fujian); 1952.10.8, 6 (Gan[su]-Ning[xia]-Qing[hai]); 1952.10.3, 3, and 1952.10.6, 6 (Guangxi); 1952.10.23, 3, and 1952.12.11 (Hubei); 1952.12.11, 3 (Hunan); 1952.10.7, 6, 1952.11.13, 3, 1952.12.11, 3, and 1952.12.13, 3 (Jiangsu); 1952.11.20, 3, and 1952.12.13, 3 (Shandong); 1952.10.30, 3 (Sichuan); 1952.10.7, 6 (Rehe); 1952.10.6, 3 (Yunnan); 1952.12.11, 3, and 1953.4.7, 4 (Zhejiang). Many notices were reprinted on two or more consecutive days; these citations refer only to the first day's notice.

riod, the physical structures of the native-place lodges were for the most part much better preserved during that period than they have been during the subsequent decades of post-Mao reform. In recent years especially, as real estate investment has transformed even the relatively unfashionable Xuannan area, more and more of the old structures have been torn down to make way for the urban landscape of twenty-first century Beijing. Although quickly disappearing, a good number of lodge sites are still extant as of the writing of this book (see the Postscript on the present state of some of these old lodges).

❦

Conclusion

In every political system, those representing the interests of the diverse localities of the country must at times be present in the capital city as part of the interaction between center and region. The state residences established for official visitors to the capital (*jundi*) of the Han dynasty and early empire, like the various regional and provincial liaison offices (*lianluo chu*) of the socialist period, demonstrate that local and regional governments in China have met this need by operating spaces in the capital for this purpose. However, the period between the fifteenth century and the early years of the Republic in the twentieth century stands out as a time during which a different institutional approach to the mediation of state/local interests in the capital prevailed. Corporate lodges independently established by the various sojourning communities present in the city became the main nexus of regional/center interaction *at* the center. That *huiguan* were corporate rather than government-operated bodies mattered on a number of different levels. The ritual worship and celebration of worthies and deities associated with the specific locality of the various lodges served to reinforce native-place solidarity. Collective ownership by an abstractly defined native-place community promoted continuity and stability over time, and the bounded autonomy accorded traditional corporate bodies such as lineages by the state was granted to the *huiguan* as well.

Over time native-place ties among scholar-officials present in the late imperial capital became increasingly woven into the governmental system. Native-place networks became important channels of information both from the center to the localities and from the localities to the center. This articulation of interests between center and periphery as mediated through compatriot metropolitan officials served as a valuable addition to the official channels of communication through memorials, petitions, the Capital Gazette, and so on. Furthermore, the state cast a broad net of mutual responsibility over scholar-officials in the capital and officially recognized native-place relationships by mandating that anyone with official business in the capital first had to acquire a *yinjie* guaranty signed by a metropolitan official from his native place. This recognition led to a standard fee for the *yinjie*, which became an indispensable source of income for otherwise impoverished metropolitan officials and incorporated native-place ties into the symbiotic relationship between the metropolitan bureaucracy and the court.

During the eighteenth century, the evolving system of native-place representation in the capital also began to shape the social space and urban ecology of the city profoundly. The proliferation of native-place lodges in the Xuannan ward resulted in the emergence of a scholar-official urban nucleus. This gathering of thousands of scholar-officials in one area prompted the emergence of the book and culture markets of Liuli chang and facilitated easy social and intellectual interaction among scholar-officials of different places. Ultimately it also encouraged sojourning scholar-officials to identify not just with their native-place compatriots but also with the imperium; participants in the social interaction of the Xuannan ward could easily envision themselves as members of the ruling elite of the empire.

It is now axiomatic among scholars that the social and political structures of late imperial China were not static and tradition bound but developed significantly over time and that not all change was a response to the challenges of the West.[1] The evolution of native-

---

1. Cohen, *Discovering History in China.*

place networks among scholar-officials in Beijing is an excellent case in point. When the *ancien régime* began to crumble in the last decades of the Qing, the response of the scholar-officials in the capital was profoundly affected by the multifaceted institutionalization of native-place ties there.

Here we see how the urban ecology of the capital affected the dynamics of political action. The dense congregation of scholar-officials in the Xuannan ward facilitated the dissemination of information, and the lodges provided space for meetings. The structure of protest actions such as the 1895 Petitioning of the Candidates (*gongche shangshu*) was greatly shaped by the mediation of interactions with the state through native-place networks. The impact of the system of native-place representation in the capital was not, however, limited to matters of space and bureaucratic practice but was reflected in intellectual developments as well. The emergence of a conception of and identification with "the nation" among scholar-officials was clearly assisted and informed by that group's long-standing identification with the imperium, which had been promoted by the ritual practices and the spatial layout of the lodges. It was neither accidental nor ironical that the meetings of Kang Youwei's Protect the Country Society (Baoguohui) were conducted in the native-place lodges of the capital, nor that so many other seminal events in the birth of Chinese nationalism had native-place network connections, including the founding of the Nationalist Party (Guomindang) in the Beijing Huguang huiguan in 1912.

As the crises of the last years of the Qing stimulated the creative rethinking of social and political structures, the possible modernities envisioned during that period found room for vital native-place lodge functions. This can be seen in Kang Youwei's call during the Hundred Days for the lodges to be used to disseminate translated information; the establishment of so many schools within lodge compounds; and the vision of a modern Beijing proudly flanked by hundreds of huiguan on the map discussed in the Introduction to this work. Earlier work has shown that there was no contradiction between modernity as broadly conceived and the continued development of native-place organizations in Shanghai. Why, then, during the Republican period did modernizing Beijing turn its back on the lodges? As we have seen, there were many causes. The abolition of the examination system in 1905 greatly reduced the periodic demand for space because of the influx of examination candidates, and the lodges increasingly gave themselves over to the residential needs of sojourning families with women and children; this undermined the respectability associated with their former all-male status. The modernizing state began to renegotiate the traditional relationship between the government and the lodges, as it moved away from the traditional autonomy delegated to the lodges and sought to penetrate and control them more systematically. With the rise of local activism and new local elites in the provinces, the political system began to shift from the extraordinarily "centered" imperial system to one in which the localities had more agency. This trend lessened the need to interface with the government in the capital. The shift in power away from Beijing, already developing for decades, culminated in the transfer of the national capital to Nanjing in 1927, an act that thoroughly ended the function of the lodges as mediators between center and region.

History should not only record what occurred and seek to explain it but also take account of what might have been. Although the native-place lodges of Beijing became associated with backwardness and were ultimately labeled "feudal remnants," things might have happened otherwise. After huiguan property was appropriated by the municipal government and the associations were abandoned, some core functions of the lodges were assumed by the *lianluo chu* established in the capital by the various regional governments. As China develops through late-stage socialism and beyond, it will be interesting to see if this latest attempt to address the need for the negotiation of center/regional interests at the center will endure.

POSTSCRIPT

Huiguan Sites Today

Fifty years after the city of Beijing appropriated native-place lodge property in the 1950s, many of the original compounds still remain. They may not last much longer, however. Ironically, despite the Maoist-era rhetoric of "destroying the old to build the new," many lodge compounds survived relatively intact up into the 1980s. After confiscation, huiguan properties were converted into residences, offices, schools, and warehouses. Furniture was carted off, altars were removed, stele inscriptions painted over, gates widened, and makeshift buildings added, but often the essential physical structures were left remarkably unchanged. When I first visited the site of the Anhui huiguan in 1994 (see Fig. 12.3), for example, most of the compound housed families who had moved in after 1949. The buildings were run down, the garden built over, and the stage hall had only recently been reclaimed after years of serving as a warehouse for a nearby factory. But despite the faded and tattered slogans left over from the Cultural Revolution on the walls and pillars, and despite the general state of neglect and disrepair, the structures were for the most part sound and unaffected. Indeed, the wholesale transformation of the urban landscape associated with the post-Mao reform policies has

Fig. 12.1   Huguang huiguan (April 2004; all photographs
in the Postscript were taken by the author)

proved a greater threat to the sites. Beginning in the 1980s and accelerating during the 1990s, state planning and profit-driven investment are, as this book goes to press, still very much in the process of replacing the horizontal city of low single-story buildings and narrow *hutong* with steel and glass shopping malls, soaring office buildings, and broad avenues designed for the ever-increasing car traffic.

Much of the built environment of old Beijing is already lost, and what is left is being demolished at an escalating rate, but a good number of former huiguan sites still retain at least some semblance of their original form. The continued existence of these sites is in part attributable to the uneven pattern of development; some areas, such as the to now relatively unfashionable Xuannan area, have been relatively neglected as areas adjacent to the major boulevards of the old Inner City and along the ring roads were targeted for investment first. Some lodge properties, however, have been preserved through the conscious efforts of farsighted city planners, who have in recent years recognized the need to preserve material

Fig. 12.2   Stage of the Huguang huiguan (June 2004)

reminders of the city that was. In a handful of cases, lodge structures have not only been preserved but been restored. The Huguang huiguan (Figs. 12.1–2) and Anhui huiguan are cases in point.

The Huguang huiguan, which was established in 1807, is now open to the public as the Museum of Chinese Opera. The present site is somewhat smaller than the original, because of street expansion on both the north and east sides. The structure that originally served as the lodge altar now serves as an exhibition hall displaying miscellanea related to China's opera history; one building has been converted into a restaurant; and the lodge stage hall, with its well-preserved majestic two-tiered stage, serves as a venue for nightly performances of Beijing opera (note the sign boards announcing upcoming performances in Fig. 12.1). The performances attract some local opera aficionados, and a good number of foreign guests as well (note the English and Chinese lyric titles in a lighted sign above the stage in Fig. 12.2). An inscribed stone monument in the courtyard in

Fig. 12.3 Stage hall of the Anhui huiguan
from the street (June 2005)

front of the stage hall informs those who stop to read it that the hall
was the site of the founding of the Nationalist Party (Guomindang)
on August 25, 1912.

The stage hall of the Anhui huiguan has also recently been refurbished (although like the Huguang huiguan only a portion of the
original compound has been restored). Established in 1870 through a
fund drive led by Li Hongzhang, Huai Army commanders, and native Anhui officials, the lodge was a frequent site of upper-level gentry banqueting and socializing and served as an important base for
the powerful network of Anhui officials and military men during
the late Qing. At the time this book went to press, the restored section of the compound was not yet open to the public. Clearly plans
are under way to open the site in the near future, although in what

Fig. 12.4   Wu-Yang huiguan (June 2004)

capacity I am not sure. (A museum dedicated to Li Hongzhang and the Huai Army would seem appropriate, but given official disapprobation of Li's role in history that is unlikely.) On a recent visit to this site, I was allowed into the compound only after much pleading with the gatekeeper and only after promising that I would take no photos; the image presented here was taken from the small lane that runs along the east side of the compound (see Fig. 12.3).

The great number of lodge sites that have been neither refurbished nor torn down to make way for more modern buildings generally stand as classic examples of Beijing *da za yuan*, or rundown "jumbled courtyard" residences. Although many of the original structures of such sites remain, the empty spaces of the original compounds tend to be filled in with ramshackle add-on shacks put up by residents in need of more living space over the years. The (Jiangsu) Wu-Yang huiguan 武陽會館 (Fig. 12.4) is one example of such a site. Indeed, the coexistence of old and new in this site is further reflected in charcoal stacked in front of nineteenth-century lodge regulations

Fig. 12.5   Charcoal stacked in front of stone plaque with
Wu-Yang lodge regulations (June 2004)

embedded in the wall addressing residency privileges of examination
candidates, rituals to be performed on the birthday of Song-period
neo-Confucian Zhu Xi, and other matters (Fig. 12.5). The Huguang
huiguan and Anhui huiguan are among the few lodges that have
been refurbished in recent years. The Zhengyi ci, a trade huiguan
established in 1667 by native bank merchants from Shaoxing in Zhejiang, is another lodge whose stage hall was recently restored. The
local government has not yet taken steps to renovate other sites, but
it has designated a certain number of former lodge properties as
"cultural preservation units," which means that, like properties with
"landmark" status in the United States, the premises may not be
fundamentally altered. Although a commendable policy, it has
proved unpopular with many who actually live on former huiguan
grounds. The "landmark" status conferred on these sites ensures that
they will not be demolished to make way for new buildings (in that
case, the residents must be given new quarters in which to live), but
with the many demands on public resources, there are no immediate
plans for most of these sites, and that leaves these properties, and
their residents, in a sort of limbo.

The Shan-Gui (AKA Shaoxing) huiguan, originally established in
1827 and in which Lu Xun lived for seven years, is a good example of

Fig. 12.6 (*left*)   Zhongshan (AKA Xiangshan) huiguan exterior
Fig. 12.7 (*right*)   Zhongshan huiguan interior
(both April 2004)

such a site, as is the Xiangshan (Zhongshan) huiguan, which was established in 1827 (see Figs. 12.6–7). Note the white plaque announcing the "cultural preservation status" of the site beside the entrance to the compound. The lodge was expanded in 1879 and then again in 1891 with money donated by Tang Shaoyi 唐紹儀 (1860–1938), who later became the Republic of China's first premier. After a subsequent expansion in the Republican period, the site occupied 122.5 jian of total building area and 6.06 mu in total area, making it one of the largest lodge compounds in Beijing. Not all of the original compound remains, but much is left intact, including the impressive meeting and banqueting hall pictured here, long since divided up into tiny residential quarters for a number of families. The Zhongshan huiguan represented Sun Yatsen's native county, and indeed the name was changed from Xiangshan to Zhongshan when the county also changed its name in 1925 in order to commemorate Sun. Sun visited the site frequently.

Fig. 12.8 (*top*)   Entrance to Nanhai huiguan
Fig. 12.9 (*bottom*)   Man han fang courtyard,
where Kang Youwei once lived
(both April 2004)

The (Guangdong) Nanhai huiguan is another example of a former lodge site now used as a residential compound, as is reflected in the public service announcement written in colored chalk by the local residential committee alerting the neighborhood to the symptoms of SARS, which happened to be posted when I visited the site in the spring of 2004 (see Figs. 12.8–9). The lodge was first constructed in 1824–25 and is best known as the former residence of Kang Youwei. Inside the compound, the courtyard where Kang lived, the so called Qi shu tang (Seven Tree Hall), is still extant (see Fig. 12.9). The building on the left, somewhat obscured by more recent structures, is the Man han fang (Perspiration-filled boat), where Kang lived, and which later lent its name to Kang's collected poems. Kang not only lived in this lodge but also actively organized here. Kang established the Yuexuehui (Guangdong study society), an important precursor of the Qiangxuehui, on these grounds. Kang also helped found China's first private newspaper, the *Wan guo gongbao* (which later changed its name to *Zhong wai jiwen*).

The Liuyang huiguan, established in 1872, is another site of interest (Fig. 12.10). The well-known philosopher and reform activist Tan Sitong lived in this lodge on and off from his childhood. Indeed,

Fig. 12.10   Liuyang huiguan, where Tan Sitong once lived (April 2004)

Fig. 12.11   Guizhou huiguan (April 2004)

the site originally served as the private residence of Tan's father, who donated the property to the Liuyang huiguan when he left Beijing for a post elsewhere. The building in the back is the Mang cang cang zhai (Mistless studio), which lent its name to Tan's collected works. Following the failure of the 1898 Hundred Days Reform, Tan was arrested on this site.

Although we do not know for sure when the Guizhou huiguan (also known as the Guizhou laoguan) was established, it was in operation by 1788, when the first independent mention of it is found (see Fig. 12.11). This site once boasted an opera stage, but it has since been dismantled. Although the front of the building is now faced with brick, the original structure remains intact. This site originally possessed a sizable garden. On the south side of this street, a smaller site under the administration of Guizhou huiguan offered living quarters for sojourners. Kang Youwei recorded having held the third and final meeting of the Baoguohui in April 1898 in the

Fig. 12.12 The Jingxian huiguan, where Chen Duxiu and
Li Dazhao edited the *Weekly Critic* (June 2004)

Guizhou huiguan. The meeting is said to have attracted about a hundred people. Although there were several other Guizhou lodges in the city, this one offered a suitable meeting space for a gathering that size, and it seems likely that this is the lodge to which he referred.

An example of native-place lodge space used for political purposes during the May Fourth period is found in the (Anhui) Jingxian huiguan, where Chen Duxiu (an Anhui native) and Li Dazhao established and edited the influential *Weekly Critic* (每周評論) from December 1918 to August 1919. (Fig. 12.12 shows the room from which Chen and Li are said to have overseen the project.)

It is easy to miss the sign for the Jinyang Guesthouse, which is located on the north side of the bustling commercial street Da Sha Lanr in the Qianmen, or Front Gate, section of the old Outer City. About twenty yards or so along a narrow passage leading back from

Fig. 12.13   Entrance to Linfen huiguan (April 2004)

the street is the guesthouse, which occupies the site of the former Linfen huiguan, established in the Ming dynasty (see Figs. 12.13–14). The Linfen huiguan was primarily a merchant lodge (as were most of the Shanxi lodges, and as is indicated by its location in the Qianmen area rather than the Xuannan area), but it is of particular interest because it represents one of the few huiguan sites to which a provincial government successfully laid claim. This site and five other sites escaped appropriation by the Beijing municipal government and were instead handed over to the Shanxi provincial government. This is perhaps testimony to the continuing benefits of having a *tongxiang* official in high office in the capital—the mayor of Beijing at the time was none other than Peng Zhen, a Shanxi native.

Fig. 12.14   Linfen huiguan interior (April 2004)

Ming Period Native-Place

Lodges of Beijing

The following abbreviations are used in the Appendix:

BJTSGC   Beijing tushuguan, Jinshi zu, ed., *Beijing tushuguan cang Zhongguo lidai shike taben huibian*
Hdc   Han Dacheng, *Mingdai chengshi yanjiu*
HBd   He Bingdi, *Zhongguo huiguan shilun*
JSFXZ   Zhu Yixin et al., *Jing shi fang xiang zhi*
LH   Li Hua, ed. and comp., *Ming-Qing yilai Beijing gong-shang huiguan beike xuanbian*
LZx   Lü Zuoxie, "Shilun Ming-Qing shiqi huiguan de xingzhi he zuoyong"
MZHGZ   *Minzhong huiguan zhi*

See the Bibliography, pp. 289–309, for complete citations of these and other works cited in the Appendix.

Name	Province	Location	Date established	Source of date	Reference
Changde huiguan 常德會館	Hunan	Gao miao	Wanli period (1573–1619)	*Changde fu zhi*, 8.24a–25a	HBd; LZx
Changsha junguan 長沙郡館	Hunan	Caochang shitiao hutong	Late Ming	*Chang jun huiguan zhi*, 1.5a	HBd; LZx
Changsha junguan 長沙郡館	Hunan	Inner City	Late Ming	*Chang jun huiguan zhi*, 1.5a	HBd; LZx
Dehua huiguan 德畫會館	Jiangxi	Daxi er hutong	Ming	*Dehua xian zhi*, 22.25a–26a	HBd; LZx
Dingzhou beiguan 汀州北館	Fujian	Changxiang xia er-tiao hutong	Wanli 15 (1587)	*MZHGZ*; "Dingzhou huiguan," 1a–8a	HBd; LZx
Fuliang huiguan 浮梁會館	Jiangxi	Dongheyan	Yongle period (1403–24)	HDc, 408, citing (Qianlong) *Fouliang xian zhi*, j. 7	HDc
Fuqing huiguan 福清會館	Fujian	Inner City	Wanli period (1573–1619)	*MZHGZ*; "Fuqing huiguan," 1a–2b	HBd; LZx
Fuzhou laoguan 福州老館	Fujian	Inner City	Ming	*MZHGZ*, "Fuzhou huiguan," 1–28	HBd; LZx

Name	Province	Location	Date	Source	Ref.
Gao'an erguan 高安二館	Jiangxi	Outer City	Ming	Zhu Shi, *Zhu Wenduan gong wenji*, "Gao'an xian huiguan ji," 1.54b	HBd; LZx
Gao'an yiguan 高安一館	Jiangxi	Inner City	Ming	Zhu Shi, *Zhu Wenduan gong wenji*, "Gao'an xian huiguan ji," 1.54b	HBd; LZx
Guangzhou huiguan 廣州會館	Guangdong	Tudi miao xiejie	Tianqi 4 (1626)	*Lingnan wenwu zhi*, 2–6	
Guanzhong nanguan 關中南館	Shaanxi (trade)	Bao'an sijie	Ming	LH, "Qianyan," 2	LH; LZx
Huaizhong huiguan 懷中會館	Jiangxi-Ji'an prefecture	Inner City: Fuxue hutong	Ming period shrine proposed Hongwu 9 (1406), used as lodge during Ming	*Di jing jing wu lüe*, 1.14. Also called Jiangyou (Jiangxi) Huaizhong huiguan	HBd
Huanggang huiguan 黄岡會館	Hubei	Caochang ertiao hutong	Jiajing period (1522–66)	(Guangxu) *Huanggang xian zhi*, 5.59b–62a	
Huazhou huiguan 莘州會館	Shaanxi	Inner City	Ming	He et al., *Beijing de huiguan*, citing *Jingshi Huazhou huiguan zhangcheng* (1919)	
Ji'an erzhong ci 吉安二忠祠	Jiangxi	Chaoshou hutong	Ming	*Jiangxi huiguan jilü*, 51a–b; see also 15a–16b for 1649 ref.	

Name	Province	Location	Date established	Source of date	Reference
Jiangshan huiguan 江山會館	Zhejiang	Unknown	By Tianqi period (1621–27)	HDc, 408, citing Tianqi period *Jiangshan xian zhi, juan* 2	HDc
Jiaxing huiguan 嘉興會館	Zhejiang	Unknown	Wanli period (1573–1619)	Shen Defu, *Wanli yehuo bian*, 24.608–9	HBd; LZx
Jingxian huiguan 經縣會館	Anhui	Inner City	Ming	*Jingxian zhi*, 10.32a; *Beiping Jingxian huiguan lu*, 1.1a	
Jingxian laoguan 經縣老館	Anhui	Changxiang tou-tiao hutong	Wanli 47 (1619)	*Jingxian zhi*, 10.32a; *Beiping Jingxian huiguan lu*, 1.1a	HBd; LZx
Jinhua huiguan 金華會館	Zhejiang	Xia guoqiang hutong	Ming	*JSFXZ*, 7.26	HBd
Jinling huiguan 金陵會館	Jiangsu	Unknown	Ming	HDc, 408, citing Zhang Yi, *Sou wen xu bi, juan* 1	HDc
Jishan huiguan 稽山會館	Shaoxing, Zhejiang	Xi Zhushi kou dajie	Ming	*Di jing jing wu lüe*, 4.180–81	HBd; LZx
Jiujiang huiguan 九江會館	Jiangxi	Xi Zhushi kou dajie	Tianqi period (1622–27)	*Dehua xian zhi*, 22.26a	

Name	Province	Location	Period	Source	Codes
Leping huiguan 樂平會館	Jiangxi	Changxiangchang sitiao hutong	Wanli 36 (1608)	*Leping xian zhi,* 4.89b–92b	HBd; LZx
Linfen dongguan 臨汾東館	Shanxi (trade)	Damochang	Ming	*BJTSGC,* 72: 107; LH, "Chongxiu Linfen dongguan ji," 86–87	LH; LZx
Linfen xiguan 臨汾西館	Shanxi (trade)	Dashalanr	Ming	LH, "Qianyan," 2, 106–7	LH; LZx
Lingnan huiguan 嶺南會館	Guangdong	Shengou	Jiajing 45–Longqing 4 (1566–70); abandoned mid-Qing; last record, 1718	*Beijing Lingnan wenwu zhi,* "Chongxiu Shengou Lingnan huiguan ji," 1–2	
Lu'an huiguan 潞安會館	Shanxi (trade)	Lushengyan	Ming	*Chen yuan shi lüe,* 9.9a; LH, "Qianyan," 3	HBd
Luzhou huiguan 盧州會館	Anhui	Unknown	Ming; est. by Grand Secretary Li Wending	*(Xuxiu) Luzhou fu zhi,* 17.80b	
Macheng huiguan 麻城會館	Hubei	Caochang toutiao hutong	Ming (Wanli?)	*Macheng xian zhi,* 2.37a–10b	HBd; LZx
Nanchang xianguan 南昌縣館	Jiangxi	Changxiang xiatoutiao	Longqing-Wanli period (1567–1619)	*Nanchang xian zhi,* 2.7a–10b	HBd; LZx
Nanling huiguan 南陵會館	Anhui	Caochang santiao hutong (west side)	Wanli period (1573–1619)	*Nanling xian zhi,* 10.7, 41.28–29b	LH; LZx

Name	Province	Location	Date established	Source of date	Reference
Pingyao huiguan 平遙會館	Shanxi (trade)	Beilu caoyuan	By Wanli period (1573–1619)	LH, "Qianyan," 2; Kato, "On the Hang," 76–77	
Poyang huiguan 鄱陽會館	Jiangxi	Xinkai hutong (Qianmen wai)	Ming	*Poyang xian zhi*, 8.7b–8b	HBd; LZx
Puyang huiguan 蒲陽會館	Fujian	Chongxing si hutong	Ming	MZHGZ, "Puyang huiguan," 1a–9 (LZx lists as Putian huiguan)	HBd; LZx
Qingyang huiguan 青陽會館	Anhui	Inner City	Wanli 26 (1598)	*Qingyang guanlu*, *juan* 1, "Fang qi," 1a–3b	
Qingyang huiguan 青陽會館	Anhui	Shijia hutong	Chongzhen 3 (1630)	*Qingyang guanlu*, *juan* 1, "Fang qi," 1a–3b	
Quan Chu huiguan 全楚會館	Hunan/ Hubei	Shengjiang hutong (*Beijing huiguan zhi-gao*, 11–14, places it Chengxiang hutong)	By Wanli period	Shen Defu, *Wanli yehuo bian*, *juan* 24, 608–9	LZx

Name	Province	Location	Date	Source	
Sanyuan huiguan 三原會館	Shaanxi	Wudao miao	Wanli period (1573–1619)	*Sanyuan xian xinzhi*, 2.6a	HBd; LZx
Sanzhong ci 三忠祠	Shanxi	Shangxie jie	Tianqi 4 (1624), as shrine	*BJTSGC*, 73.150 (Jing 9505)	
Shang-Hunan huiguan 上湖南會館	Hunan	Caochang shitiao hutong	Wanli 21 (1593)	*Shang Hunan huiguan zhuanshu*, 1.3a	HDc
Shang-Xin huiguan 上新會館	Jiangxi	Caochang hutong; moved to Changxiang sitiao hutong, 1607	Before Wanli 29 (1601)	*Shanggao xian zhi*, 3.42a–53a, esp. 45b–47a; LZx mistakenly lists one huiguan at each site	LZx
Shanyou huiguan 山右會館	Shanxi (trade)	Xiaoshi dajie	Ming	LH, "Qianyan," 21	LH; LZx
Shaowu huiguan 邵武會館	Fujian	Caochang ertiao hutong	Wanli 34 (1606)	*MZHGZ*, "Shaowu huiguan," 1–17a	HBd; LZx
Shexian huiguan 歙縣會館	Anhui	Caishi kou; moved to location west of Zhengyang men	Before Jiajing 39 (1560)	*Chongxiu Shexian huiguan lu*, "Xulu jiecun yuanbian jixu," 1.1b	HBd; LZx
Shidai huiguan 石埭會館	Anhui	Daxi er hutong (east side)	Tianqi 4 (1624)	*Shidai beizhi bubian*, 1.16	
Tiezhu gong 鐵柱宮	Jiangxi	Damo chang	Jiajing period (1522–66)	*JSFXZ*, 8.2a	

Name	Province	Location	Date established	Source of date	Reference
Tongan yiguan 同安邑館	Fujian	Inner City; a Ming period cemetery was located on Zhuan'er hutong in Outer City	Ming	*Tongan xian zhi*, 40.9b–10; *MZHGZ*, "Tongan huiguan," 1b; QL 22 (1757) stele inscription	LZx
Wuhu huiguan 蕪湖會館	Anhui	Gao miao	Yongle period (1403–24)	*Wuhu xian zhi*, 13.1a	HBd
Xiangling beiguan 襄陵北館	Shanxi	Xi Heyan, Shejia hutong	Late Ming	*Xiangling xian zhi*, 24b.11b–14a	
Xincheng dongguan 新城東館	Jiangxi	Changxiang shang sitiao hutong	Jiajing period (1522–66)	*Xincheng xian zhi*, 2.8a–10a	HBd; LZx
Xinjian dongguan 新建東館	Jiangxi	Changxiang xiatou-tiao hutong	Ming	*Xinjian xian zhi*, 18.7b–12a	HBd; LZx
Xiuning yiyuan 休寧義園	Anhui	Unknown	Wanli 20 (1592)	*Jingshi Xiuning huiguan gongli gongyue*, 51	HDc
Xuancheng huiguan 宣城會館	Anhui	Changxiang toutiao (later during Ming moved to Inner City, Yuhe Qiao)	Ming	*Xuancheng xian zhi*, 31.376–78	

Name	Province	Location	Date	Source	
Yanping junguan 延平郡館	Fujian	Fenfang Liuli jie	Wanli period (1573–1619)	*MZHGZ*, "Yangping junguan," 1a–2b	HBd; LZx
Yingcheng huiguan 應城會館	Jiangxi	Caochang ertiao hutong	Wanli period (1573–1619)	*Yingcheng xian zhi*, 4.27a–28a	HDc
Yinxian huiguan 鄞縣會館	Zhejiang (trade)	Guojia jing (You'an men nei)	Ming	LH, 96–98	LH; LZx
Yuanzhou huiguan 袁州會館	Jiangxi	Caochang qitiao hutong	Ming	*Pingxiang xian zhi*, 2.19b	HBd; LZx
Yuedong huiguan 粵東會館	Guangdong	Guangqu men nei	Yongle period (1403–24)	Stele inscription, "Chongxiu Guangdong Juyiyuan ji," *BJTSGC*, 87.190	HDc
Yuexi huiguan 粵西會館	Guangxi	Unknown	Ming	HDc, 408, citing Zhang Yi, *Sou wen xu bi, juan* 1	HDc
Yugan huiguan 餘干會館	Jiangxi	Changxiangchang sitiao hutong	Before Wanli 38 (1608); site sold to Leping huiguan at that time	*Leping xian zhi* (1870), 4.89b–92b	HBd; LZx
Yunnan huiguan 雲南會館	Yunnan	Qianmen wai, Zhushi kou	Ming	*BJTSGC*, 69.80 (1740 stele inscription)	

Name	Province	Location	Date established	Source of date	Reference
Yunnan huiguan 雲南會館	Yunnan	Inner City, Chaoyang men area	Ming (1628)	Wang Shiren et al., *Xuannan hongxue tuzhi*, 151	
Yunnan huiguan 雲南會館	Yunnan	Inner City, Xuanwu men nei	Ming	*BJTSGC*, 69.80 (1740 stele inscription)	
Yuyao xiangci 餘姚鄉祠	Zhejiang	Houtiechang	Jiajing period (1522–66)	*JSFXZ*, 10.18b; *JSFXZ* (BJ), 253	LZx
Yuzhang dongguan 豫章會館	Jiangxi	Changxiang shang sitiao hutong	Longqing–Wanli period (1567–1619)	*Nanchang xian zhi*, 2.7a–10b	
Zhangzhou huiguan 漳州會館	Fujian	Bingjiao hutong	Ming	*MZHGZ*, "Zhangzhou huiguan"	HDc
Zhongzhou huiguan 中州會館	Henan	Inner City, Dong Jiangmi xiang	Ming period	*BJTSGC*, 75.185	
Zhongzhou huiguan 中州會館	Henan	Inner City, western section, Taipu sijie	Ming	*BJTSGC*, 75.185	

Reference Matter

Bibliography

Huiguan Annals and Other Materials
Printed by Native-Place Lodges

Anhui huiguan zhi 安徽會管志. Comp. Li Jingming 李景銘. 1943 (Minguo 32). "Chao ben"; 23 of 26 *juan* extant. 3 vols. There also exists a 1944 printed edition in 4 vols.

Beijing Changsha junguan zhilüe 北京長沙郡館志略. Comp. Yuan Dexuan 袁德宣 et al. Beijing: Zhongguo yinshuju, 1924.

Beijing Hunan Huiguan zhilüe 北京湖南會館志略. Comp. Yuan Dexuan 袁德宣 et al. 1924.

Beijing Lingnan wenwu zhi 北京嶺南文物志. Ed. Beijing shi Guangdong sheng huiguan caichan weiyuanhui 北京市廣東省會館財產委員會. Beijing: The editor, 1954.

Beijing shi Guangdong sheng huiguan caichan guanli weiyuanhui 1953 nian quanniandu huiwu gongzuo zong jie baogao 北京市廣東省會館財產管理委員會 1953 年全年度會務工作總結報告. Comp. Beijing shi Guangdong sheng huiguan caichan guanli weiyuanhui 北京市廣東省會館財產管理委員會. 1954.

Beijing shi Guangdong sheng huiguan caichan guanli weiyuanhui choubei hui di'i jie weiyuanhui gongzuo baogao 北京市廣東省會館財產管理委員會籌備會第一屆委員會工作報告. Comp. Beijing shi Guangdong sheng huiguan caichan guanli weiyuanhui choubei hui 北京市廣東省會館財產管理委員會籌備會. 1952.

Beiping Fujian Quanjun huiguan zhi 北平福建泉郡會館志. Ed. Xu Qitian 許其田 et al. 1937.

Beiping Huguang huiguan zhilüe 北平湖廣會館志略. Comp. Shi Rongzhang 石榮暲. 1945. Another edition is entitled *Huguang guan zhi* 湖廣館志. 1947. Reprinted in Beijing shi duiwai wenhua jiaoliu xiehui 北京市對外文化交流協會 et al., eds., *Beijing Huguang huiguan zhigao* 北京湖廣會館志稿. Beijing: Beijing yanshan chubanshe, 1994.

Beiping Jingxian huiguan lu 北平涇縣會館錄. Ed. Xu Shaolie 徐紹烈. 4 vols. 1933.

Chang jun guan zhi 長郡館志. 1825. Hunan Provincial Library.

Guangdong lüjing tongxiang hui gongzuo gaikuang 廣東旅京同鄉會工作概況. Comp. Du Zhiying. 1930.

[Chongxiu] Hejian huiguan ji 重修河間會館記. Ed. Shu Chenglong 舒成龍. 1771.

Huguang huiguan dongshihui wenjian yi ban 湖廣會館董事會文件一斑. Ed. Huguang huiguan dongshihui 湖廣會館董事會. 1927. Reprinted in Beijing shi duiwai wenhua jiaoliu xiehui 北京市對外文化交流協會 et al., eds., *Beijing Huguang huiguan zhigao* 北京湖廣會館志稿. Beijing: Beijing yanshan chubanshe, 1994.

Jiangsu huiguan shoucang mulu 江蘇會館收藏目錄. Ed. Xia Qingyi 夏清貽. Beijing: Caizhengbu, Yinshuaju, 1935.

Jiangxi huiguan jilüe 江西會館級略. Comp. Huang Zantang 黃贊湯. 1933. Includes appendix "Er zhong ci jilüe" 二忠祠級略.

Jingcheng Anhui huiguan cunce 京城安徽會館存冊. Comp. Wu Tingdong 吳廷棟. 2 vols. 1886.

Jingdu Baoqing guan zhi 京都寶慶館志. 2 *juan*. 1887.

Jingdu Baoqing guan zhi 京都寶慶館志. 2 *juan*. 1903.

Jingshi Changsha junguan zhi 京師長沙郡館志. Comp. Hu Yuanyuan 胡遠源 et al. 5 vols. 1835–99.

Jingshi Guangdong xuetang shucang juanshu mulu 京師廣東學堂書藏捐書目錄. Beijing, 1909. Held in the library of the Chinese Academy of Sciences in Beijing.

Jingshi Henan quansheng huiguan guanli zhangcheng 京師河南全省會館管理章程. Rev. Zhao Zhi'an 趙智庵. Beijing: Jinghua yinshuju, 1913.

Jingshi Xiuning huiguan gongli guiyue 京師休寧會館公立規約. Rev. Zhu Zhaolin 朱兆麟 et al. 1922.

Lüchao Dinglong huiguan zhi 旅潮汀龍會館志. Ed. Qiu Fu 丘復 et al. 1916.

Lüjin Anhui tongxiang lu 旅津安徽同鄉錄. 1917. Printed for the Tianjin Anhui huiguan by the Tianjin huaxin yinshuaju.

Lüping Chaozhou tongxiang lu 旅平潮州同鄉錄. 1928.

Minzhong huiguan zhi 閩中會館志. Ed. Li Jingming 李景銘. 1943.

Qingyang guan lu 青陽館錄. Comp. Beijing Qingyang huiguan 北京青陽會館. 4 vols. N.d. (DG 12 [1832] is last date recorded in text.)

Shang Hunan huiguan zhuanshu 上湖南會館傳書. Written by Ouyang Houjun 歐陽厚均; ed. Shang Hunan huiguan. 3 vols. 1814. There is also a one-volume 1882 edition printed with movable type.

Shanhua guan zhi 善化館志. Ed. and comp. Gong Zhenxiang 龔鎮湘. 1888 (GX 14). 2 vols. Beijing Municipal Archives.

Shaoxing xianguan jilüe 紹興縣館級略. Ed. Ding Caisan 丁采三 and Ma Jisheng 馬吉生. 1920.

(*Chongxu*) *Shexian huiguan lu* 重續歙縣會館錄. Comp. Xu Shining 虛世寧 et al.; recopied by Xu Shangyong 徐上鏞. 1834.

(*Shoudu*) *Yangxian yiguan luocheng jinian kan* 首都陽羨邑館. Ed. Qian Zhuolun 錢桌倫. Nanjing, 1933.

Yongxin lüjing tongxianghui kan 永新旅京同鄉會刊. Comp. Li Yuanxi 李元熙. 1926.

Yue ci jilüe 越祠級略. Ed. Ding Caisan 丁采三 and Ma Jisheng 馬吉生. 1920.

"Zhejiang huiguan guan shengdi jun jueshi zhenjing" 浙江會館關聖帝君覺世眞經. Beijing Municpal Archive, 19: 1.2.1.

Local Gazetteers

Changde fu zhi 常德府志. 1813.

Dehua xianzhi 德化縣志. 1872.

Dongguan xian zhi 東莞縣志. 1921.

Huaining xian zhi 懷寧縣志. 1825.

Huaining xian zhi 懷寧縣志. 1915.

Huanggang xian zhi 黃岡縣志. 1879.

Huizhou fu zhi 徽州府志. 1827.

Huoshan xian zhi 霍山縣志. 1905.

Ji'an fu zhi 吉安府志. 1870.

Jianning xian zhi 建寧縣志. 1919.

Jingxian zhi 涇縣志. 1914.

Leping xian zhi 樂平縣志. 1870.

Lianzhou fu zhi 廉州府志. 1833.

Longyan xian zhi 龍巖縣志. 1920.

[Xuxiu] Luzhou fu zhi 續修盧州府志. 1885.

Macheng xian zhi 麻城縣志. 1934.

Nanchang xian zhi 南昌縣志. 1870.

Nanhai xian zhi 南海縣志. 1910.

Nanling xian zhi 南陵縣志 . 1924.

Nanxiong zhili zhou zhi 南雄直隸州志. 1819.

Panyu xian xu zhi 番禺縣續志. 1911.
Panyu xian zhi 番禺縣志. 1871.
Pingxiang xian zhi 萍鄉縣志. 1872.
Poyang xian zhi 鄱陽縣志. 1824.
Qiongzhou fu zhi 瓊州府志. 1891.
Sanyuan xian zhi 三原縣志. 1880.
Shanggao xian zhi 上高縣志. 1870.
Shexian zhi 歙縣志. 1936.
Shidai beizhi huibian 石埭縣志. 1938.
Shunde xian zhi 順德縣志. 1929.
Tongan xian zhi 同安縣志. 1928.
Wuhu xian zhi 蕪湖縣志. 1807. Reprinted 1913.
Wuhu xian zhi 蕪湖縣志. 1919.
Wuyuan xian zhi 婺源縣志. 1883.
Xiangling xian zhi. 襄陵縣志. 1881.
Xiangshan xian zhi 香山縣志. 1923.
Xincheng xian zhi 新城縣志. 1871.
Xinjian xian zhi 新建縣志. 1871.
Xiuning xian zhi 休寧縣志. 1815.
Xuancheng xian zhi 宣城縣志. 1888.
Yangjiang xian zhi 陽江縣志. 1925.
Yingcheng xian zhi 應城縣志. 1882.
Yixian zhi 黟縣志. 1870.
Zhongxiang xian zhi 鍾祥縣志. 1867.

Maps

Jing dushi neiwaicheng ditu 京都市內外城地圖. 1916.
Lao Beijing hutong xiangxi tu 老北京胡同詳細圖. Beijing: Zhongguo hua-bao chubanshe, n.d.
Xince shiyong Beiping dushi quantu 新測實用北平都市全圖. Shanghai, 1930.
Zui xin xiangxi dijing yutu 最新詳細帝京輿圖. Beijing: 1909.

Other Materials

Alabaster, E. *Notes and Commentaries on Chinese Criminal Law and Cognate Topics, with Special Relation to Ruling Cases, Together with a Brief Excursus on the Law of Property.* London, 1899.
Alford, William P. "Of Arsenic and Old Laws: Looking Anew at Criminal Justice in Late Imperial China." *California Law Review* 74 (1984): 1180–256.

———. *To Steal a Book Is an Elegant Offense: Intellectual Property Law in Chinese Civilization.* Stanford: Stanford University Press, 1995.

Arlington, L. C., and William Lewisohn. *In Search of Old Peking.* Oxford: Oxford University Press, 1987.

Armentrout-Ma, L. Eve. "Fellow-Regional Associations in the Ch'ing Dynasty: Organizations in Flux for Mobile People. A Preliminary Survey." *Modern Asian Studies* 18, no. 2 (1984): 307–30.

———. "Urban Chinese on the Sinitic Frontier: Social Organizations in United States Chinatowns, 1849–1898." *Modern Asian Studies* 17, no. 1 (1983): 107–35.

Batiste-Maybon, Pierre. *Essai sur les associations en Chine.* Paris: Librairie Plon, 1925.

Beijing shi dang'anguan 北京市檔案館, ed. *Beijing huiguan dang'an shiliao* 北京會館檔案史料. Beijing: Beijing chubanshe, 1997.

Beijing shi renmin zhengfu. Minzhengju 北京市人民政府民政局. "1949 nian Beijing huiguan qingkuang diaocha baogao" 1949 年北京會館情況調查報告. *Beijing dang'an shiliao* 1988, no. 2: 32–41. Originally dated Nov. 15, 1949, and entitled "Huiguan diaocha gongzuo baogao" 會館調查工作報告. Also reprinted in Beijing shi dang'anguan, ed., *Beijing huiguan dang'an shiliao* (q.v.), 1066–76.

Beijing Tongrentang shi bianwei hui 北京同仁堂史編委會 et al., eds. *Beijing Tongrentang shi* 北京同仁堂史. Beijing: Renmin ribao chubanshe, 1993.

Beijing tushuguan. Jinshi zu 北京圖書館金石組, ed. *Beijing tushuguan cang Zhongguo lidai shike taben huibian* 北京圖書館藏中國歷代石刻拓本匯編. Beijing, 1991. Cited as *BJTSGC*.

Beiping shehui diaocha suo 北平社會調查所. *Beiping shehui gaikuang tongji tu* 北平社會概況統計圖. 1932.

Beiping zhinan 北平指南 (Guide to Beiping). Beiping: Beiping min she, 1929.

Belsky, Richard D. "Beijing Scholar-Official Native-Place Lodges: The Social and Political Evolution of *Huiguan* in China's Capital City." Ph.D. diss., Harvard University, 1997.

———. "Bones of Contention: The Siming Gongsuo Riots of 1874 and 1898." *Papers on Chinese History* 1, no. 1 (Spring 1992): 56–73.

BJTSGC, see Beijing tushuguan. Jinshi zu, ed.

Bradstock, Timothy. "Craft Guilds in Ch'ing Dynasty China." Ph.D. diss., Harvard University, 1984.

Bredon, Juliet. *Peking.* New York: Oxford University Press, 1982.

Brook, Timothy. *Geographical Sources of Ming-Qing History.* Ann Arbor: Center for Chinese Studies, University of Michigan, 1988.

Brunnert, H. S., and V. V. Hagelstrom. *Present Day Political Organization of China*. Beijing: Chinese Maritime Service, 1911.

Burgess, John S. *The Guilds of Peking*. New York: Columbia University Press, 1928.

Cao Zixi 曹子西 et al., eds. *Beijing tongshi* 北京通史. 10 vols. Beijing: Zhongguo shudian, 1994.

Chan, Hok-Lam. "The Chien-wen, Yung-lo, Hung-hsi, and Hsüan-te reigns, 1399–1435." In *The Cambridge History of China*, vol. 7, pt. I, *The Ming Dynasty, 1368–1644*, ed. Frederick W. Mote and Denis Twitchett. Cambridge, Eng.: Cambridge University Press, 1988, 182–304.

Chan, Wellington K. K. "Merchant Organizations in Late Imperial China: Patterns of Change and Development." *Journal of the Hong Kong Branch of the Royal Asiatic Society* 15 (1975): 28–42.

Chang Chong-li. *The Chinese Gentry: Studies on Their Role in Nineteenth-Century Chinese Society*. Seattle: University of Washington Press, 1967.

Chang, Hao. "Intellectual Change and the Reform Movement." In *Cambridge History of China*, vol. 11, pt. II, *Late Ch'ing, 1800–1911*, ed. by Denis Twitchett and John K. Fairbank. Cambridge, Eng.: Cambridge University Press, 1980, 274–338.

———. *Liang Chi-Chao and Intellectual Transition in China, 1890–1907*. Cambridge, Mass.: Harvard University Press, 1971.

Chang, Peng. "The Distribution and Relative Strength of the Provincial Merchant Groups in China, 1842–1911." Ph.D. diss., University of Washington, Seattle, 1958.

Chang, Sen-dou. "The Morphology of Walled Capitals." In *The City in Late Imperial China*, ed. G. William Skinner. Stanford: Stanford University Press, 1977, 75–100.

Chen Jiaji 陳家驥. "Jiangxi huiguan yijiu" 江西會館憶舊. *Yandu* 燕都, no. 25 (1989, no. 4): 47.

Chen Zhengxiang (Chen Cheng-siang) 陳正祥. *Beijing de dushi fazhan* 北京的都市發展. Research Report no. 73. Hong Kong: City University of Hong Kong, 1974.

Chen Zongfan 陳宗蕃, ed. *Yandu congkao* 燕都從考. Beijing: Beijing guji chubanshe, 1991.

Cohen, Paul A. *Discovering History in China: American Historical Writing on the Recent Chinese Past*. New York: Columbia University Press, 1984.

Cole, James. "Competition and Cooperation in Late Imperial China as Reflected in Native Place and Ethnicity." In *Remapping China: Fissures in Historical Terrain*, ed. Gail Hershatter et al. Stanford: Stanford University Press, 1996, 156–63.

——. *Shaohsing: Competition and Cooperation in Nineteenth-Century China*. Tucson: University of Arizona Press for the Association for Asian Studies, 1986.

Crampton, William G. *Flag*. New York: Alfred A. Knopf, 1989.

Crissman, Lawrence W. "The Segmentary Structure of Urban Overseas Chinese Communities." *Man* 2, no. 2 (June 1967): 185–204.

Crossley, Pamela Kyle. *Orphan Warriors: Three Generations and the End of the Qing World*. Princeton: Princeton University Press, 1990.

Da Qing fagui daquan 大清法規大全. Beijing: Zhengxue she, 1909.

Dai Yi 戴逸. *Qianlong di ji qi shidai* 乾隆帝及其時代. Beijing: Zhongguo renmin daxue, 1992.

Dai Yi 戴逸 et al., eds. *Wuxu bairi zhi* 戊戌百日志. Beijing: Yanshan chubanshe, 1998.

Deglopper, Donald R. "Social Structure in a Nineteenth-Century Taiwanese Port City." In *City in Late Imperial China*, ed. G. William Skinner. Stanford: Stanford University Press, 1977, 633–50.

Ding Wenjiang 丁文江. *Liang Rengong xiansheng nianpu changbian chugao* 梁任公先生年譜長編初稿. Taipei: Shijie shuju, 1959.

Ding Yan 丁晏. *Shiting jishi* 石亭紀實. In *Yi zhi zhai cong shu* 頤志齋叢書, ce 19. Shanyang: Ding shi liu yi tang, 1862.

Dong, Madeleine Yue. "Communities and Communication: A Study of the Case of Yang Naiwu, 1873–1877." *Late Imperial China* 16, no. 1 (June 1995): 79–119.

Dou Jiliang 竇季良. *Tongxiang zuzhi zhi yanjiu* 同鄉組織之研究. Chongqing: Zhengzhong shuju, 1943.

Dou Zongyi 竇宗一. *Li Hongzhang nian (ri) pu: Jindai Zhongguo xuelei shishi jiyao* 李鴻章年(日)譜: 近代中國血淚史實紀要. Hong Kong: You lian, 1968.

Dray-Novey, Alison Jean. "Policing Imperial Peking: The Ch'ing Gendarmerie, 1650–1850." Ph.D. diss., Harvard University, 1981.

——. "Spatial Order and Police in Imperial Beijing." *Journal of Asian Studies* 52 (1993): 885–922.

Duara, Prasenjit. "Superscribing Symbols: The Myth of Guandi, Chinese God of War." *Journal of Asian Studies* 47, no. 4 (1988): 778–95.

Eberhard, Wolfram. *A Dictionary of Chinese Symbols: Hidden Symbols in Chinese Life and Thought*. New York: Routledge, 1986.

Elvin, Mark, and G. William Skinner, eds. *The Chinese City Between Two Worlds*. Stanford: Stanford University Press, 1974.

Fairbank, John King. *China: A New History*. Cambridge, Mass.: Belknap Press, Harvard University Press, 1992.

Fan Xiangyong 范祥雍. *Luoyang qielan ji jiaozhu* 洛陽伽藍記校注. Shanghai: Shanghai guji chubanshe, 1978.

Favier, Alphonse. *Péking: histoire et description*. Beijing: Imprimerie des Lazaristes au Pé-T'ang, 1897.

Fewsmith, Joseph. "From Guild to Interest Group: The Transformation of Public and Private in Late Qing China." *Comparative Studies in Society and History* 25, no. 4 (Oct. 1983): 617–40.

———. *Party, State and Local Elites in Republican China: Merchant Organization and Politics in Shanghai, 1890–1930*. Honolulu: University of Hawai'i Press, 1985.

Fincher, John. "Political Provincialism and the National Revolution." In *China in Revolution: The First Phase, 1900–1913*, ed. Mary Clabaugh Wright. New Haven: Yale University Press, 1968, 185–226.

Fitzgerald, C. P. *China: A Short Cultural History*. London: Cresset Press, 1935.

Folsom, Kenneth E. *Friends, Guests, and Colleagues: The Mu-fu System in the Late Ch'ing Period*. Berkeley: University of California Press, 1968.

Franck, Harry A. *Wandering in Northern China*. New York: Century, 1923.

Freedman, Maurice. *Chinese Lineage and Society: Fukien and Kwangtung*. London School of Economics Monographs on Social Anthropology, no. 33, London: Athlone, 1966.

———. "Immigrants and Associations: Chinese in Nineteenth-Century Singapore." *Comparative Studies in Society and History* 3, no. 1 (Oct. 1960): 25–48.

———. *Lineage Organization in Southeastern China*. London School of Economics Monographs on Social Anthropology, no 18. London: Athlone, 1958.

Fu Gongyue 傅公鉞. "Beijing huiguan de yan'ge yu fazhan" 北京會館的沿革與發展. *Shoudu bowuguan wenji* 首度博物館文集, no. 5 (1990): 66–73.

Gamble, Sidney. *Peking: A Social Survey*. New York: George H. Doran, 1921.

Geiss, James P. "Peking Under the Ming (1368–1644)." Ph.D. diss., Princeton University, 1979.

Golas, Peter. "Early Ch'ing Guilds." In *The City in Late Imperial China*, ed. G. William Skinner. Stanford: Stanford University Press, 1977, 555–80.

Goodman, Bryna. "Creating Civic Ground: Public Maneuverings and the State in the Nanjing Decade." In *Remapping China: Fissures in Historical Terrain*, ed. Gail Hershatter et al. Stanford: Stanford University Press, 1996, 164–77.

———. "The Native-Place and the City: Immigrant Consciousness and Social Organization in Shanghai, 1853–1927." Ph.D. diss., Stanford University, 1990.

———. *Native Place, City and Nation: Regional Networks and Identities in Shanghai, 1853–1937.* Berkeley: University of California Press, 1995.

———. "New Culture, Old Habits: Native-Place Organization and the May Fourth Movement." In *Shanghai Sojourners*, ed. Frederic Wakeman, Jr., et al. Berkeley: University of California, 1992.

Gottdiener, Mark. *The Social Production of Urban Space.* Austin: University of Texas Press, 1994.

Gu Wei 贾维. "Tan Sitong zaonian ji qi jiazu ziliao *Tan shi jia shu* jianxi" 谭嗣同早年及其家族资料《谭氏家书》简析. *Jindai shi ziliao* 近代史资料 no. 101 (2001): 295–321.

Guo Chunyu 郭春愉. *Bing lu riji* 邴盧日記. N.p., 1935.

Han Dacheng 韩大成. *Mingdai chengshi yanjiu* 明代城市研究. Beijing: Zhongguo renmin daxue, 1991.

———. "Mingdai de Beijing" 明代的北京. In *Jinghua jiushi cunzhen* 京華舊事存真, ed. Su Tianjun 蘇天鈞. Beijing: Beijing guji chubanshe, 1992, 125–57.

He Bingdi (Ho Ping-ti) 何炳棣. "The Geographic Distribution of Hui-Kuan (Landsmannschaften) in Central and Upper Yangtze Provinces, with Special Reference to Interregional Migrations." *Tsing Hua Journal of Chinese Studies* 5, no. 2 (Dec. 1966): 120–52.

———. *The Ladder of Success in Imperial China: Aspects of Social Mobility, 1368–1911.* New York: Columbia University, 1962.

———. *Zhongguo huiguan shilun* 中國會館史論. Taipei: Xuesheng shuju, 1966.

Heng Lan 恆蘭. "Fengtian huiguan zhi youlai" 奉天會館之由來. *Wenshi ziliao xuanbian* 文史資料选编, no. 25 (1985): 268.

Honig, Emily. "Native Place and the Making of Chinese Ethnicity." In *Remapping China: Fissures in Historical Terrain*, ed. Gail Hershatter et al. Stanford: Stanford University Press, 1996, 143–55.

Hou Junxia 侯俊俠 and Wang Ruiqi 王瑞琪. "Beijing Liuli chang wenhua jie ji" 北京琉璃廠文化□記. In *Jingdu shengji* 京都胜迹, ed. Hu Yuyuan 胡玉遠 et al. Beijing: Beijing Yanshan chubanshe, 1996, 350–51.

Hsu, Immanuel C. Y. "Late Ch'ing Foreign Relations, 1866–1905." In *Cambridge History of China*, vol. 11, pt. II, *Late Ch'ing, 1800–1911*, ed. Denis Twitchett and John K. Fairbank. Cambridge, Eng.: Cambridge University Press, 1980, 70–141.

Hu Chunhuan 胡春煥 and Bai Hequn 白鶴群. *Beijing de huiguan* 北京的會館. Beijing: Zhongguo jingji chubanshe, 1994.

Hu Sijing 胡思敬. "Wuxu lü shuang lu" 戊戌履霜錄. In *Wuxu bianfa* 戊戌變法, ed. Zhongguo shixue hui 中國史學會. Shanghai: Shanghai renmin chuban she, 1957, vol. 1, 357–406.

Huang Liuhong 黃六鴻. *A Complete Book Concerning Happiness and Benevolence (Fu-hui ch'üan-shu): A Manual for Local Magistrates in Seventeenth-Century China.* Trans. and ed. Djang Chu. Tucson, Arizona: University of Arizona Press, 1984.

———. *Fu hui quan shu* 福惠全書. 1694. Reprinted—n.p.: Sha tu yuan shu heng, 1893.

Hummel, Arthur W. *Eminent Chinese of the Ch'ing Period.* 2 vols. Washington, D.C.: United States Government Printing Office, 1943, 1944.

Imahori Seiji 今堀誠二. *Chūgoku no shakai kōzō; anshan rejīmu ni okeru "kyōdōtai"* 中國の社會構造；アンシャンレジームにおける「共同體」. Tokyo: Hikaku, 1953.

———. *Peipin shimin no jichi kōsei* 北平市民の自治構成. Tokyo: Bunkyūdō, 1947.

Jacobs, J. Bruce. "The Concept of *Guanxi* and Local Politics in a Rural Chinese Cultural Setting." In *Social Interaction in Chinese Society,* ed. Sidney L. Greenblatt et al. New York: Praeger Publishers, 1982, 209–36.

Jian Enpei 簡恩霈. "Ji citang nian xiangxian" 記祠堂念鄉賢. In *Wenshi ziliao xuanbian,* no. 36 (1986): 241–44.

———. "Yunnan ren zai Beijing" 雲南人在北京. *Yandu* 燕都, no. 22 (1989, no. 1): 47–48.

[*Qin ding*] *Jiaoping Yuefei fanglüe* 欽定剿平粵匪方略. Ed. Yixin 奕訢 et al. N.p.: Guangxu era? (1875–1908).

Johnson, Linda Cooke. "Yingguo huiguan: Yingguo shangren zai Shanghai de daoda, 1843–1850" 英国会馆：英国商人在上海的到达. Trans. Wang Shuo, Qinghua University. *Zhongwai lishi yanjiu* 中外历史研究 1994: 1–26.

K. "Chinese Guilds and Their Rules." *China Review* 12 (July–Aug. 1883): 5–9.

Kang Youwei. "Chronological Autobiography of K'ang Yu-wei." Trans. Jung-pang Lo. In *K'ang Yu-wei: A Biography and a Symposium,* ed. Jung-Pang Lo. Tucson: University of Arizona Press, 1967, 17–174.

Karl, Rebecca, and Peter Zarrow, eds. *The 1898 Reforms and the Origins of Modernity in China.* Cambridge, Mass.: Harvard University Asia Center, 2001.

Katō Shigeshi 加藤繁. "On the Hang or the Associations of Merchants in China, with Especial Reference to the Institution in the T'ang and Sung Periods." Trans. H. Kodama. *Memoirs of the Research Department of the Toyo Bunko,* no. 8 (1936): 45–83.

———. "Shindai ni okeru Pekin no shōnin kaikan ni tsuite" 清代に於ける北京の 商人會館に就いて. *Shigaku zasshi* 史學雜誌 53, no. 2 (Feb. 1942): 1–31.

Kirby, William C. "China Unincorporated: Company Law and Business Enterprise in Twentieth-Century China." *Journal of Asian Studies* 54 (Feb. 1995): 43–63.

Kleeman, Terry F. *A God's Own Tale: The Book of Transformation of Wenchang, the Divine Lord of Zitong*. Albany: State University of New York Press, 1994.

Kong Xiangji 孔祥吉. *Kang Youwei bianfa zouyi yanjiu* 康有為變法奏議研究. Shenyang: Liaoning jiaoyu chubanshe, 1988.

———. *Wuxu weixin yundong xintan* 戊戌维新运动新探. Changsha: Hunan renmin chubanshe, 1988.

Kong Xiangji 孔祥吉, ed. *Jiuwang tucun de lantu: Kang Youwei bianfa zouyi ji zheng* 救亡圖存的藍圖: 康有為變法奏議輯證. Taipei: Lianhe baoxi wenhua, 1998.

Kuhn, Philip A. "Ideas Behind China's Modern State." *Harvard Journal of Asiatic Studies* 55 (1995): 295–337.

———. *Origins of the Modern Chinese State*. Stanford: Stanford University Press, 2002.

———. *Rebellion and Its Enemies in Late Imperial China: Militarization and Social Structure, 1796–1864*. Cambridge, Mass.: Harvard University Press, 1970.

Kui Yingtao 隗瀛涛 et al., eds. *Sichuan Xinhai geming shiliao* 四川辛亥革命史料. Chengdu: Sichuan renmin chubanshe, 1981.

Kwong, Luke S. K. *A Mosaic of the Hundred Days: Personalities, Politics and Ideas of 1898*. Cambridge, Mass.: Harvard University, Council on East Asian Studies, 1984.

———. *T'an Ssu-T'ung, 1865–1898: Life and Thought of a Reformer*. Leiden: E. J. Brill, 1996.

Lei Luqing 雷祿慶. *Li Hongzhang xinzhuan* 李鴻章新傳. Jindai Zhongguo shiliao congkan xuji. Taipei: Wenhai chubanshe, 1983.

Lessing, Ferdinand Diederich. *Yung-Ho-Kung: An Iconography of the Lamaist Cathedral in Peking*, vol. 1 Stockholm: Elanders Boktryckeri Aktiebolao, 1942. Reprinted—London: Curzon, 1993.

Levenson, Joseph. "The Province, the Nation, and the World: The Problem of Chinese Identity." In *Approaches to Modern Chinese History*, ed. Albert Feuerwerker et al. Berkeley: University of California Press, 1967, 268–87.

Li Chang 李暢. "Huiguan xilou shangcun de san lou" 會館戲樓尚存的三樓. *Yandu* 燕都, no. 24 (1989, no. 3): 9–10.

———. "Tantan Yangping huiguan juchang" 談談陽平會館劇場. *Beijing wanbao* 北京晚報, Nov. 21, 1993, 6.

Li Ciming 李慈銘. *Yueman tang riji* 越縵堂日記. Taipei: Wenhai chubanshe, 1963.

Li Guoxiang 李國祥 et al., eds. *Ming shilu leizuan: Beijing shiliao juan* 明實錄類纂: 北京史料卷. Wuhan: Wuhan chubanshe, 1992.

Li Hua 李華. "Ming Qing liangdai de Beijing huiguan" 明清兩代的北京會館. *Yandu* 燕都, no. 25 (1989, no. 4): 32–33.

Li Hua 李華, ed. and comp. *Ming-Qing yilai Beijing gongshang huiguan beike xuanbian* 明清以來北京工商會館碑刻選編. Beijing: Wenwu chubanshe, 1980.

Li Hongruo 李虹若. *Chao shi cong zai* 朝市叢載. Beijing Song zhu zhai, 1886.

Li Jiarui 李家瑞. *Beiping fengsu leizheng* 北平風俗類徵. Shanghai: Shangwu yinshuguan, 1937.

Li Pengnian 李鵬年 et al., eds. *Qingdai liubu chengyu cidian* 清代六部成語詞典. Tianjin: Tianjin renmin chubanshe, 1990.

Li Qiao 李喬. "Anhui huiguan: Huaijun jituan de yige judian" 安徽會館: 淮军集團的一個據點. *Beijing shiyuan* 北京史苑 1983, no. 1: 326–28.

——. "Ming-Qing yilai tongxiang huiguan de xiangtu xing ji qi shehui lishi beijing" 明清以来同乡会馆的乡土性及其社会历史背景. *Beijing shiyuan* 北京史苑 1988, no. 4: 117–32.

——. *Zhongguo hangye shen chongbai* 中國行業神崇拜. Beijing: Zhongguo Huaqiao chuban, 1990.

Li Zhengzhong 李正中. " 'Gongche shangshu' xin jie" "公車上書"新解. *Jindai shi yanjiu* 近代史研究 1984, no. 2: 299.

Liang Qichao 梁啓超. *Wuxu zhengbian ji* 戊戌政變記. Shanghai: n.p., 1936.

——. *Yinbingshi heji* 飲冰室合集. Beijing, Zhonghua shuju, 1996.

Lillywhite, Bryant. *London Coffee Houses: A Reference Book of Coffee Houses of the Eighteenth and Nineteenth Centuries.* London: George Allen and Unwin, 1963.

Lin Keguang 林克光. "Beijing Qiangxuehui yizhi" 北京強學會遺址. In *Jindai jinghua shiji* 近代京華史跡, ed. idem et al. Beijing: Zhongguo renmin daxue chubanshe, 1985, 257–68.

——. *Gexinpai juren Kang Youwei* 革新派巨人康有爲. Beijing: Zhongguo renmin daxue chubanshe, 1990.

——. "Songyun an yu gongche shangshu" 嵩筠庵與公車上書. In *Jindai jinghua shiji* 近代京華史跡, ed. idem et al. Beijing: Zhongguo renmin daxue chubanshe, 1985, 244–56.

Lin Xiaojuan 林孝胜, ed. *Xinjiapo huiguan shukan mulu huibian* 新加坡會館書刊目錄匯編. Singapore: Xinjiapo zongxiang huiguan lianhe zonghui, 1989.

Lin Yutang. *My Country and My People.* New York: Reynal & Hitchcock, 1935.

Liu Boji 劉伯驥. *Guangdong shuyuan zhidu* 廣東書院制度. Taipei: Zhong-hua congshu, 1958.

Liu Guangdi 劉光第. *Liu Guangdi ji* 劉光第集. Beijing: Zhonghua shuju, 1986.

Liu, Hui-chen Wang. "An Analysis of Chinese Clan Rules: Confucian Theories in Action." In *Confucianism in Action*, ed. David S. Nivison and Arthur F. Wright. Stanford: Stanford University Press, 1959, 63–96.

———. *The Traditional Chinese Clan Rules*. Locust Valley, N.Y.: J. J. Augustin, 1959.

Liu, Kwang-Ching. "Chinese Merchant Guilds: An Historical Inquiry." *Pacific Historical Review* 57, no. 1 (1988): 1–23.

———. "Li Hung-chang in Chihli: The Emergence of a Policy, 1870–1875." In *Approaches to Modern Chinese History*, ed. Albert Feuerwerker et al. Berkeley: Univiversity of California, 1967, 68–104.

———. "The Limits of Regional Power in the Late Ch'ing Period: A Reappraisal." *Ch'ing-hua hsüeh-pao* 10, no. 2 (July 1974): 192–223.

Liu Tong 劉侗 and Yu Yizheng 于奕正. *Di jing jing wu lüe* 帝京景物略. 1635. Reprinted—Beijing: Beijing guji chubanshe, 1992.

Liu Wu-chi et al., eds. *K'uei Hsing: A Repository of Asian Literature in Translation*. Bloomington: Indiana University Press, 1974.

Lu Baozhong 陸寶忠. *Lu Wenshen gong (Baozhong) nianpu* 陸文慎公(寶忠) 年譜. 1923. Reprinted—*Jindai Zhongguo shiliao congkan*. Taipei: Wenhai chubanshe, 1970, 58: 576.

Lu Xun 魯迅 (Zhou Shuren 周树人). *Lu Xun quanji* 魯迅全集. 16 vols. Beijing: Renmin chubanshe, 1993.

Lü Zuoxie 呂作燮. "Ming-Qing shi Suzhou de huiguan he gongsuo" 明清時蘇州的會館和公所. *Zhongguo shehui jingji shi yanjiu* 中國社會經濟史研究 (Xiamen) 1984, no. 2: 10–24.

———. "Shilun Ming-Qing shiqi huiguan de xingzhi he zuoyong" 試論明清時期會館的性質和作用. In *Zhongguo zibenzhuyi mengya wenti lunwenji* 中國資本主義萌芽問題論文集, ed. Nanjing daxue, Lishixi, Ming-Qing shi yanjiushi 南京大学历史系明清史研究室. Jiangsu renmin chubanshe, 1983, 172–211.

Lyell, William A., trans. *Lu Xun: Diary of a Madman and Other Stories*. Honolulu: University of Hawai'i Press, 1990.

Ma Jiannong 馬建農. "Beijing shu si fazhan shi kaolüe" 北京書肆發展史考略. *Beijing shehui kexue* 北京社會科學, 1988, no. 2 (no. 10), 108–16.

Ma Shutian 馬書田. "Sichuan ying yu Qin Liangyu" 四川營與秦良玉. *Beijing shiyuan* 北京史苑 1983, no. 1: 352–54.

Ma Tiehan. "Yinhao huiguan: Zhengyi ci" 銀號會館: 正乙祠. *Yandu* 燕都, no. 24 (1989, no. 3): 12–13.

Ma Zhixiang 馬芷庠. *Beiping lüxing zhinan* 北平旅行指南 (Beiping travel guide). Beiping: n.p., 1935, 1936. (Note: unless otherwise indicated, page numbers cited in the notes refer to the 1936 edition.)

MacGowan, D. J. "Chinese Guilds or Chambers of Commerce and Trade Unions." *Journal of the North China Branch of the Royal Asiatic Society* 1886, no. 21: 133–92.

Mackerras, Colin P. *The Rise of Peking Opera, 1780–1870: Social Aspects of the Theatre in Manchu China.* Oxford: Clarendon Press, 1972.

Mann, Susan. *Local Merchants and the Chinese Bureaucracy, 1750–1950.* Stanford: Stanford University Press, 1987.

Maybon, Pierre. *Essai sur les associations en Chine.* Paris: Librairie Plon, 1925.

Meyer, Jeffrey F. *The Dragons of Tiananmen: Beijing as a Sacred City.* Columbia: University of South Carolina Press, 1991.

Michael, Franz. "Introduction: Regionalism in Nineteenth-Century China." In Stanley Spector, *Li Hung-chang and the Huai Army: A Study in Nineteenth-Century Chinese Regionalism.* Seattle: University of Washington Press, 1964, xxxix–xliii.

[Qing] Minzheng bu. Minzhi si. Huji ke [清] 民政部民治司戶籍科. "Minzheng bu guanyu diaocha jing waicheng huiguan, pu hu, miaoyu de biaoce" 民政部關於調查京外城會館, 鋪戶, 廟宇的表冊. China Number One Historical Archives, Minzheng bu an juan mu lu, 530/21-2, no. 28 (undated). Reprinted as "Qingmo Beijing waicheng xunjing youting huiguan diaochao biao (1906 nian)" 清末北京外城巡警右庭會館調查表 (1906 年). In *Beijing huiguan dang'an shiliao* 北京會館檔案史料, ed. Beijing shi dang'anguan 北京市檔案館. Beijing: Beijing chubanshe, 1997, 798–818. [Note the date given in the title of the reprint is based on the establishment of the Minzheng bu in that year.]

Morse, Hosea Ballou. *The Gilds of China.* London: Longmans Green, 1909.

———. *The Gilds of China, with an Account of the Gild Merchant or Co-hong of Canton.* New York: Russell & Russell, 1932. Reprinted—Taipei: Ch'eng-wen Publishing, 1972.

Mote, Frederick W. "A Millennium of Chinese Urban History: Form, Time and Space Concepts in Soochow." *Rice University Studies* 59 (1973): 35–65.

———. "The Transformation of Nanking." In *The City in Late Imperial China*, ed. G. William Skinner. Stanford: Stanford University Press, 1977, 101–53.

———. "Yuan and Ming." In *Food in Chinese Culture: Anthropological and Historical Perspectives*, ed. K. C. Chang. New Haven: Yale University Press, 1977, 193–257.

Murphey, Rhoads. "City as a Mirror of Society." In *The Chinese: Adopting the Past, Facing the Future*, ed. Robert F. Dernberger, Kenneth J. De-Woskin, Steven M. Goldstein, Rhoads Murphey, and Martin K. Whyte. Ann Arbor: University of Michigan, Center for Chinese Studies, 1991: 133–37.

Naquin, Susan. "The Peking Pilgrimage to Miao-Feng Shan: Religious Organizations and Sacred Site." In *Pilgrims and Sacred Sites in China*, ed. Susan Naquin and Chün-fang Yü. Berkeley: University of California Press, 1992, 333–77.

———. *Peking: Temples and City Life, 1400–1900*. Berkeley, California, University of California Press, 2000.

Nathan, Andrew J. *Peking Politics, 1918–1923: Factionalism and the Failure of Constitutionalism*. Berkeley: University of California Press, 1976.

Negishi Tadahi 根岸佶. *Chūgoku no girudo* 中國のギルド. Tokyo: Nihon hyōronsha, 1951.

———. *Shanhai no girudo* 上海のグルド. Tokyo: Nihon hyōronsha, 1951.

———. *Shina girudo no kenkyū* 支那ギルドの研究. Tokyo: n.p., 1933.

Ng, Wing Chung. "Urban Chinese Social Organization: Some Unexplored Aspects in Huiguan Development in Singapore, 1900–1941." *Modern Asian Studies* 26, no. 3 (July 1992): 469–94.

Niida Noboru 仁井田陞. *Chūgoku no shakai to girudo* 中國の社會とギルド. Tokyo: Iwanami shoten, 1951.

———. "The Industrial and Commercial Guilds of Peking and Religion and Fellow Countrymanship and Elements of Their Coherence." Trans. M. Elder. *Folklore Studies* 9 (1950): 179–206.

———. *Pekin kōshō girudo shiryō shū* 北京工商ギルド資料集. 6 vols. Tokyo: Tōkyō daigaku, Tōyō bunka kenkyūjo, 1975–83. (Note: the more recently released vol. 7 concerns Tianjin *huiguan*.)

———. "Zai Beijing huiguan mulu" 在北京會館目錄. Beijing, n.d. (1911–44).

Niu Ruchen 牛汝辰. "Hutong mingcheng de yahua" 胡同名稱的雅化. *Yandu* 燕都, no. 23 (1989, no. 2): 43.

North-China Herald and Supreme Court and Consular Gazette. Shanghai, weekly.

Orb, Richard A. "Chihli Academies and Other Schools in the Late Qing: An Institutional Survey." In *Reform in Nineteenth Century China*, ed. Paul A. Cohen and John E. Schrecker. Cambridge, Mass.: Harvard University, East Asian Research Center, 1976, 231–40.

Polachek, James. *The Inner Opium War*. Cambridge, Mass.: Harvard University, Center for East Asian Studies, 1992.

Qi Rushan 齊如山. *Qi Rushan huiyi lu* 齊如山回憶錄. Beijing: Zhongguo xiju chubanshe, 1989.

Qing huidian shili 清會典事例. 1899. Reprinted in 12 vols. Beijing: Zhonghua shuju, 1991.

Qing shilu 清實錄 (original title: *Da Qing lichao shilu* 大清歷朝實錄). 60 vols. Beijing: Zhonghua shuju, 1986.

Quan Hansheng 全漢昇. *Zhongguo hanghui zhidu shi* 中國行會制度史. Taipei: Shihuo chubanshe, 1978.

Rankin, Mary Backus. *Elite Activism and Political Transformation in China: Zhejiang Province, 1865–1911*. Stanford: Stanford University Press, 1986.

Rao Shangdong (Niew Shong Tong) 饒尚東. *Wenlai Huazu huiguan shilun* 汶萊華族會館史論. Singapore: Singapore Society of Asian Studies, 1991.

Rowe, William T. *Hankow: Commerce and Society in a Chinese City, 1796–1889*. Stanford: Stanford University Press, 1984.

———. *Hankow: Conflict and Community in a Chinese City, 1796–1895.* Stanford: Stanford University Press, 1989.

———. "Introduction: City and Region in the Lower Yangzi." In *Cities of Jiangnan in Late Imperial China*, ed. Linda Cooke Johnson. Albany: State University of New York Press, 1993, 1–16.

Rozman, Gilbert. *Urban Networks in Ch'ing China and Tokugawa Japan.* Princeton: Princeton University Press, 1973.

Sangren, P. Steven. "Traditional Chinese Corporations: Beyond Kinship." *Journal of Asian Studies* 43, no. 3 (May 1984): 391–415.

Schultz, William Rudolph. "Lu Hsün: The Creative Years." Ph.D. diss., University of Washington, 1955.

Serruys, Henri. *Sino-Mongol Relations During the Ming*, II, *The Tribute System and Diplomatic Missions (1400–1600)*, vol. 14 of *Mélanges chinois et bouddhiques*. Brussels: Institut Belge des hautes etudes chinoises, 1967.

Sewell, William H. *Work and Revolution in France: The Language of Labor from the Old Regime to 1848*. Cambridge, Eng., and New York: Cambridge University Press, 1980.

She Youzhi 佘幼芝. "Guanyu Yuan Chonghuan cimu qingkuang de jieshao" 關於袁崇煥祠墓情況的介紹. In *Proceedings of the Conference on the Achievements of Historical Figures in South China During the Late Ming and Early Ch'ing*, ed. Law Ping-min and Lau Kin-ming. Hong Kong: Chinese University of Hong Kong, History Department, 1993, 298–300.

Shen Defu 沈德符. *Wanli yehuo bian* 萬曆野獲編. Beijing: Zhonghua shuju, 1980 (1959).

Shiba Yoshinobu. "Ningpo and Its Hinterland." In *The City in Late Imperial China*, ed. G. William Skinner. Stanford: Stanford University Press, 1977, 391–439.

[Zeng ding] Shiyong Beijing zhinan 增訂實用北京指南. 4th ed. Shanghai: Shangwu yinshuguan, 1926.

Sit, Victor F. S. *Beijing: The Nature and Planning of a Chinese Capital City.* Chichester, Eng.: John Wiley and Sons, 1995.

Skinner, G. William. "Introduction: Urban Development in Imperial China." In *The City in Late Imperial China* (q.v.), 3–31.

———. "Introduction: Urban Social Structure in Ch'ing China." In *The City in Late Imperial China* (q.v.), 521–53.

———. "Mobility Strategies in Late Imperial China: A Regional Systems Analysis." In *Regional Analysis*, vol. 1, *Economic Systems*, ed. Carol A. Smith. New York: Academic Press, 1976, 327–64.

Skinner, G. William, ed. *The City in Late Imperial China.* Stanford: Stanford University Press, 1977.

Spector, Stanley. *Li Hung-chang and the Huai Army: A Study in Nineteenth-Century Chinese Regionalism.* Seattle: University of Washington Press, 1964.

Spence, Jonathan D. *The Gate of Heavenly Peace: The Chinese and Their Revolution, 1895–1980.* Middlesex, Eng.: Penguin Books, 1987.

Strand, David. *"Civil Society" and "Public Sphere" in Modern China: A Perspective on Popular Movements in Beijing, 1919–1989.* Working Papers in Asian/Pacific Studies. Durham, N.C.: Duke University, Asian/Pacific Studies Institute, 1990.

———. *Rickshaw Beijing: City, People and Politics in the 1920s.* Berkeley: University of California Press, 1989.

Sun Baoxuan 孙宝瑄. *Wang shan lu riji* 忘山廬日記. Beijing: Shanghai guji chubanshe, 1983.

Sun Chengze 孫承澤. *Tian fu guang ji* 天府廣記. Beijing: Beijing chubanshe, 1963.

Sun, E-tu Zen. *Ch'ing Administrative Terms: A Translation of the Terminology of the Six Boards with Explanatory Notes.* Cambridge, Mass.: Harvard University Press, 1961.

Swallow, Robert W. *Sidelights on Peking Life.* Beijing: China Booksellers, 1927.

Tan Sitong 譚嗣同. *Tan Sitong quanji* 譚嗣同全集. Ed. Cai Shangsi 蔡尚思 and Fang Xing 方行. Beijing: Zhonghua shuju, 1981.

Tang Jincheng 汤錦程. *Beijing de huiguan* 北京的會館. Beijing: Zhongguo qinggongye chubanshe, 1994.

Teng, Ssu-yü, and John K. Fairbank. *China's Response to the West: A Documentary Survey.* Cambridge, Mass.: Harvard University Press, 1954.

Terada Takanobu 寺田隆信. "Guanyu Beijing Shexian huiguan" 關於北京歙縣會館. Trans. Pan Hongli 潘宏立. *Zhongguo shehui jingji shi yanjiu* 中國社會經濟史研究 1991, no. 1, 28–38.

———. "Qingdai Beijing de Shanxi shangren 清代北京的山西商人." In *Zheng Tianting jinian lunwenji* 郑天挺纪念论文集, ed. Wu Tingqiu 吴庭璆. Beijing: Zhonghua shuju, 1990, 561–82.

Tian Yunjin 田蘊瑾. [*Zui xin*] *Beiping shi zhinan* [最新]北平市指南. Shanghai: Ziqiang shuju, 1936.

Tōa dōbunkai 東亞同文會. *Shina shōbetsu zenshi* 支那省別全誌. 18 vols. Tokyo, 1917–20.

Tong Xun 佟洵. "Liuyang huiguan Mang cang cang zhai" 瀏陽會館莽蒼蒼齋. In *Jindai jinghua shiji* 近代京華史跡, ed. Lin Keguang 林克光 et al. Beijing: Zhongguo renmin daxue chubanshe, 1985, 277–86.

Van de Sprenkel, Sybille. *Legal Institutions in Manchu China: A Sociological Analysis.* London: University of London, Athlone Press, 1962.

———. "Urban Social Control." In *The City in Late Imperial China*, ed. G. William Skiner. Stanford: Stanford University Press, 1977, 609–32.

Wakeman, Frederic, Jr. *The Great Enterprise: The Manchu Reconstruction of Imperial Order in Seventeenth-Century China.* 2 vols. Berkeley: University of California Press, 1985.

Wang Canchi 王燦熾. "Qingmo Minchu Beijing huiguan dizhi xinjiu diming duizhaobiao" 清末民初北京會館地址新舊地名對照表 and "Qingmo Minchu Beijing gongshang huiguan (bufen) dizhi xinjiu diming duizhaobiao" 清末民初北京工商會館(部分)地址新舊地名對照表. *Beijing shiyuan* 北京史苑, no. 4 (1988, no. 5). Reprinted in *Wang Canchi shizhi lunwen ji* 王燦熾史誌論文集. Beijing: Yanshan chubanshe, 1991, 358–88 and 389–91.

———. "Sun Zhongshan yu Beijing Huguang huiguan" 孫中山與北京湖廣會館. In *Beijing Huguang huiguan zhi gao* 北京湖廣會館志稿, ed. Beijing shi duiwai wenhua jiaoliu xiehui 北京市对外文化交流协会 et al. Beijing: Yanshan chubanshe, 1994, 29–54.

Wang Rigen 王日根. "Ming-Qing shidai huiguan de yanbian" 明清時代會館的演變. *Lishi yanjiu* 歷史研究 1994, no. 4: 47–62.

———. *Xiangtu zhi lian: Ming Qing huiguan yu shehui bianqian* 鄉土之鏈: 明清會館與社會變遷. Tianjin: Tianjin renmin chubanshe, 1996.

Wang Shijing 王士菁. "Lu Xun zai Beijing juzhuguo de difang" 魯迅在北京居住過的地方. *Yandu* 燕都, no. 34 (1991, no. 1): 18–20.

Wang Shiren 王世仁 et al., eds. *Xuannan hongxue tuzhi* 宣南鴻學圖志. Beijing: Zhongguo jianzhu gongye chubanshe, 1997.

Watson, James. "Chinese Kinship Reconsidered: Anthropological Perspectives on Historical Research." *China Quarterly*, no. 92 (1982): 589–622.

———. "Standardizing the Gods: The Promotion of T'ien Hou ('Empress of Heaven') Along the South China Coast, 960–1960." In *Popular Culture in Late Imperial China*, ed. David Johnson, Andrew J. Nathan, and

Evelyn S. Rawski. Berkeley: University of California Press, 1985, 292–324.

Weber, Max. "Citizenship." In idem, *General Economic History*. Glencoe, Ill.: Free Press, 1950, 315–51.

———. *The City*. New York: Free Press, 1958.

———. *The Religion of China: Confucianism and Taoism*. New York: Free Press, 1951.

Wei Jingzhao 韋經照. "Nanhai huiguan chunqiu" 南海會館春秋. In *Jindai jinghua shiji* 近代京華史跡, ed. Lin Keguang 林克光 et al. Beijing: Zhongguo renmin daxue chubanshe, 1985, 269–76.

Wen Hai 文海. "Wuxu weixin yundong shiqi de xuehui zuzhi" 戊戌維新運動時期的學會組織. *Beijing shiyuan* 北京史苑 1983, no. 1: 30–53.

Wen Tingshi 文廷式. *Wen Tingshi ji* 文廷式集. Comp. Wang Shuzi 汪叔子. Beijing: Zhonghua shuju, 1993.

Weng Tonghe 翁同龢. *Wong Tonghe riji paiyin ben, fu suoyin* 翁同龢日記排印本, 附索引. 6 vols. Ed. Zhao Zhongfu 趙中孚. Taipei: Chengwen chubanshe, 1970.

Wright, Mary Clabaugh, ed. *China in Revolution: The First Phase, 1900–1913*. New Haven: Yale University Press, 1968.

Wu Changyuan 吳長元. *Chen yuan shi lüe* 宸垣識略. 1788. Reprinted— Taipei: Wenhai chubanshe, 1972.

Wu Jianyong 吳建雍. "Qing qianqi jingshi Xuannan shixiang" 清前期京師宣南士鄉. *Beijing shehui kexue* 北京社會科學 1996, no. 3: 58–66.

Wu Jianyong 吳建雍 and He Xiaolin 赫曉琳. *Xuannan shixiang* 宣南士鄉. Beijing: Beijing chubanshe, 2000.

Wu Jingzi 吳敬梓. *Rulin waishi* 儒林外史. Beijing: Renmin wenxue chubanshe, 1975.

Wu Zhezheng 吳哲征. "Beijing Huguang huiguan" 北京湖廣會館. *Shoudu bowuguan wenji* 首度博物館文集, no. 7 (1992): 125–26. A more-or-less identical version of this article was published in *Yandu* 燕都, no. 43 (1992, no. 4): 26–28.

———. "Huiguan." In *Beijing wangshi tan* 北京往事談, ed. Zhongguo renmin zhengzhi xieshang huiyi 中国人民政治协商会议 et al. Beijing: Beijing chubanshe, 1988, 84–93.

Wu Zhezheng 吳哲征 et al. "Nie Er zai Beijing" 聶耳在北京. *Yandu* 燕都, no. 41 (1992, no. 2): 13–14.

Xu Dingxin 徐鼎新. "Shanghai gongshang tuanti de jindaihua" 上海工商團體的近代化. In *Jindai Shanghai chengshi yanjiu* 近代上海城市研究, ed. Zhang Zhongli 张仲礼. Shanghai: Shanghai renmin chubanshe, 1990, 509–91.

Xuanwu qu diming zhi bianji weiyuanhui 《宣武區地名志》編輯委員會, ed. *Beijing shi Xuanwu qu diming zhi* 北京市宣武區地名志. Beijing: Beijing chubanshe, 1993.

Yang, C. K. "Some Thoughts on the Study of Chinese Urban Communities." Paper prepared for the Seminar on Problems of Micro-Organization in Chinese Society, sponsored by the Subcommittee on Research on Chinese Society of the ACLS-SSRC Joint Committee on Contemporary China, Bermuda, Jan. 1963.

Yang Jingting 楊靜亭. "Dumen huiguan" 都門會館. Cataloged independently in the Beijing Academy of Social Science library. Dated 1911. (Note: this edition contains minor variations from the huiguan section in the *Xinzeng dumen jilüe*; see second entry below.)

———. *Dumen zhuzhi ci* 都門竹枝詞. Beijing, 1877.

———. *Xinzeng dumen jilüe* 新增都門紀略. Revised and augmented by Xu Yongnian 徐永年. 8 *juan*. Beijing, 1907. (Note: the 1907 edition is held in the library of the Academy of Science in Beijing; Harvard has a 1909 edition with only minor variations.)

Yang Liansheng 楊聯陞. "Keju shidai de fukao lüfei wenti" 科舉時代的府考旅費問題. *Qinghua xuebao* 清華學報 n.s. 2, no. 2 (June 1961): 116–30.

Yang, Mayfair Mei-hui. *Gifts, Favors, and Banquets: The Art of Social Relationships in China.* Ithaca: Cornell University Press, 1994.

Ye Zufu 叶祖孚. *Beijing fengqing zatan* 北京風情雜談. Beijing: Zhongguo chengshi chubanshe, 1995.

Young, James Sterling. *The Washington Community, 1800–1828.* New York: Columbia University Press, 1966.

Yu Heping 虞和平. "Yapian zhanzheng hou tongshang kou'an hanghui de jindaihua" 鴉片戰爭後通商口岸行會的近代化. *Lishi yanjiu* 歷史研究 1991, no. 6: 122–35.

Yuan Huiyu 袁誨余. "Tongchuan huiguan" 潼川會館. *Yandu* 燕都, no. 37 (1991, no. 4): 30–32.

Yuan Shuyi 苑書義. *Li Hongzhang zhuan* 李鴻章傳. Beijing: Renmin chubanshe, 1991.

Zeng Guofang 曾國藩. *Zeng Guofan jiashu quanbian* 曾國藩家書全編. 4 vols. Beijing: Zhongguo huaqiao chubanshe, 2000.

———. *Zeng Guofan riji (quanben zhushi)* 曾國藩日記(全本注釋). 4 vols. Tianjin: Tianjin renmin chubanshe, 1995.

Zhang Dechang 張德昌. *Qing ji yige jingguan de shenghuo* 清季一個京官的生活. Hong Kong: Xianggang Zhongwen daxue, 1970.

Zhang Jixin 张集馨. *Dao Xian huan hai jian wen lu* 道咸宦海見聞錄. Beijing: Zhonghua shuju, 1981.

Zhang, Li. *Strangers in the City: Reconfigurations of Space, Power, and Social Networks Within China's Floating Population.* Stanford: Stanford University Press, 2001.

Zhang Xiaoxin 張孝訢. "Beiping huiguan diaocha" 北京會館調查. Senior thesis, Yenching University, School of Law, Sociology Department, 1936. Held in the unpublished documents section of the Beijing University Library.

Zhang, Yingjin. *The City in Modern Chinese Literature and Film: Configurations of Space, Time, and Gender.* Stanford: Stanford University Press, 1996.

Zhao Lingyu 趙令瑜. "Zhongguo huiguan zhi shehuixue de fenxi" 中國會館之社會學的分析. Senior thesis, Yenching University, School of Law, Sociology Department. 1937. Held in the unpublished documents section of the Beijing University Library.

Zhongguo huiguan zhi bianzuan weiyuanhui 中國會館志編纂委員會, ed. *Zhongguo huiguan zhi* 中國會館志 Beijing: Fangzhi chubanshe, 2002.

Zhongguo renmin zhengzhi xieshang huiyi 中国人民政治协商会议 et al., eds. *Beijing wangshi tan* 北京往事談. Beijing: Beijing chubanshe, 1988.

Zhongguo shixue hui 中國史學會, ed. *Wuxu bianfa* 戊戌變法. Shanghai: Shanghai renmin chubanshe, 1957.

Zhou Lianggong 周亮工. *Min xiao ji* 閩小記. Shanghai: Shanghai guji chubanshe, 1985.

Zhou Xiashou 周遐壽 (Zhou Zuoren 周作人). *Lu Xun de gu jia* 魯迅的故家. Shanghai: Shanghai chuban, 1953.

Zhou Zongxian 周宗賢. *Xue nong yu shui de huiguan* 血濃於水的會館. Taipei: Xingzhengyuan, Wenhua jianshe weiyuanhui, 1985.

Zhu Shi 朱軾. *Zhu Wenduan gong wenji* 朱文端公文集. N.p.: Gutang Zhu shi. 1873.

Zhu Yixin 朱一新 and Miao Quansun 繆荃孫. *Jing shi fang xiang zhi* 京師坊巷志. 10 *juan*, with an additional *juan* of textual commentary by Liu Chenggan 劉承幹. Beijing: Nan lin Liu shi Qiuyuan zhai, 1918.

———. *Jing shi fang xiang zhi gao* 京師坊巷志稿. Reprinted—Beijing: Guji chubanshe, 1983.

———. "Jing shi zhi: fang xiang" 京師志: 坊巷. In *Guangxu Shuntian fu zhi* 光緒順天府志, *juan* 13-14. Beijing, 1884–86.

Zhuang Zexuan 莊澤宣 and Chen Xuexun 陳學恂. "Zhongguo tongxiang tuanti de yanjiu (chugao)" 中國同鄉團體的研究(初稿). *Lingnan xuebao* 嶺南學報 6, no. 4 (June 1941): 50-73.

Index

Harvard East Asian Monographs
(* out-of-print)

Harvard East Asian Monographs

Harvard East Asian Monographs

Harvard East Asian Monographs

Harvard East Asian Monographs

Harvard East Asian Monographs

Harvard East Asian Monographs

Harvard East Asian Monographs

Harvard East Asian Monographs

Harvard East Asian Monographs

Harvard East Asian Monographs